SIKKIM
DAWN OF
DEMOCRACY

G.B.S. SIDHU

SIKKIM
DAWN OF DEMOCRACY

THE TRUTH BEHIND
THE MERGER WITH INDIA

PENGUIN
VIKING
An imprint of Penguin Random House

VIKING

USA | Canada | UK | Ireland | Australia
New Zealand | India | South Africa | China | Singapore

Viking is part of the Penguin Random House group of companies
whose addresses can be found at global.penguinrandomhouse.com

Published by Penguin Random House India Pvt. Ltd
4th Floor, Capital Tower 1, MG Road,
Gurugram 122 002, Haryana, India

First published in Viking by Penguin Random House India 2018

ISBN 9780670090648

Typeset in Adobe Garamond Pro by Manipal Digital Systems, Manipal
Printed at Replika Press Pvt. Ltd.

www.penguin.co.in

This is a legitimate digitally printed version of the book and therefore might not
have certain extra finishing on the cover.

This book is dedicated to my late wife, Iqbal, who battled leiomyosarcoma with fortitude and equanimity till the end

Contents

Contents

Preface

It was in August 1973, a day before I left for Gangtok to take charge as the Officer on Special Duty (Police)—OSD (P)—that I called on the legendary Rameshwarnath Kao (also called R.N. Kao), the then head of India's external intelligence agency, i.e. the Research & Analysis Wing (R&AW), which he had founded just five years ago. My visit to his South Block office was short and brief. Kao asked me if P.N. Banerjee, then joint director, Calcutta (now Kolkata), and Ajit Singh Sayali, my predecessor in Gangtok, had briefed me adequately about the requirements of the job. I replied in the affirmative. He then told me that I had been hand-picked in consultation with Banerjee for a very important operation and that he was confident I would be able to live up to his expectations. I was also told that though I would be the man taking decisions to handle unforeseen developments, Banerjee and he would always be there to help me in every way required. Thanking Kao for the confidence he reposed in me, I promised to do everything possible within my means to achieve the desired results.

After my briefings in Calcutta and Gangtok, I had realized the historical importance of the job assigned to me. Meeting Kao convinced me further that in Sikkim I would witness the unfolding of an important chapter in India's history. This prompted me to start maintaining a diary in which I recorded notes about important developments, events and interactions as they took place during that period. I felt that these notes would be useful reference as and when I decided to write about the merger of Sikkim with India. Despite Kao's suggestion to me in 1988 to write precisely such a book elaborating the R&AW's role in the merger, I could not undertake this project for a number of reasons—both official and personal. From May 2011, when my wife's leiomyosarcoma was detected, my time and energy were entirely devoted to her treatment. After the initial positive response, the cancer resurfaced. She faced the ailment boldly and there was no regret or pain on her face till the end, which came in January 2017.

Meanwhile, a number of books on Sikkim had begun appearing, many of which selectively depicted the ground realities in the period leading up to and including the merger. In some cases these books sought to underplay, or even ignore, the existence of a popular grassroots-level movement in Sikkim that favoured a merger with India. In other cases, the merger itself was incorrectly labelled an annexation, conveniently ignoring the fact that it took place through a resolution passed in April 1975 with an overwhelming majority in a popularly and democratically elected Assembly. There were also instances of certain writers resorting to unsubstantiated speculation on the nature, extent and commencement of the R&AW's role in merger-related operations. That these writers were engaging in mere speculation may be gauged from the fact that they didn't even appear to be aware of the presence of an officially approved (by the Chogyal) R&AW office in Gangtok—headed by an OSD (P) to begin with.

The period immediately after the merger also caught my attention. What surprised me the most was the speed with which Kazi Lhendup Dorji's (popularly called Kazi or Kazi Sahib) hold over his party started crumbling in the immediate aftermath of the merger. Kazi, who had devoted his life for the sake of Sikkim's freedom from the Chogyal's yoke, was accused of selling his 'country' (he was called a *desh bechoa*) to India, by those who had lost their power, perks and privileges with this merger. In fact, Kazi and his party lost the 1979 elections to those very forces that could not secure a single seat in the pre-merger elections of April 1974.

It is in the context outlined above that I began writing this book in the middle of 2017, in equal parts to fulfil a promise made to Kao in 1988, to put on record how (and, even more importantly, why) the R&AW's operation to facilitate the merger of Sikkim with India was conceived and executed, and finally to investigate the circumstances that contributed to the rapid decline in Kazi's fortunes and prestige after I left Gangtok in early 1976.

Getting to the actual merger-related operations, they were not ordinary intelligence operations in which there is a clear nexus between the source or asset and its handler, where the source is duly compensated in one way or the other for the services rendered. They were more of a collaborative effort between the R&AW and the pro-democracy and pro-reform forces in Sikkim, who were previously repeatedly let down by India due to its policy of appeasement of the maharaja/Chogyal at the cost of their democratic aspirations. The R&AW was assigned the task of undoing that historical damage by providing these pro-democratic forces a level-playing field against the all-powerful and manipulating Chogyal, at a time when diplomacy had ceased yielding the desired results. I felt I was dealing with the remnants of Sikkim's freedom fighters who were unfortunately left to fend for themselves after the rest of the India attained independence in August 1947. Under the circumstances, I considered myself to be a sort of political assistant to the Kazi, sent by the Government of India (GoI) to help him achieve his lifelong dream of Sikkim's merger with India. The sophistication of the operation itself may be judged from the fact that even its main target—the former Chogyal—whom I met frequently to brief him about Tibet- and China-related intelligence matters, could not identify my link with the operation. Till the end, he and his family continued to blame the Intelligence Bureau (IB) for their troubles.

In closing, at its heart this book is a first-hand narration of what a three-man R&AW special operations team (spl ops) in Gangtok, headed by myself as OSD (P), did in response to then Prime Minister Indira Gandhi's directions to R.N. Kao in December 1972, asking him to 'do something about Sikkim'. I hope the readers find it interesting.

Acknowledgements

Information about the R&AW's merger-related special operations in Sikkim forms the heart of this book. It is primarily based on the entries that I made in a diary I started maintaining soon after my arrival in Gangtok in August 1973. Though I had decided much earlier to use the diary for writing this book, the inspiration came from the late R.N. Kao when I met him at his residence in 1988. I am extremely grateful to him for reposing confidence in a junior officer like me, who had barely served for nine years (with only eighteen months in the R&AW) at that time, for handling such a sensitive operation of national importance and then asking me to write this book. I wish I had accepted his offer of a short note, which he wanted to give me to include in this book as the first chapter. Nonetheless, he narrated its contents to me.

In addition to the role played by the other two members of my spl ops team, Padam Bahadur Pradhan and Myngma Tshering, the diary contains details of my meetings with the Chogyal, the political officer (PO), Kazi Sahib and some other senior Sikkim Congress leaders, and other persons with access to information of our interest. For the role played by the R&AW's operational team before my arrival in Gangtok (between February and May 1973, when the 8 May agreement was signed), I drew upon my pre-assignment briefings from the late P.N. Banerjee in Calcutta, and discussions with my predecessor in Gangtok and later my boss in New Delhi, A.S. Sayali, as well as Padam Bahadur, who is now enjoying a retired life in his home town, Kalimpong, near Gangtok. My special thanks to both of them. In addition, the late B.S. Das's book *Sikkim Saga* proved to be extremely useful in understanding the developments of that period in the correct perspective. Unfortunately, he died a few years ago, otherwise I would have surely called on him to seek his views on developments of our interest.

Before I commenced writing the book, it was essential to transcribe the contents of my diary. Surprisingly, it did not take me long to refresh my memory about what I had written forty-five years ago and to correlate its contents with the actual developments that took place. Having done so, I started dictating its contents to my daughter, Harmeeta. The whole process of reviewing and transcribing was over in less than a month. Thereafter, I continued to seek her help as and when I had to dictate my handwritten notes. This process continued till the end. When I started writing this book, my son, Gagan, provided valuable inputs at various stages to make it understandable for the readers. Some background information on Sikkim, before I came to the operational part of the book, was incorporated especially at his suggestion. I am thankful to both of them for their support.

My special thanks to Ambassador Bajpai, the then PO, for being extremely helpful to me both in Gangtok and during the last few months in New Delhi. In Gangtok, he shared all important information with me at regular intervals. In New Delhi, during my recent meetings with him, he shared whatever information of my interest that he had. I wished he and Mr Das had stayed in Gangtok longer. Had that been the case, things would not have come to such a pass as would require the disarming of the Sikkim Guards by the Indian army, that too one day before the state Assembly passed the merger-related resolutions.

I was always aware of the utility of the combined civil services foundation course at the National Academy of Administration, Mussoorie. But its real importance was understood when I landed in Gangtok. Three of my batchmates—Sudhir Devare and Gurdip Bedi from the Indian Foreign Service (IFS) and Krishan Murari Lal from the Indian Administrative Service (IAS)— were already posted there. In addition, two IAS officers from the 1965 batch of the West Bengal cadre—Jayant Sanyal and D.K. (Devi) Manavalan—also came to Sikkim along with Murari in April 1973 and were posted as OSDs in charge of districts to help B.B. Das run the administration in Sikkim. In addition to helping me settle down in Gangtok, they were a valuable source of information about what was happening in the state at that time. Devare was replaced by another of my batchmates from the IFS, Ranjit Gupta, in May 1974.

Fortunately for me, all the people mentioned above settled down in the National Capital Region (New Delhi), making it easier for me to have regular discussions with them to recapitulate developments of that crucial period. Devare wrote a six-page note which came in handy for me to understand the prevailing situation on the eve of the April 1973 agitations. In addition to sharing with me whatever he could recollect, Gupta helped me locate books of interest. I also met Kishan S. Rana, the then director (north) who had been sent by Foreign Secretary Kewal Singh to help PO Gurbachan Singh in the first half of April 1975. His input about his two visits to New Delhi during that period, to participate in discussions about the holding of a referendum on 14 April 1975, was rather useful. I had been meeting Murari, Sanyal and Manavalan regularly as they are neighbours. However, after preparing a specific brief for each of them with regard to the information required for my book, I also met them separately to seek information of my interest, which they shared willingly. I am grateful to all of them for their help.

From Sikkim, I am especially thankful to Karma Topden (who passed away on 8 August 2018), the former head of the Chogyal's intelligence set-up, who despite his illness took the trouble of coming to my residence during one of his consultation visits to New Delhi. He helped in clearing some doubts about his role and activities during that period. I was lucky to establish contact with the still going strong Nar Bahadur Khatiwada, who as the then adopted son of the Kazini played a significant role in mobilizing public demonstrations in Sikkim, especially in Gangtok, in April 1973 and thereafter. During one of his visits to New Delhi, he came to my residence for lunch. He clarified certain aspects of that fateful period. My special thanks to him for taking this trouble.

Lt Gen. Depinder Singh (retd), former GOC-in-C (southern command), as commander of the 64 Mountain Division oversaw the disarming operation of the Sikkim Guards on 9 April 1975. I had a two-hour session with him at the Gymkhana Club. Special thanks to him for sharing with me information on the decision, planning and execution of that operation. Now settled in Panchkula near Chandigarh, he was always available on the phone for further clarifications.

Once the skeleton of the book was ready, I started discussing parts of it with my old friends, Gurdip Bedi and Yogesh Tiwari (IFS, 1966), during my regular rounds of golf at Delhi Golf Club. Both of them contributed towards fine-tuning the description of some events and made several useful suggestions, many of which have been incorporated in the book. My special thanks to all those who might have helped me but whose names I am unable to mention here.

The ministry of external affairs' (MEA) old and declassified documents available at the National Archives, New Delhi, helped me understand the genesis of India's policy towards the Chogyal and Sikkim's pro-democracy and pro-reform parties. Further, a couple of visits to the Nehru Memorial Museum and Library at Teen Murti, New Delhi, helped me find two very useful documents from P.N. Haksar's papers, which have been quoted at appropriate places.

In addition, books like *Sikkim and Bhutan* by V.H. Coelho, *Indira Gandhi, the 'Emergency', and Indian Democracy* by P.N. Dhar, *Sikkim: Requiem for a Himalayan Kingdom* by Andrew Duff and *Smash and Grab* by Sunanda K. Datta-Ray came in handy to fill in the gaps from a historical perspective.

Also, special thanks to my editor, Ranjana Sengupta, and her colleague, Aditya Jha, from Penguin Random House, for their constant support throughout the writing process, as well as their valuable suggestions at the editing stage. They made me aware of the difference in the writing styles of an intelligence report and an assessment, comprising reliable and acceptable information without any constraints, and the need to exercise caution by a former intelligence officer in his post-retirement writing meant for public consumption. A good lesson for the future, provided I have the time to write a second book.

Introduction

The merger of Sikkim with India in May 1975 was a historic event in more than one way. Firstly, it undid the wrong done by India to the people of Sikkim by denying them the right to accede to, and finally merge with, the Union of India through the signing of the Instrument of Accession, as was the case with the rest of the 565 Indian princely states, which like Sikkim, were also members of the Chamber of Princes and the Constituent Assembly of India, before the country attained independence on 15 August 1947.

Secondly, to protect its strategic interests in this vulnerable and heavily defended sector along the Sino–Indian border, India no longer had to depend upon the whims and fancies, and the growing unpredictability, of the Chogyal who had long cherished the ambition to secure an independent status for Sikkim like that of neighbouring Bhutan. Imagine the implications of a dissatisfied, sulking or even a revolting Chogyal in the background of a Doklam-like face-off between China's People's Liberation Army (PLA) and the Indian army, with the Communist Party of China's People's Daily publication, *Global Times,* threatening to incite revolt in Sikkim against India.

Thirdly, through it, India's international borders achieved a finality, which will continue to remain the same unless minor adjustments, if any, are made based on mutual agreements with some of our neighbouring countries with whom we have festering territorial disputes. Though seven more states have been added to the list of member states comprising the Republic of India since 1975 (taking the total from twenty-two to twenty-nine), these were carved out through internal realignments of existing boundaries.

R&AW's operation relating to the merger of Sikkim continued to remain shrouded in mystery since it was first conceived by legendary spy and R&AW's founder head Rameshwarnath Kao sometime towards the end of December 1972. It was approved by then Prime Minister Indira Gandhi and launched in early February 1973. It was a unique operation, unlike any other of this magnitude and significance. Within the department, knowledge of its existence was confined to three people: Kao in New Delhi; P.N. Banerjee, joint director and regional head of R&AW's office in Calcutta; and the OSD (P) Gangtok, who was head of the R&AW's set-up in Sikkim. In Sikkim, initially, only Kazi, president of the Sikkim National Congress (SNC); and S.K. Rai, general secretary of the K.C. Pradhan-led Janata Congress, were taken into confidence about the scope of this operation. They were clearly told that the GoI had finally decided to lift its protective hand from the head of the Chogyal. Unlike in the past, when Tashi Tshering's (president of the Sikkim State Congress) 'no tax', 'no rent' campaign launched in 1949 was sabotaged by India, it would no longer stand in the way of the pro-democratic and pro-reform demands of the parties that had been fighting for political, administrative and other reforms since India's independence.

However, Kazi was the only one who was told that India would accept the demand for the merger of Sikkim in case he was able to build overwhelming support in its favour, both amongst the general public and in the yet-to-be-elected Assembly. Kazi, to his credit, did not share this information with anyone else till the last moment.

When I started writing this book, some of my friends advised me against mentioning the role of the R&AW in the merger of Sikkim. I did not know how such a book could be written or what useful purpose it would serve. Appreciating their suggestion made in good faith, I told them that it was Kao himself who had asked me to write this book in 1988. Had there been any chance of me disclosing any information that could go against the interests of national security, an extremely security-conscious person like Kao would not have asked me to write about the R&AW's role in Sikkim's merger in the first instance. Actually, there are situations where withholding such information from the public domain any longer becomes counterproductive and allows certain parties or individuals to push forward their predetermined conclusions in the hope that such facts as could counter their hypothesis would continue to remain buried under the thick cover of secrecy. It was over forty-three years ago that Sikkim merged with India. It is high time that the truth behind the merger be brought out. That would help remove the cobwebs of doubt, or even confusion, created in the minds of the people by some others to make them believe that there was no popular demand for Sikkim's merger and that the state was 'annexed' against the popular will of the majority of Sikkimese people, which was not the case.

The truth must be revealed, if nothing else, at least to redeem Kazi who devoted his lifetime to free Sikkim from the Chogyal's yoke, but was unfortunately accused of selling his 'country' to India. The worst part of all this was that while Kazi was being accused in the immediate aftermath of the merger, of selling his country to India, no Indian agency or person in authority could—or they chose not to—do anything to neutralize such false and motivated propaganda. Instead, they continued to remain mute witnesses to Kazi's agony.

As our operations in Gangtok related mostly to the careful handling of political figures of various hues and giving advice to the PO, as and when required, on the most suitable way of handling law-and-order problems resulting from the frustration of the Chogyal, it would be relevant to mention here, very briefly, my experience while performing my duties as an Indian Police Service (IPS) officer in Uttar Pradesh. After serving as a lecturer of history at the Government Ripudaman College, Nabha, Punjab, for two years, I joined the IPS in 1964 and was allotted to the Uttar Pradesh cadre. After passing out from the then Central Police Training College in Mount Abu as the best all-round probationer of my batch, and being awarded the Prime Minister's baton and the Home Minister's revolver, I was posted as assistant superintendent of police (ASP) Kanpur. I was able to squeeze in a month each in the summers of 1966 and 1967 to do the basic and advanced mountaineering courses at the newly opened Nehru Institute of Mountaineering in Uttarkashi.

As per past practice, the Uttar Pradesh Police were to hold the Annual Police Week celebrations in Lucknow in December 1967. I was called from Kanpur to participate in the ceremonial parade as the Uttar Pradesh Police's flag-bearer. Other than rehearsals for the parade in the mornings, the rest of the day used to be fun. But that was not to be this time. Rehearsals for the parade were stopped on the fourth day due to a strike, of which the Lucknow University campus was the nerve centre. While local police officers were assigned duties in the city and one of my batchmates was manning the control room, I was given one company of the

Provincial Armed Constabulary (PAC) and asked to stop the students from exiting the campus. Through an unorthodox and somewhat unauthorized action that followed, we were able to force the students to call off their strike by the evening of the third day. We were back on the parade ground the next morning. Fortunately, nothing serious happened at the university, otherwise I would have faced a judicial inquiry for trying to solve a problem in the capital city of Uttar Pradesh, where I had gone to participate in a ceremonial parade.

Thereafter, I was promoted and posted as Commandant (CO) of one of the PAC battalions in Sitapur. Within a few months of my reaching Sitapur, in the early summer of 1968, the visiting Inspector General of Police (IGP) Jia Ram asked me to proceed to Haridwar at a day's notice to assist the Superintendent of Police (SP) Ardh Kumbh Mela, R.K. Mishra, in his duties. It was a three-month assignment. The day went into supervising preparations and arrangements for the Kumbh Mela, and the evenings were spent listening to learned scholars of ancient Hindu scriptures, especially on the Bhagavad Gita and Ramayana.

In an otherwise caste-ridden society, with the bias reflected in government services too, as a Sikh and as an outsider, I enjoyed a privileged status both within the service and amongst the general public. While I was still posted in Sitapur, it was this privileged position that landed me a job which made me live literally out of a suitcase for two weeks, hopping from one dak bungalow to another to spend whatever was left of the night. Due to political uncertainty in Uttar Pradesh, the state was placed under President's rule in February 1968. There was a bitter struggle for power between the C.B. Gupta-led Indian National Congress (INC) and the Chaudhary Charan Singh-led Bharatiya Kranti Dal (BKD). This rivalry particularly manifested its ugly head in two western districts of Uttar Pradesh—Meerut and Muzaffarnagar—

which were considered strongholds of Chaudhary Charan Singh. After almost one year of President's rule, fresh elections to the UP Assembly were called on 5 February 1969. In the above-mentioned two districts, there was likelihood of sectarian violence and obstruction to scheduled-caste voters exercising their franchise.

It was under these circumstances that I was asked by IGP Jia Ram to report to the Deputy Inspector General (DIG), Meerut Range, to be used at his discretion as a standby firefighter. One day, I got a call from the DIG to report to SP (Muzaffarnagar) Banerjee immediately and help him control a potentially explosive situation. When I reached Muzaffarnagar a couple of hours later, I found Banerjee and the District Magistrate (DM) huddled in a meeting at the local Police Lines. I was told that a Congress candidate of a particular constituency (perhaps Shamli) had been assassinated, allegedly by BKD party workers. As a result, some heavily armed BKD leaders who had gathered at the house of a prominent party leader were under siege by equally well-armed Congress supporters. A small incident or accidental firing could lead to a massacre. I took one company of the PAC from the Police Lines with me, in addition to my personal guards, to the spot. Seeing a Sikh IPS officer, the pro-Congress crowd allowed me to enter the house of the BKD leader. There, I saw about twenty-five men, all armed with single- and double-barrel twelve-bore guns and a huge pile of cartridges, ready to defend their citadel. After a prolonged discussion, they agreed to return to their homes only if the crowd outside moved away. Similar persuasion and a personal assurance that the law would catch up with the culprits worked on the pro-Congress crowd. They started retreating gradually. However, a large contingent of the PAC, under the charge of local police officers, stayed back in the area for a few more days to ensure peace in the neighbourhood.

I got married in May 1969. I had been transferred to Agra as Additional SP, where I joined soon after the wedding. While in Sitapur I was riding horses in the morning and playing games in the evening; in Agra, I had to chase dacoits, mostly at odd hours. Thereafter, I was posted as SP (Barabanki), where I stayed for a little over two years until I opted for deputation to the R&AW. Those were the times when there was practically no political interference in police work. Recommendations would come in from the political leaders, but these were dealt with on merit and there were no complaints from their side on such an action.

The R&AW had been created in September 1968. I thought it would offer me better prospects for promotion, and in the process, I would be able to see some parts of the world by serving in Indian missions abroad. Being the best all-round IPS probationer of my batch, it should not have been difficult for me to join the R&AW had I personally met the senior officer concerned in this connection. But I preferred an easier and quicker way out. I requested my father-in-law, Sardar Swaran Singh, the then foreign minister of India, to recommend my case to R.N. Kao. This was the only occasion I ever used my connection with him insofar as my service matters were concerned. Later, I was gratified to know that after the merger of Sikkim with India, Kao personally thanked my father-in-law for recommending my name for deputation with the department.

I joined the R&AW in February 1972. After completing my training, I was posted as JAD (Joint Assistant Director, a post equivalent to that of an undersecretary) in charge of two of the personnel branches. I finally landed in Gangtok to take charge as the OSD (P) Gangtok on 27 August 1973.

Insofar as operational work was concerned, before the merger-related spl ops were launched, the R&AW's main role in Sikkim was to collect Tibet- and China-related intelligence. This had to be shared by the OSD (P) with the Chogyal, Palden Thondup Namgyal, through personal meetings at regular intervals. However, given the new requirements of planning and implementing the spl ops, my predecessor, A.S. Sayali had, in early February 1973, constituted a three-member team comprising himself, Senior Field Officer (SFO—equivalent in rank to a deputy superintendent of police) Padam Bahadur Pradhan (a Nepalese) and Deputy Field Officer (DFO—equivalent to a sub-inspector) Myngma Tshering (a Bhutia) for the job.

By the time I took over as OSD (P), the developments that followed the anti-Chogyal and pro-democracy demonstrations in April 1973—in Sikkim in general and in Gangtok in particular—had already forced the Chogyal to sign the 8 May 1973 tripartite agreement with the then Foreign Secretary Kewal Singh and the leaders of the major political parties. This agreement had significantly curtailed the powers of the Chogyal and laid the grounds for holding fresh elections in April 1974 under the aegis of the Election Commission of India (ECI).

The April 1974 elections resulted in a landslide victory for Kazi's Sikkim Congress (thirty-one seats out of thirty-two). Based on this, the next phase of the spl ops had to be planned and executed. While we awaited directions from New Delhi, we had to ensure that the Sikkim Congress Legislature Party remained a single solid block behind Kazi, and that he was able to withstand or block any Chogyal-inspired move to create dissension within its ranks.

In that context, while the magnitude of the Sikkim Congress's victory reduced the probability of any serious dissidence within the party, we had to be careful about the moves of some of the senior leaders of this party; such as the mercurial K.C. Pradhan[*] and the shifty B.B. Gurung.[**] Also, the Sikkim Congress's newly developed proximity (encouraged by the R&AW) with the Lepcha group led by Rinzing Lepcha[***] had to be nurtured and strengthened. In addition to that, it was important to know how the Chogyal would react to the new political realities arising out of the poor performance of the

---

[*] K.C. Pradhan belonged to a well-known Nepalese family from Sikkim. His elder brother, Keshav Chander Pradhan, was the chief conservator of forests during my stay at Gangtok. K.C. Pradhan was close to the Chogyal and was one of his Mahjong partners. During one of his meetings with the Chogyal, he was pulled up in the presence of his elder brother for wasting time on frivolous things. Pradhan walked out of the meeting in a huff and soon formed the Janata Congress that contested the January 1972 elections. His party won only two seats. He was one of Padam Bahadur's 'friends' (a term we used for all our operational contacts from the Sikkim Congress). Pradhan was stubborn and self-centred, and that made him difficult to handle. But he could be made to fall in line on occasion, either through the influence of his party general secretary S.K. Roy or even through saner advice favourable to his own political future.

[**] B.B. Gurung joined politics early in his life. A senior leader known for party-hopping from time to time, Gurung was also known for maintaining clandestine contact with the Chogyal. He was one of my 'friends' about whom I have given detailed comments at an appropriate place in this book.

[***] Rinzing Togden Lepcha was a well-known leader of the Lepcha community. As a representative of the pro-Chogyal National Party, he was a member of the executive council (cabinet) formed after the 1970 elections. He was also one of my 'friends', and we encouraged him to break ranks with the Chogyal-controlled National Party and join hands with Kazi to put forth a joint front against the Chogyal-inspired parties or individuals who contested the April 1974 elections. He and his followers finally joined the Sikkim Congress before that.

pro-Chogyal National Party. It was also important to keep an eye
on some other pro-Chogyal groups and individuals, especially the
carefully selected and cultivated Nar Bahadur Bhandari, who was
the young Nepalese face of the pro-Chogyal and anti-Kazi party
Sikkim United Independent Front (SUIF) that was propped up on
the eve of the April 1974 elections but failed miserably.

Subsequent to these elections, my first major move was to meet
the Chogyal to ascertain his views on the outcome under cover of
briefing him about trans-border intelligence. I called on him on
the afternoon of 20 April 1974. The meeting lasted for about
thirty-five minutes. For a change, he was not drinking. Briefing
him about the trans-border developments, I said that nothing
significant had been noticed in Tibet during the last couple of
months. As if he was not bothered about what was happening in
Tibet, he told me that he knew that but was concerned about a
lot of activities in Sikkim. In that context, he said the following:

> Let us see what happens next. It would have been better had
> the Government of India placed more faith in me. Although I
> know, I had in the past acted rashly but I have learnt a lot of
> lessons from my experience and now expect the Government of
> India to take a better view of me.
>
> The recent elections in Sikkim have created a communal
> feeling amongst various communities and my work of last
> twenty years has been undone. I had nursed Sikkim to a place
> of abundance with communal harmony but certain people are
> out to destroy it. I had been pleading with the Government of
> India right from the beginning that there should be a check
> over the movements of the Nepalese into Sikkim, so that
> they may not create a problem later on. But nobody listened
> to me. I had established a system whereby a Nepalese had to
> take permission from the local police even for moving from

one place to another in Sikkim. But that arrangement was made ineffective and it finally led to the present problem. The Government of India needs to be extremely vigilant about the growth of pan-Nepalese feelings in this area, including the activities of the Nepalese in Darjeeling district.

My thirty-five years of achievements in the economic field, of which I was rather proud, have been undone within the last one year. I had brought economic prosperity to the Sikkimese people by sheer hard work but now I cannot see the same being destroyed by certain incompetent persons.

Kewal Singh (foreign secretary) recently told one of our common friends that there was absolute peace in Sikkim but I asked him, 'Where is the peace?' Anti-social elements are taking advantage of the situation. Rustomji (an Indian Civil Service officer and a friend of the Chogyal who had served as a diwan in Sikkim in the 1950s) once told me that Sikkim was as small as a subdivision of an Indian district. Therefore, it should not be very difficult for all the administrators there to establish law and order, if they so desired.

What the Government of India did not have in Sikkim, I do not understand. Defence, foreign affairs, telecommunications, etc. What more does it want? We should be told so that details of the same can be worked out to mutual benefit. I will be going to Delhi sometime in May, to discuss matters of mutual importance and also to decide about my future. If the response is favourable, I will be happy, but if not, I have been running the show for the past thirty-five years and am now a bit tired, and would look forward to rest and lesser responsibilities.

I do not understand why certain people based in Gangtok (possibly referring to PO K.S. Bajpai) misunderstood me. I am rather sorry that I am being misquoted. It is my misfortune that I speak too much, but people who speak too much are

always good at heart and should not be looked down upon
with suspicion. People say that I have been talking to the press
irresponsibly. It is a fact that I did say something to the press
in the past, but most of the information was added by the
reporters on their own as per their habit.

As would be evident from the above, the Chogyal had by then
realized that only abject surrender to Prime Minister Indira Gandhi
could help him save his position, howsoever diluted it might be
in comparison to his previous exalted status. He obviously wanted
me to convey his significantly changed position to the prime
minister through Kao, which I did. But little did he realize that it
was too late for him and that no amount of pleading at that stage
would cut ice with her as she had already decided to accept the
demand for the merger of Sikkim with India, as and when it was
received from the popularly elected government. He was to be the
last Chogyal that Sikkim would see. Despite the difference in our
age and status, he was extremely courteous to me. I felt rather bad,
but was helpless in not being able to do anything for him. On the
contrary, we were the ones who were hastening his eclipse.

One would wonder how things came to such a pass that a
man who controlled Sikkim with an iron fist, and who was not
willing to negotiate with India on anything less than sovereign and
independent status for Sikkim as recently as September/October
1972, was trying to use my position to convey to Indira Gandhi
that he would be satisfied with much less than what was granted
to him through the Indo–Sikkim Treaty of 1950. Also, what had
the R&AW done that the Chogyal was using my services to make
desperate pleas to Indira Gandhi for forgiveness for his past acts
of omission and commission? These are some of the hitherto
unanswered questions that I have sought to address through this
book, in order to set the records straight.

Before I do so, it would be important to explain the background to how these operations were conceived and initiated, why a comparatively junior officer like me without any intelligence experience in the department was selected for the job, what was Sikkim's position during the British rule in India, how it escaped being absorbed in the Union of India as was the case with many other princely states that were similarly placed, what was independent India's approach towards Sikkim and why the carefully crafted Indian policy of appeasement of the Chogyal at the cost of democratic aspirations of a large majority of Sikkimese people underwent a sudden 180-degree turn in the middle of March 1973 (as far as the MEA's official position was concerned), and lastly, what were the constraints under which the three-member R&AW team headed by the OSD (P), especially created to implement merger-related operations, had to work. This has been clarified in the first six chapters.

Chapter I

Kao's Call

Sometime in September 1988, when I was posted at the R&AW headquarters in New Delhi as a joint secretary, I received a call from Kao who had retired in 1977. He wanted me to select some books on Sikkim and its merger with India. I picked up three to four volumes and got those delivered to his residence in New Delhi's upscale Vasant Vihar.

A month later, Kao called me again to ask about certain aspects of the R&AW's spl ops relating to the merger of Sikkim. It was not difficult for me to answer his questions. He complimented me on my capacity to retain minute details even though fifteen years had elapsed. I told him that it was mainly due to the fact that whilst at that time he was guiding the destiny of the whole of R&AW, I was dealing with the developments in a tiny place like Sikkim. Talking to Kao on the phone felt great. Given that he was the head of the department, we were in awe of him. In any case, our meetings with him were few and far between, and even during those brief interactions, we used to be sitting on the edge of our chairs, always conscious of our presence before a man of his stature.

In November 1988, I got another call from Kao. This time he wanted me to see him at his residence. I guessed the context but was not aware of what lay in store for me. At the entrance to his house, I was received by former SFO Saihgal, who had continued his close association with Kao even after retirement. With a broad grin, Saihgal, whose mannerisms had not changed over the years, said that 'sahib' had called me for an important 'assignment'. He left it to Kao to explain the details and ushered me into the study on the first floor where Kao was waiting. After making me feel comfortable, he got straight to the point.

Kao said that within a few years of the R&AW's creation, after the bifurcation of the IB in September 1968, the newly created department was able to launch two major successful operations. In fact, he described these operations as the crowning achievements of the nascent 'department' (a term often used by us old hands when referring to the R&AW). The first was the liberation of Bangladesh in December 1971, and the second was to do with the merger of Sikkim with India through resolutions passed in the Sikkim Assembly with an overwhelming majority in April 1975. He pointed out that the significant role played by the R&AW, and its creation Mukti Bahini, in the liberation of Bangladesh was fairly well known by then. However, the nature and extent of its spl ops relating to the merger of Sikkim with India had remained a closely guarded secret. That was because only three or four persons were involved in it. These included Kao, P.N. Banerjee (who was my immediate boss during my posting in Gangtok) and the OSD (P), Gangtok. According to Kao, not even his close confidant and his second in command, K. Sankaran Nair, was kept in the loop.

Continuing further, Kao said that as Banerjee had died—on 24 July 1974 due to a massive heart attack during one of his clandestine visits to Dhaka—and he himself was getting old, it would be better if I started writing a book on the role that the R&AW had played in the merger of Sikkim with India, particularly as most of the crucial developments on the ground took place during my tenure as OSD (P). In this context, he added that he had already written a note of about eighteen pages, covering the background and the circumstances under which this operation was conceived and launched. He added that he would be happy to give it to me, and that it could form the first chapter of my book. I thanked Kao for the confidence he reposed in me, but being extremely busy at that time, I expressed my inability to undertake the task. I, however, promised that one day after my retirement I would surely fulfil his wish. Kao appreciated my compulsions but added that he would, nevertheless, like to share with me some crucial information, which could be incorporated in the book as and when I decided to write it.

According to Kao, it was sometime towards the end of December 1972 that the then Prime Minister Indira Gandhi called him and her Principal Secretary, P.N. Haksar, to her office to discuss Sikkim. She mentioned that the Chogyal was being difficult, as he wanted to accept the offer of Permanent Association with India (with the possibility of India sponsoring Sikkim's membership of some UN-related organizations in the future) only if he was allowed to enter into this arrangement with the full sovereign rights of his state. This offer was personally carried to Gangtok for the last time in September 1972 by the then foreign secretary and a friend of the Chogyal, T.N. Kaul. Due to India's strategic interests in Sikkim, it could not have agreed to Sikkim entering into any such arrangement in its 'full sovereign rights', as the Chogyal's legal adviser from England had advised him to do. In view of that, Indira Gandhi pointedly asked Kao, 'Can you do something about Sikkim?' Kao told her that he would get back after a fortnight.

The timing of this meeting between the prime minister, Haksar and Kao, which resulted in a 180-degree turnaround in India's policy towards the Chogyal, was rather interesting. Foreign Secretary Kaul had retired in the first week of December 1972 to take up his new assignment as India's ambassador to the US. Kaul had been a close friend of the Chogyal since his days as maharaj kumar and had played a significant role in the formulation and implementation of India's policy of continued appeasement of the Chogyal, even at the cost of the democratic aspirations of the Sikkimese people, since his days as a joint secretary (MEA) in the early 1950s. While Kaul, as foreign secretary, was promoting a new treaty relationship of permanent association with Sikkim, offering the Chogyal much more liberal terms than contained in the treaty of 1950, Haksar was opposed to such a policy of capitulation to the Chogyal's whims and fancies.[1] He, however, did not mind minor concessions beyond what had been guaranteed to Sikkim through the 1950 treaty. While the merger of Sikkim with India was still unthinkable, Haksar was of the view that the Chogyal, who wanted nothing less than independence, could be made to accept whatever India wanted within the existing treaty relationship in a period of two years, if India handled the pro-democratic and anti-Chogyal forces properly. Indira Gandhi, who was aware of Haksar's views, somehow allowed Kaul to see if he could convince the Chogyal to accept the new permanent association relationship in lieu of the protectorate status which Sikkim enjoyed as per the 1950 Indo–Sikkim Treaty. Despite his persistent efforts till the end, Kaul failed to convince the Chogyal to agree to this new proposal.

Kaul was succeeded by a non-partisan foreign secretary, Kewal Singh. He did not suffer from any past hangover and agreed with Haksar's approach towards the Chogyal. It appears that Haksar might have consulted Singh and Kao before he set up the meeting with Indira Gandhi.

In this context, the remarks of P.N. Dhar—who succeeded Haksar as principal secretary to the prime minister—in his book *Indira Gandhi, the 'Emergency' and Indian Democracy* are rather interesting:[2]

> Kewal Singh was a shrewd officer who knew that the prime minister was dissatisfied with the way his predecessor had handled the Chogyal. He had no interest of his own to defend and had no difficulty co-operating with R.N. Kao, the head of R&AW. With Kewal Singh as Foreign Secretary and Kao as head of the intelligence and PMO as the clearing house of policy, Indira Gandhi was able to stay in constant touch with the situation in Sikkim.

After meeting Indira Gandhi along with Haksar, Kao summoned P.N. Banerjee to New Delhi and informed him of the prime minister's decision. He was asked to work out a suitable plan that would either get the Chogyal to agree to what was being offered or for a complete merger of Sikkim with India. Banerjee promised to work out an operational plan of action in consultation with the then OSD (P), Gangtok, A.S. Sayali, and get back to him as soon as possible.

Banerjee returned to Calcutta, but to Kao's surprise he was back in New Delhi along with Sayali in ten days. Banerjee told Kao that he could convey to the prime minister with confidence that it would be possible for us to deliver the desired results. However, the R&AW would need clear instructions as to what their final goal would be and the time frame within which the results were to be delivered. By this time, an operation, which was originally planned as a tactic to build pressure on the Chogyal to make him sign a new agreement or treaty, had assumed the role of an operation leading to the complete merger of Sikkim with India.

Kao, accompanied by Haksar, met the prime minister again and told her about the information he had got from Banerjee. He received on the spot clearance for launching the spl ops, with the final aim of facilitating the merger of Sikkim as an Indian state. The prime minister, however, told Kao that the operation had to be carried out in close collaboration with Kewal Singh, without of course disclosing any details to him.

I came to know what happened during those ten days—from the time Banerjee was first called by Kao to when he, along with Sayali, met Kao with their final operational plan—during a recent meeting with Sayali.[3] After his first meeting with Kao, Banerjee called Sayali on the phone from New Delhi and asked him to meet him in Calcutta. There, Banerjee and Sayali discussed the general outline of the operation. Sayali, who till then did not know the purpose for which he had been called, suggested that the anti-Chogyal and pro-reform political parties—which were, of course, dominated by the Nepalese—could be used to build pressure on the Chogyal to make him fall in line and compel him to do what the prime minister desired. As Banerjee's main focus till then was Bangladesh, he told Sayali to return to Gangtok and discuss the matter in detail with his SFO, Padam Bahadur Pradhan, and be ready for another brainstorming session with him at Gangtok. Sayali did as advised and was ready for more discussion on the subject with Banerjee, who came to Gangtok within three days of Sayali's return. Banerjee had a detailed discussion with Sayali and Padam Bahadur. Based on this, Sayali was asked to prepare a short note incorporating the various facets of the proposed operation, including an all-out merger of Sikkim as an Indian state. Banerjee visited New Delhi again. Sayali was also called to be present during the operational discussions with Kao. It was after that meeting that Kao and Haksar met the prime minister again, and she conveyed her clearance to launch this special operation with the ultimate aim of facilitating Sikkim's merger with India. The scope of this operation, and the various stages through which it actually passed during the subsequent twenty-seven months (February 1973 to April 1975), is discussed later in this book.

After final approval from Kao, Sayali withdrew two members of the R&AW's staff dealing with trans-border operations and formed a three-man special operation cell comprising himself, SFO Padam Bahadur and DFO Myngma Tshering. Padam Bahadur and Myngma were suitably briefed about the outlines of this operation without disclosing its ultimate aim, i.e., the merger. Sayali took Kazi into full confidence, but requested him not to share the details with anyone else lest the Chogyal was alerted. Padam Bahadur contacted his friend S.K. Rai, who was the general secretary of the K.C. Pradhan-led Janata Congress, and told him that the GoI was planning to lift its protective cover from over the Chogyal's head and extend full support to the anti-Chogyal parties to help them secure the political, economic and democratic reforms they had been fighting for. As Padam Bahadur was not told about the final goal, he did not tell this to Rai at this stage.

That the subject of Sikkim's merger with India was dear to Kao's heart became evident from the information that I received a couple of years ago from Rana Banerjee (an IAS officer of the Assam cadre, but no relative of P.N. Banerjee), former R&AW

special secretary.[4] Rana told me that in June 2000, a few days
before he proceeded to Kolkata to take charge as commissioner in
charge of the R&AW office there (a post earlier held by the late
P.N. Banerjee as joint director), he called on Kao at his residence
in New Delhi. Kao advised him to use this opportunity to gain
some knowledge about the operations Banerjee had carried out.
In this context, Kao specifically told Rana to study files about
my role during Sikkim's merger-related operations from 1973 to
1975, which he described as substantial.

During his two-year tenure in Kolkata, Rana studied files
relating to Bangladesh's liberation struggle and the merger-related
operations in Sikkim. Regarding my role, Rana told me that
Banerjee, in his correspondence with Kao, had made a number of
complimentary references. Rana completed his tenure in Kolkata
in July 2002 but could not thank Kao for having encouraged him
to read the old files as Kao had passed away by then.

Due to my inability to undertake the task of writing this book
in 1988, the note that Kao wanted to hand over to me eventually
made its way to the Nehru Memorial Museum and Library in
New Delhi in 2000, when Kao handed over seven short notes on
his recollections of certain events during his career. At the time
of submission of these notes to the library, the Sikkim note was
clubbed with two other notes, one on Bangladesh and the second
on a more sensitive subject—Indira Gandhi's assassination. As
per Kao's instructions, these three notes will be opened for public
consultations in 2027, twenty-five years after his death in 2002.

As mentioned in the previous chapter, I joined the R&AW in
February 1972. Sometime in early July 1973, I got a call from

Shivraj Bahadur, staff officer to Kao, the then R&AW secretary, to see him in his office in South Block. When I met Bahadur the next day, he wanted to know whether I would like to go to Sikkim as OSD (P), Gangtok. He said he was asking because Kao, in consultation with Banerjee, had shortlisted me for a very sensitive and important Sikkim-related operation. It was a bit of a pleasant surprise as this was the first time that somebody had sought my availability for any assignment or posting, and that too for a post normally given to officers more senior than me. I readily agreed, but some doubts continued to linger in my mind. One thing was obvious: my consent was being sought as I was the son-in-law of the then foreign minister, a senior member of Indira Gandhi's cabinet and one of her close confidants. With such a background, Kao might have felt that I may like to be posted to North America or Europe rather than Gangtok.

Another thing that I could not understand was that with only a little over a year's experience in the R&AW, and that too in the personnel branches, what was so special about me that I was shortlisted for a sensitive operation like that. However, I came to know the real reason only after reaching Gangtok, and that too after meeting some of our 'friends' from the political parties involved in furthering the cause of this operation. The reason was that the anti-Chogyal political leadership in Sikkim and their cadre, who had launched the April 1973 agitations under the R&AW's encouragement (leading to the signing of the 8 May 1973 agreement), were highly suspicious of the GoI's intentions. The majority was apprehensive that India might be using them to bring the recalcitrant Chogyal to his senses, enter into a deal with him and finally ditch them.

That India had let down their popular leader Tashi Tshering in 1949 was still fresh in the minds of the pro-democracy leaders in Sikkim.[5] Even the Chogyal exploited that situation by continuously feeding the Sikkim Congress leaders information that India was working out a compromise formula with him. In fact, during my meeting with Kazi and youth leader Nar Bahadur Khatiwada at my residence in April 1974, when they came over to discuss the Government of Sikkim Bill of 1974, Khatiwada specifically told me that a number of Sikkim Congress leaders were still apprehensive of India's true intentions. I, thereafter, had to assure Khatiwada in Kazi's presence that as long as I was the OSD (P), nothing of that sort would happen. I had the advantage of two important connections to assure the Sikkim Congress leaders that they would not be let down this time. I was a part of the cabinet secretariat directly under the charge of the prime minister. Second, I was the son-in-law of the foreign minister. The posting of a person of my background and the assurances I gave them that, unlike in 1949, this time there would be no going back and that we would extend support to them till the end, went a long way in assuaging their apprehensions, which was very crucial to the success of the R&AW's operation.

Chapter II

Namgyals and the British Imperialism

Originally, Sikkim was inhabited by three tribes: the Naong, Mon and Chang. The Lepchas, who came from somewhere along the borders of Tibet and Burma through Assam, were assimilated with the earlier inhabitants. They speak a Tibeto-Burman language and have accepted Mahayana Buddhism, although the pre-Buddhist Lepcha religious practices have also influenced Sikkimese Buddhism to some extent.[1]

The Tibetans, including the Namgyals, who later came to be known as Bhutias, started coming into Sikkim from the thirteenth century. They previously lived a pastoral life on the plateaus of Tibet, especially in the Kham area. They belonged to the Rnying Ma Pa (The Old Order), a liberal sect of Mahayana Buddhism.[2] Most of them settled down as farmers, although some still preferred to live in the high valleys of northern Sikkim, herding yaks and sheep. They named the territory they occupied Ren-jong (also called Den-jong or 'the valley of rice').

The other tribes are either indigenous to Sikkim or have lived here for centuries. The latter includes the Magars and Tsongs who entered Sikkim from the trans-Himalayan region in the prehistoric period. The largest migration into Sikkim took place between the mid-eighteenth and nineteenth centuries, when various tribes entered from northern and eastern Nepal. The first

Nepalese group was the Newar, a Tibeto-Burman people skilled in metalwork. They were followed by the Gurungs, Tamangs and Rais. They entered Sikkim via Tibet and were adept in farming at high altitudes. Other groups that migrated from Nepal included clans of Chhetris, Bahuns, Bishus, Karmas, etc. The various Nepalese-origin tribes spoke their own languages—at present, most of them speak Nepalese, which is also called Gorkhali.

According to the Limbu tradition, the name 'Sikkim' was a corruption of the Limbu word 'sukhim' meaning the 'happy house' or 'new house'.

At one point, Sikkim's borders extended as far as Ilam in Nepal. In a series of wars that lasted nearly a century, Nepal occupied part of western Sikkim but was obliged to relinquish most of it in 1793 and the rest in 1816 due to British intervention.

The majority of educated Sikkimese of Nepalese origin are of the view that their description as 'Nepalese' is misleading, as that makes them feel like 'foreigners' in their own state (Sikkim) and country (India). They consider themselves the Gürkhas of Sikkim, on the same lines as the Gurkhas of West Bengal, including Darjeeling, and also of Nepal.[3] According to them, Nepalese-speaking Sikkimese belong to both the ethnic groups of Gurkhas namely the Khas (of Caucasian lineage who originally migrated from Central Asia and include the Chhetris, Bahuns, Kamis and Sarkis, etc.)—and the Kiratas (the original inhabitants of the Himalayan and the sub-Himalayan regions, which include the Limbus (Tsongs), Rais, Magars, Gurungs, Tamangs and Newars, etc.).[4]

They are also of the view that the origin of the word 'gurkha' can be traced to Guru Gorakhnath, who inducted the Khas people into Hinduism in the eleventh century AD. Thereafter, the Khas started getting divided into castes and sub-castes. Some others feel that as the Khas were originally nomadic, engaged in cattle

herding and fiercely protective of cows, they came to be known
as 'gau rakhas'.[5] According to them, the religious divide amongst
various sections of Sikkimese society was deliberately escalated by
the Sikkim durbar for political gains and to maintain its hold over
the Sikkimese population.

The twelfth and last Chogyal* from the Namgyal dynasty, Palden
Thondup Namgyal (1963–75), and his predecessors claimed
their lineage to the legendary Khye Bumsa, 'the superior of
10,000 heroes', who came to Sikkim in the thirteenth century.
Originally from Chumbi Valley, Bumsa came in close contact
with the Lepchas and signed a blood brotherhood treaty with
Thekong Tek, a Lepcha chieftain, in Kabi Lungchok, north of
Gangtok. This treaty established new ties of brotherhood between
the Lepchas and the Bhutias. While Bumsa returned to Chumbi
Valley and died there, one of his descendants, Phuntsog Namgyal,
was later installed as the first Chogyal (1642–70) of Sikkim at
Yuksom in 1642. Phuntsog Namgyal divided his kingdom into
twelve 'dzongs' or districts and appointed a dzongpen in charge
of each of these districts. The second Chogyal, Tensung Namgyal
(1670–1700), moved his capital from Yuksom to Rabdentse and
elevated many of these dzongpens to the rank of councillors to
the king.[6] Later, these councillors came to be known as kazis, who

---

* The title of Chogyal means 'dharamraja' or religious and temporal head
  of a kingdom. It fell into disuse during the British rule as they started
  addressing the king first as Sikkimputee Raja (Treaty of Titalia, 1817,
  and Darjeeling Grant, 1835) and later as Maharaja (Treaty of 1861).
  The title of Chogyal was restored after repeated requests by Thondup to
  the GoI, a few days before his coronation in April 1965.

enjoyed immense power and privileges. Much later, some of the Lepchas were also given the title of kazi, but most Lepcha kazis were in charge of collecting land revenue and other taxes for the Chogyal and enjoyed lesser power and prestige as compared to their Bhutia counterparts.

During the rule of the fourth Chogyal, Gyurmed Namgyal (1717–33), the capital town of Rabdentse was fortified due to constant fear of Gurkha and Bhutanese raids. However, the Nepalese on their own, and in collaboration with the Bhutanese, continued to occupy Sikkimese territories. Bhutan captured all the area east of the river Teesta, but withdrew to present frontiers after a negotiation. A peace treaty was signed with Nepal in 1775, and the Gurkhas promised to abstain from further attacks and collaboration with the Bhutanese. But the Gurkhas later violated the treaty and occupied large areas of western Sikkim. The seventh Chogyal, Tsugphud Namgyal (1793–1863), shifted the capital from Rabdentse to Tumlong as it was farther away from Nepal.

In the initial stages, common interests against the expansionist kingdom of Nepal brought the British closer to Sikkim. Thereafter the kingdom of Sikkim became important for the British as it provided easy access to Tibet through Chumbi Valley. Sikkim had already lost some territory to Nepal in the south and west districts, and the British did not like the expansionist moves of the Shahs of Nepal in that region. This clash of interests led to the Anglo-Nepal war of 1814–16 in which Sikkim provided logistical support to the British. The signing of the Treaty of Sagauli with Nepal in 1815 and the Treaty of Titalia with Sikkim in 1817 resulted in Nepal returning a major portion of Sikkimese territory.

With both Nepal and Sikkim satisfied with this relationship, the British established themselves as peacekeepers in this region.

The growing British proximity to Sikkim in the aftermath of the treaty of 1817 resulted in the seventh maharaja, Tsugphud Namgyal, ceding 'all the land south of the Great Rangeet River, east of the Balsan, Kahil and little Rangeet rivers and west of the Rungpo and Mahanadi rivers' to the British in 1835. This transfer, better known as the Darjeeling Grant,[7] was secured by the British through dubious and unethical means, for use as a sanatorium or hill station, without any reciprocal transfer of areas, which the Sikkimese expected. Prolonged correspondence about compensation by the British in the form of territory proved futile. Finally, in 1841, the British agreed to pay an annuity of Rs 3000 from the date of announcement which was raised to Rs 9000 in 1868 and to Rs 12,000 in 1874. This annuity was temporarily stopped in 1849 when two British nationals, Dr Campbell and Dr Hokier, were maltreated by the Sikkimese.

With Darjeeling as a base, the East India Company started planning the opening of the crucial Chumbi Valley trade route with Tibet. However, the dubious and unethical manner in which the Darjeeling Grant was secured continued to be a bone of contention between the two. This simmering discontent led to the British sending a 1800-strong armed contingent to teach Sikkim a lesson. However, before anything serious could happen, the Sikkimese sued for peace and the Anglo-Sikkim treaty of peace and friendship was signed at Tumlong in March 1861. As Tsugphud refused to return from Chumbi Valley this treaty was signed by his son Sidkeong on his behalf. This was the first time that the title of maharaja was used by the British for Sikkim's ruler. Through the Treaty of Tumlong, the British also secured trading rights through Sikkim. This treaty, which superseded the 1817 Treaty of Titalia, laid the foundation of the Anglo-Sikkim relations for as long as the British ruled India. It even continued to be in force after India's independence till a new relationship with Sikkim was formed with the signing of the December 1950 Indo-Sikkimese Treaty, which recognized Sikkim as a protectorate of independent India.[*]

Tsugphud Namgyal's seventy-year rule (1793–1863) was the longest by any Namgyal ruler of Sikkim. He married five times. His eldest surviving son, Sidkeong, from his second wife was born in 1819 and was the eighth maharaja (1863–74). After his death in 1874, Sidkeong was succeeded by his half-brother, Thotub Namgyal (1874–1914).

During the rule of the ninth maharaja, Thutob Namgyal (1874–1914), a number of important developments took place. Using Sikkim as a base, the British opened a trade route to Tibet. This invited retaliation from Tibet when, in 1888, they occupied some territory in the Lingthu area of Nathang Valley on this side of Jelep La and constructed a small fort about 20 km inside Sikkimese territory. With the maharaja vacillating, and even overlooking growing Tibetan influence in this area, a British contingent was sent to Lingthu. In the battle that followed, the Tibetans were defeated and forced to retreat across Jelep La. With the British campaign finally ending in September 1888, Sikkim virtually came under the supervision and control of the first British PO, John Claude White, who was

---

[*] As per the treaty of 1861, which governed the relations between the British government and the Sikkim durbar, the latter was entitled to collect an ad valorem duty up to 5 per cent on all goods passing through Sikkim out of Tibet, Bhutan and Nepal. But Sikkim had refrained from exercising this right, despite the fact that by 1947, when India gained independence, the total value of annual trade had reached Rs 1 crore. Information sourced from the National Archives (Ministry of States PR Branch file no. 5–PR/47).

appointed in 1889 to look after the British interests in Sikkim, Bhutan and Tibet.

Thotub Namgyal had three sons. Two of them—Tshodak and Sidkeong Tulku (who were born in 1878 and 1879, respectively)—were from his first wife while the third one—Tashi Namgyal (who was born in 1893)—was from his second wife.

Despite protests from the maharaja, Sidkeong Tulku was brought to Darjeeling and placed under the charge of a private tutor. The British felt that the eldest son of the maharaja, Tshodak Namgyal, who was studying in Tibet, had to be brought back to keep him away from the anti-British Tibetan influence, to which the maharaja did not agree. This led to a three-year exile for the maharaja in 1892, to Kurseong near Darjeeling. Meanwhile, in 1894, the capital of Sikkim was shifted from Tumlong to Gangtok. Though the maharaja returned to Gangtok in 1895, only partial power was restored to him in 1905, due to Sikkimese support during the 1904 Younghusband expedition. In the following year, i.e., 1906, the affairs of the state of Sikkim were transferred from the government of Bengal to the GoI.

It was during Thutob Namgyal's rule that the simmering dispute between Sikkim and Tibet ended, with representatives of the British and Chinese governments signing the Anglo-Chinese Convention of Calcutta in March 1890. The interesting part of this convention was that the main stakeholders—Sikkim, Bhutan and Tibet—were not taken on board during the course of negotiations or even at the time of signing the convention document. This convention recognized British and Chinese interests in Sikkim and Tibet, respectively. It had eight articles. The first three and important articles are reproduced below:

The boundary of Sikkim and Tibet shall be the crest of the mountain range separating the waters flowing into the Sikkim Teesta and its affluents from the waters flowing into the Tibetan Mochu and northwards into other rivers of Tibet. The line commences at Mount Gimpochi on the Bhutan frontier and followed the abovementioned water-parting to the point where it meets Nepal territory.

It is admitted that the British Government, whose protectorate over the Sikkim State is hereby recognized, has direct and exclusive control over the internal administration and foreign relations of that State, and except through and with the permission of the British Government, neither the Ruler of the State nor any of its officers shall have official relations of any kind, formal or informal, with any other country.

The Government of Great Britain and Ireland and the Government of China engage reciprocally to respect the boundary as defined in Article I, and to prevent acts of aggression from their respective sides of the frontier.

A protocol to the convention of 1890 was signed in December 1893, which regulated trade, communications and pasturage.

The exact location of the tri-junction—where the boundaries of the three countries meet in this area—had remained a point of dispute between China on one side and India and Bhutan on the other since India's independence. The seventy-three-day standoff in June 2017 between the PLA and the Indian army in Doklam has to be viewed in this context. There appear to be three reasons for the PLA's transgression into the Doklam area. Firstly, China wanted to assert its right to settle its boundary dispute with Bhutan bilaterally through a package deal. According to this deal, Beijing would cede about 500 sq. km of territory in the Jakurlung and Pasamlung valleys in northern Bhutan in return for Bhutan ceding control of Doklam area, which includes the Jampheri Ridge that overlooks India's militarily vulnerable Siliguri Corridor, also called 'chicken's neck'—the only, and very narrow corridor connecting the Northeast with the rest of India. Secondly, it wanted to see whether, under pressure from China, Bhutan could be forced to come out of the comfort of its special relationship with India and agree to settle its boundary dispute with China on a bilateral basis. Thirdly, China wanted to test India's guts and gauge how far it would go to assist Bhutan, that too at a time when its own strategic interests in the region were being threatened by China.

Bhutan did not recognize the Indo-China convention, as it was not a party to it. But beginning 1988—when a status quo agreement was signed with the Chinese—till now, the Bhutanese have had twenty-four rounds of talks with the Chinese to settle their boundary dispute. On the Indian side, due to Bhutan's special relations with India, this matter is also being discussed between the special representatives (SRs) of India and China as part of the overall border dispute between the two countries. The twentieth round of SR talks was held at New Delhi on 22 December 2017. During the 2012 talks, it was agreed that the dispute in this area would be resolved in consultation with the third party (Bhutan) involved. Though the Chinese claimed that the Doklam issue was not discussed at the latest round of talks between the two SRs, according to some reports, the standoff was a part of the discussions, with the two sides exchanging ideas on how to avoid recurrence of such incidents.

During my posting as OSD (P), Gangtok, I visited our forward post Kupup a number of times. Kupup abuts Jelep La. From there, we could clearly observe the Doklam area. On being asked to identify the tri-junction in this area, the officers posted at Kupup used to point towards Batang La. According to Claude Arpi, a well-known French scholar on Sikkimese affairs,[8] as per Sikkimese records Gipmochi is a part of Batang La and is about 4 km north of the Indian army-manned Doka La post. If that is the case, Doklam, which is south of Batang La, belongs to Bhutan, and the Chinese claim over Doklam falls flat. The standoff resulting from the road-building activity in there by the PLA troops, which was noticed on 16 June 2017, was stopped after the intervention of the Indian troops.

During the course of this seventy-three-day standoff, the Communist Party of China-controlled media tried to whip up anti-India feelings. The 5 July issue of *Global Times*, published by the Communist Party's People's Daily, called for teaching a 'bitter lesson' to India by making it suffer losses heavier than 1962. In the next day's issue, this paper commented that 'although China had recognized in 2003, India's annexation of Sikkim, it can readjust its stance on the matter . . . as long as there are voices in Chinese society supporting Sikkim's independence, the voices will spread and fuel pro-independence appeal in Sikkim.'

The standoff came to an end as a result of an hour-long meeting on 5 September 2017, on the sidelines of the BRICS summit in Xiamen. During this meeting, Prime Minister Narendra Modi and President Xi Jinping decided to 'shelve differences' and make further efforts to enhance mutual trust. It was also decided to maintain strong contacts between the two defence forces and strengthen security mechanisms to avoid recurrence of such situations and maintain peace and tranquillity on the borders. But due to the very nature of the border dispute, claims and counterclaims by the contesting parties would continue in one form or the other, as long as there is no formal agreement amongst them. Meanwhile, the PLA had constructed military infrastructure, such as helipads, in the northern Doklam area already under their control and stationed about 1600 troops for the first time during the ensuing winter.

With the establishment of the residency or the political office in Gangtok, British presence in Sikkim assumed greater significance as they started using it to influence events in Tibet and even in Bhutan. To avoid the mounting pressure from the Chinese, the Dalai Lama escaped from Tibet to Gangtok in 1911 and spent about two years in Darjeeling before returning to Lhasa. This marked the beginning of the growing British influence on the Dalai Lama. The same year, i.e., 1911, the maharaja of Sikkim was honoured by the Imperial Delhi Durbar and officially granted a fifteen-gun salute, far greater than what was warranted.

The PO was also instrumental in sidelining the claim of succession of the designated heir and the eldest son of Maharaja Thotub Namgyal, Tshodak Namgyal, who had refused to return from Tibet. As a result, his younger brother Sidkeong Tulku was installed as the tenth maharaja in 1914 after the death of his father. Sidkeong died in December 1914, within ten months of ascending the throne, under the most bizarre circumstances. A British doctor who was sent to him gave him an extra dose of brandy and covered him with thick quilts, and a charcoal heater was put under his bed.[9] The result of such treatment was a foregone conclusion. Sidkeong had been educated in England and had spent one year at Oxford. He was a very intelligent man, and the people of Sikkim had great expectations from him. It was not known if the British wanted to get rid of him—to replace him with his more pliable half-brother Tashi Namgyal as the eleventh maharaja (1914–63).

Full powers were restored to the maharaja only in 1918. In 1935, Sikkim became a member of the Chamber of Princes. Tashi Namgyal's elder son and designated heir, Prince Paljor, who had joined the Royal Indian Air Force, died in Peshawar when his aircraft crash-landed in December 1941. Tashi Namgyal's rule lasted for almost fifty years—he died in 1963, sixteen years after India became independent. Saddened by the death of his eldest son, Tashi Namgyal had left the affairs of the state in the hands of his second son, Palden Thondup Namgyal, who was just eighteen years old when his brother died. Thondup succeeded his father in 1963, and after repeated requests to the GoI, he was bestowed the title of Chogyal, a few days before his coronation in April 1965.

On the eve of India's independence, the British Empire in India comprised some directly administered provinces and around 600 princely states with whom they had established relations over a period of 100 years through subsidiary alliances. In addition, there were some colonial enclaves under French and Portuguese control. The decision of the British to leave India resulted in the formation of two separate countries: India and Pakistan. It was easy to transfer the provinces directly administered by the British to the successor governments in India and Pakistan, but dealing with the princely states was a difficult task. Of the 600 such states, approximately 566, including Sikkim, were linked to India and the remaining to Pakistan.[10]

When the British finally decided to leave India and hand over power to the successor government/governments, the then Viceroy of India, Lord Wavell, issued a declaration in May 1946 on behalf of the British government. It indicated that in the wake of the planned transfer of power, subject states will have to enter into 'a federal relationship with the successor government or governments in British India or, failing this, enter into particular political arrangements with it or them'. The Indian Independence Act of 1947 formally ended the British paramountcy over these princely states. According to this Act, on transfer of power on 15 August 1947, all the princely states were free to join either India or Pakistan, or could choose to become independent.

These states, with a large population, occupied more than half of emerging India's territory. Therefore, Indian political leaders and senior officials involved in the transfer of power felt that unless a single federal structure with a strong government at the centre was in place, India would always be susceptible to political, military and social conflicts. All these states, including Sikkim, had two things in common. They were members of the Chamber of Princes created by the Government of India Act of 1935 and also of the Constituent Assembly of India, established to frame the Constitution. Sikkim, an Indian state with an area of 2818 square miles (7298.5 sq. km) and a population of just 1,21,520, was also represented in these institutions. In view of that, like any other princely state, a Sikkimese delegation led by Maharaj Kumar Thondup landed in New Delhi soon thereafter and started consultations with other members of the Chamber of Princes and the leaders of the impending successor government of India. However, Thondup's efforts to secure any assurance about Sikkim's special status from the concerned British officers, through meetings arranged directly or through the then PO Arthur John Hopkinson, failed to elicit a satisfactory response.

The Constituent Assembly of India had 229 members elected by the provincial assemblies comprising British-ruled areas. In addition, princely states had a quota of seventy members. Bigger states had more than one member in the Assembly, but the smaller states were grouped together to let them have a joint single representation. In that category, Cooch Behar represented a group of some small states, including Sikkim, in the Constituent Assembly. The interim government of India (known as the Viceroy's Executive Council) was formed on 2 September 1946 out of the members of this Constituent Assembly. Sardar Vallabhbhai Patel was given the charge of home and minister of states. Jawaharlal Nehru was vice president of this council and member in charge of external affairs and Commonwealth relations. The Constituent Assembly met for the first time on 9 December 1946.

Fortunately for India, Sardar Patel, popularly known as the Iron Man of India, was the minister of home and states affairs of the interim government. Patel was ably supported by an outstanding civil servant, V.P. Menon, whom Patel had appointed as secretary in charge of his ministry. They were able to enlist support even from Lord Mountbatten, the last British Governor General of India, in assuring the princes of the good faith in which these negotiations were being carried out.

The Government of India Act of 1935 had introduced the concept of the instrument of accession, wherein the ruler of a princely state could accede to the federation of India. The instrument of accession was a legal document designed to bring about accession of the consenting princely states and was to be executed by the GoI on the one hand and by the rulers of each of the princely states, individually, on the other.

Patel started meeting these princes in groups, and sometimes individually, from May 1947. While these negotiations were taking place, on 5 July 1947, Patel unveiled his government's policy based on the concept of instrument of accession. Through the signing of a bilateral instrument of accession, the states were to accede to India on three subjects—foreign affairs, defence and communication—leaving all other issues to the states to administer, although at a later stage they would be encouraged to hand over power to an elected government. To hasten the process of signing the instrument of accession to meet the deadline of 15 August 1947, the day of transfer of power by the British to the Indian government, Patel assured the princes that the Congressmen, irrespective of their political ideology, were not their enemies, but would respect their rights to property and estates and civil liberties. He also assured them that their loss of income would be adequately compensated through the grant of privy purses. The last assurance had been granted in the face of opposition from the socialist group of the Congress, including Nehru, who did not like that Patel had bypassed the cabinet on this important decision. But Patel saw to it that the provision was incorporated in the Constitution. Later, in 1971, the Congress government under Indira Gandhi repealed this proviso by bringing in a constitutional amendment. Patel also played upon their patriotic feelings and allowed and encouraged them to contest for public office.

Patel's effort paid dividends. By 15 August 1947, as many as 562 of the 566 Indian princely states had signed the instrument of accession. Only Sikkim and three other states—Junagadh, Hyderabad and Kashmir—continued to resist. The last three were finally made to join the Union of India through coercion, threat of and even use of force. With the promulgation of the Constitution of India on 26 January 1950, the Union of India became a modern and contemporary republic, replacing the Government of India Act of 1935 as the country's fundamental governing document. The integration of the princely states was finally complete in 1956, when the States Reorganization Act, redrawing the boundaries of these states on linguistic lines, was implemented.

As Sikkim fulfilled the basic criterion of signing the instrument of accession with India, Sardar Patel and B.N. Rau— constitutional adviser to the Constituent Assembly—were in favour of treating it on a par with the other princely states, like any other member state of the Chamber of Princes, making it enter into a bilateral instrument of accession with India. Nehru, on the other hand, due to his idealism, Pan-Asia vision and sensitivity to the Chinese concerns in this region, wanted Sikkim to be treated as a special case.

It was in this context that Nehru moved the following resolution on Sikkim and Bhutan in the Constituent Assembly meeting held on 22 January 1947, in the Constitution Hall, with Rajendra Prasad (the first President of the Republic of India after the Indian Constitution was promulgated) acting as chairperson.

> . . . this Assembly resolves that the Committee constituted by its Resolution of December 21 1946 (to confer with the Negotiation Committee set up by the Chamber of Princes and with other representatives of Indian States for certain specified purposes), shall in addition, have powers to confer with such persons as the Committee thinks fit for the purpose of examining the special problems of Bhutan and Sikkim and to report to the Assembly the results of such examinations.

While describing the purpose for which the above-mentioned committee was formed, Nehru significantly remarked that, 'Bhutan is in a sense an independent state under the protection of India. Sikkim is in a sense an Indian state but different from others.'

This resolution was finally adopted.

That Nehru's decision to treat Sikkim as a special case was a mistake was recognized by Prime Minister Indira Gandhi. She shared her views on this matter with Principal Secretary P.N. Dhar during the course of the R&AW's spl ops undertaken to facilitate the merger of Sikkim with India. Dhar, in his book *Indira Gandhi, the 'Emergency' and Indian Democracy*, noted that:[11]

> She told me in very clear terms that her father had made a mistake in not heeding the Sikkimese demand for accession to India in 1947. She said she never asked him about his decision in the matter, but her guess was that he had assumed that the

Chinese would leave Tibet's autonomy undisturbed and, in anticipation of this, he had perhaps thought it fit to do nothing in Sikkim that would provoke them. She had no hesitation in admitting that in retrospect Sardar Patel's instinctive reaction seemed correct. The short point that emerged was that we should undo our earlier mistake and support the people of Sikkim in their struggle against the Chogyal which they had launched in 1973.

In furtherance of the resolution adopted by the Constituent Assembly on 22 January 1947, a meeting was held in the chamber of V.P. Menon, the secretary in the states department (present-day home ministry) on 3 June 1947.[12] In addition to Menon, it was attended by Maharaj Kumar Palden Thondup Namgyal, T.D. Densapa and Roop Narayan from Sikkim, and J.D. Dorji as the representative of Bhutan. The MEA was represented by Joint Secretary P.A. Menon.

Sikkim's case was presented by Roop Narayan, the maharaja's legal adviser. He said that in view of its geographical location, cultural and other affinities with the people of Tibet and Bhutan, Sikkim was unlike any other Indian state and would not fit into the Union of India. Though he specifically accepted that Sikkim had so far been treated as an Indian state, he said he would now like it to be placed on the same footing as Bhutan.

As the decision to give special status to Sikkim had already been taken at Nehru and Patel's level, without examining the merits of the case presented by Roop Narayan, Menon, on his own, mentioned that Sikkim could adopt one of the following two courses:

a) To accede to India on the three subjects: defence, external affairs and communication, or,

b) Without accession, enter into an agreement on these subjects with India.

Menon did not question the Sikkimese delegation as to how just 12 per cent of the population of the state, comprising Bhutias of Tibetan origin, could represent the interest of its entire population, and how the remaining 88 per cent (13 per cent Lepchas and 75 per cent Nepalese) could have religious and cultural affinity with Tibet and Bhutan. Menon straightaway accepted that the position of Sikkim was different from that of any other Indian state and approximated more closely to that of Bhutan. He did not, therefore, feel that it would be necessary for Sikkim to enter the Union of India and voluntarily suggested that both Sikkim and Bhutan might adopt the second of the two courses listed above.

Bhutanese representative Dorji said that he did not have the authority to commit on this subject at the time. The representatives of Sikkim expressed their thanks and said that they were satisfied with the explanation the secretary gave. Menon then made it clear that, pending the conclusion of the new agreement, it would be necessary for Sikkim to sign a standstill agreement for the maintenance of status quo. A copy of the draft agreement was handed over to the representatives of Sikkim, and they were asked to come back with their proposal on the subject in due course. Menon also said that he did not consider it necessary for Sikkim to be represented at the states' conference called by his department on 25 July 1947. It was also agreed that till such time as the standstill agreement was signed, the relationship with Sikkim would continue to be conducted by the GoI's department of external affairs.

I had the pleasure of meeting T.D. Densapa—the father of Jigdal Densapa and secretary to the Chogyal during my tenure in Gangtok—when he invited me and Bali (my wife) for dinner at his residence. Also known as Athing La or Burmeok Kazi (after his family estate), he enjoyed the title of Rai Sahib. He always dressed in the typical Tibetan way and had long braids on either side of his face, giving an impression of a Tibetan nobleman. This appearance might have come in handy to impress the Indian officials and political leaders about Sikkim's cultural and religious affinity with Tibet.

From the very beginning, the Bhutia–Lepcha (12 per cent and 13 per cent, respectively, of Sikkim's population) alliance was a marriage of convenience to further the cause of the Namgyal dynasty in Sikkim. In the post-1947 period, Thondup used it to ward off threats from the pro-democracy forces comprising mainly the Nepalese population, but led by some enlightened Bhutia and Lepcha leaders. Further, to maintain their exclusivity, the Namgyals (both men and women), including Thondup, mostly intermarried with Tibetan nobility. The Lepchas were aware that the better-educated Bhutias were taking advantage of the 50 per cent quota reserved for this group in political and other institutions. But they could not do much to improve their lot. The Lepchas were only considered good enough to provide women from their tribe to serve as mistresses or concubines. Thondup himself had a Lepcha girl as his mistress before he got married, with whom he had two children. The R&AW spl ops team fully exploited these grievances amongst some senior Lepcha leaders like Rinzing Lepcha by weaning them away from the pro-Chogyal Sikkim National Party and encouraging them to join Kazi's SNC just before the April 1974 elections, which finally led to a landslide victory for the latter.

Having secured a written assurance from the secretary of the states department about the special status of his state, Thondup shifted his energies towards securing some sort of commitment from the British before they left, about the return of Darjeeling hills and other territories ceded to them as a part of the Darjeeling Grant in 1835.[13]

Betraying the trust reposed in him and his father by Nehru, by accepting their pleas of special identity for Sikkim, and with just fifteen days left for the British to leave India, Thondup wrote two separate letters dated 1 August 1947. One was under the name of Maharaja Tashi Namgyal and the other under his own name, requesting the British for the 'retrocession' (return) of the areas transferred to them through the Darjeeling Grant of 1835. The letter, signed by Thondup, was addressed to Sir George Abell, Viceroy's House, New Delhi. In this letter, Thondup thanked Abell for his help during his last visit to New Delhi and informed him that his father was sending another letter through a special messenger enclosing therewith the 'Sikkim memorandum'. He requested him to place that memorandum before the Viceroy. That memo was a thirty-page booklet containing a legal case prepared by D.K. Sen, barrister-at-law, for the restoration of the Darjeeling hill areas to Sikkim.

The second letter, written by Maharaja Tashi Namgyal, was addressed to the honourable member, foreign affairs and Commonwealth department, GoI. In this letter, Tashi Namgyal drew attention to paragraph nine of the above memorandum, in which a specific request for the 'retrocession' of Darjeeling areas, and reasons thereof, was made. It would be obvious that Thondup wanted some sort of positive response, if not a firm commitment, on this issue from the British before they left India so that he could follow up his case with the succeeding government in India. But the British were intelligent enough not to oblige Thondup at this late a stage of their withdrawal.

The file containing these two letters (MEA file no. 7(7) NEF 1947) remained pending disposal. After India's independence, the case was examined in detail with a background note prepared by V.M.M. Nair, undersecretary (MEA), on 6 November 1947. This note was put before D.S. (X) Hareshwar Dayal and was finally seen by P.A. Menon, joint secretary. It was then decided that as the two letters were actually addressed to the viceroy and his staff, no further action on their contents needed to be taken (by post-Independence Indian authorities) and the case was closed. This important issue should have been brought to the notice of the foreign minister. Nehru handled this charge himself till his death in 1964. It appears that Menon had shown this file to Nehru without making any note on it.

Chapter III

The Sikkim of Tashi Tshering's Dreams (1947–53)

India's conscious decision to treat Sikkim as a special case and not ask it to sign the bilateral instrument of accession left very little scope for the pro-democracy and anti-durbar political forces in Sikkim to fight for its merger with India. Meanwhile, India's policy towards Sikkim started taking a definitive shape. As reflected through some of the declassified papers of the MEA—available with the National Archives of India at New Delhi—former PO V.H. Coelho's book *Sikkim And Bhutan* and my discussion with former PO K.S. Bajpai, all facets of this policy became clear by 1953.

This policy, which continued to be followed by the MEA till the end of 1972, revolved around one cornerstone and three fundamental beliefs. The cornerstone was that if India wanted to protect its strategic interests in Sikkim, the maharaja had to be supported under all circumstances to allow him to maintain a firm hold over the administration.

Keeping that in view, the first fundamental belief was that anti-durbar agitations had to be curbed, contained and controlled to a certain extent so as to preclude any possibility of the so-called instability spreading in this strategically located state. Secondly, the efforts of the Nepalese-dominated parties, even though led by enlightened Bhutia and Lepcha leaders, to bring about significant changes in the political and administrative system of Sikkim should not be allowed to succeed beyond a point, as that could lead to similar political demands from the Nepalese of neighbouring Darjeeling and Siliguri. That, in turn, could also generate feelings of pan-Nepalism in this sensitive region. Thirdly, if Bhutia–Lepcha interests were ignored, and they felt threatened by the success of the Nepalese-dominated parties, they could look towards Tibet or China for help.

In view of the above, the word 'merger' soon became a sort of *varjit swar* (prohibited musical note), to borrow a term from Indian classical music. Also, any pro-merger demand or agitation on the part of the anti-durbar parties would have been seen as a criticism of Nehru's decision, which they could not afford at the time. Therefore, pro-democracy and pro-reform parties in Sikkim had to remain content with such demands as accession to India; land, political and administrative reforms to secure equal rights for people of different ethnic groups; and party-to-party relations with the INC, etc.

In short, India's policy towards Sikkim till the end of December 1972 can be described as a policy of 'apparent appeasement and cautious containment'. This meant kid-glove treatment for the maharaja through protection of his interests and cautious containment of the pro-democratic and progressive forces fighting against his autocratic rule. However, in curbing, controlling and containing the anti-durbar activities of these parties, the MEA and its PO in Gangtok took care that these parties did not get totally marginalized. A somewhat healthy existence of anti-durbar parties was essential to contain the growing ambitions of Palden Thondup Namgyal, first as the maharaj kumar and later as the maharaja/chogyal and the pro-independence charter of Thondup's creation, the Sikkim National Party (SNP).

To sum up, the GoI's policy during this period was to maintain a delicate balance between the two conflicting interests. But in doing so, the balance of decisions made was mostly in the maharaja's favour. It was a difficult task, but once a decision was taken at the political level, it was not very difficult for the seasoned and efficient MEA officials to give such a policy shape. On the other hand, the anti-durbar parties, for whom India was the only lifeline, had little option but to accept its pro-maharaja decisions as and when the need for India's intervention or assistance arose. It thus became clear that unless India's perception of its strategic interests in this region underwent a significant change, and the maharaja/chogyal was seen to be a liability rather than an asset, there was no chance of progressive and anti-chogyal forces succeeding in their struggle for even political, economic and administrative reforms, not to speak of a merger.

Palden Thondup Namgyal in his various roles—first as maharaj kumar and then as maharaja (1963–65) and later as the Chogyal—took full advantage of India's policy of appeasement towards his family, arising out of India's security concerns in this region. In fact, he exploited these concerns to the hilt by convincing the concerned Indian authorities that they needed him in Sikkim.

In this respect, he followed a three-pronged policy. Firstly, he made the concerned Indian government policymakers firmly believe that it was only the maharaja/chogyal who could provide a stable government in Sikkim, a condition conducive to India's security interests in this region. Secondly, he convinced them that the local political leaders were a bunch of selfish and shifty characters incapable of forming a government, let alone a stable one. Lastly, Thondup fully and repeatedly exploited to his advantage the possible threat to India because of pan-Nepalism (all the Gurkhas of Sikkim, Darjeeling and contiguous areas uniting and forming a so-called Gurkhaland) if India showed any accommodation towards Nepalese interests in Sikkim. In the later stages, he also tried to convince the Indian leadership that a popular government in Sikkim may encourage the spread of communist ideology from the neighbouring state of West Bengal, which India could not afford due to the Chinese presence across Sikkim's northern and eastern borders. During my meetings with him, the Chogyal repeatedly tried to sell these ideas to me so that I could pass this information on to Kao and, through him, to Indira Gandhi.

To achieve these objectives, Thondup needed to create pro-Sikkim lobbies at appropriate levels, which could then influence the decision-making process in India. He did this through lavish entertainment and expensive gifts to senior Indian VIPs of civil, defence and political backgrounds, who were either posted in or visiting Gangtok. Some selected visitors were even invited to stay at the palace guest house as his personal guests, though some of them should have stayed at India House as the PO's guests. The most prominent of these was T.N. Kaul, whom Thondup came to know well in the early 1950s while he was posted with the High Commission of India in London. Later, Kaul held the crucial posts of joint secretary, secretary (east) and India's foreign secretary at the MEA headquarters. During these tenures, he played a crucial role in the formulation of India's policy of appeasement towards Sikkim. According to Sunanda K. Datta-Ray, a close friend of Thondup and some of his family members, 'Many snide remarks could be heard of how the highest in Delhi had pampered and indulged Coo Coo La (the Chogyal's sister); Kaul was regarded as foremost among her admirers. His attention was hardly surprising since European aristocrats, British politicians and American diplomats also paid court to the Chogyal's gifted sister.'[1]

That Kaul had a soft corner for the Chogyal would be evident from what Sudhir Devare, then first secretary in the political office, told me recently.[2] Devare recalled that soon after he joined the political office in June 1970, Kaul paid a visit to Gangtok. Kaul was a frequent visitor there and would normally stay as the Chogyal's guest in his palace. PO K.S. Bajpai had not yet joined and the post was still vacant. K.C. Johary, counsellor, was the acting PO. Around this time, a news report that criticized the Chogyal appeared in an Indian newspaper which upset the Chogyal a great deal. He brought this to the attention of the foreign secretary. Kaul came to India House the next morning and took the Indian diplomats to task for not being able to manage the press and causing the Chogyal much annoyance and discomfiture. That was also an indication of how the authorities in India were being solicitous of the Chogyal's sensitivities, as they did not wish to displease him in any way.

The subsequent paragraphs and chapters describe the various developments of interest in Sikkim and the role played, directly or indirectly, by the main players in the unfolding drama. But keeping in view the involvement of two enlightened Sikkimese leaders—one Bhutia and the other Lepcha—who dedicated their lives to the amelioration of and fulfilment of democratic aspirations of the Sikkimese people, the period between 1947 and 1972 has been divided into three chapters. Owing to the leading role played by Tashi Tshering—a Bhutia; popularly known as Tashi Babu— during 1947–53, this chapter has been named after him. The next chapter, which covers the period from 1953–66, has been named as the period of Kazi's ascendance (who replaced Tshering as president of the Sikkim State Congress [SSC] in 1953). The third period, from 1967–72, which saw hectic activity arising from Thondup's burning desire to change the nature of the treaty relationship with India, has been titled 'Demands for the Revision of the 1950 Treaty'.

On the eve of independence, political developments in India led to the formation of popular governments in the neighbouring state of West Bengal and elsewhere. This was bound to have an impact on the political activists in Sikkim, thereby raising the aspirations of popular leaders like Tashi Tshering and Kazi. In August 1947, there were a number of political parties or factions in the state, with the SSC led by Tashi Tshering having the largest number of followers.[3] In addition to the SSC, there were two other like-minded parties—Praja Sudharak Samaj led by Dhan Bahadur Chhetri, and the Kazi-led Praja Mandal whose ideologies were somewhat similar to that of the SSC. Both parties wanted abolition of landlordism, democratic reforms and a closer relationship with India. Though led by enlightened Bhutia and Lepcha leaders, the followers of these parties mainly comprised the Nepalese-speaking population of south and west Sikkim.

The fourth party—Sikkim Rajya Praja Sammelan (SRPS)—wanted an outright merger with India, with the ultimate objective of creating a new and larger Nepalese-speaking state within India comprising Sikkim, Darjeeling and other contiguous areas. However, its strength in Sikkim was limited to a few hundred.

A fifth party—SNP—was set up by Thondup as a counter to the SSC. Its membership was limited to Bhutias and Lepchas, mainly from north and east Sikkim, with some representation from the south and west. The SNP favoured the establishment of an independent Sikkim, but till such time as conditions were favourable for that, the party was willing to reach a negotiated settlement with India (such as revision of the 1950 treaty).

As Sikkim had not been incorporated into the Union of India, the leaders of the three like-minded parties—the SSC, Praja Mandal and the Praja Sudharak Samaj—had a joint meeting in Gangtok on 5 December 1947. They passed a resolution demanding the abolition of absentee landlordism, formation of an interim government till a popular government was formed and, finally, the most important, 'accession of the state of Sikkim to India if it had already not been done' by the maharaja.

It was also decided to merge the two smaller parties into the SSC, with Tashi Tshering as the president. Tshering also announced the party's desire to affiliate with the Nehru-led All-India State People's Conference that was functioning in the princely states of India.

Further, it was decided that a big rally would be organized in Gangtok in support of these demands. Before that, a delegation of these parties comprising Tshering, Kazi and some others had already met PO Hopkinson (who stayed back for some time after India's independence) and requested him to use his good offices with the maharaja for the introduction of political reforms. Failing to get any positive response from Hopkinson, the SSC leaders went ahead with the rally at Gangtok on 7 December, at the site where Paljor stadium stands today. A leaflet titled 'A Few

Facts about Sikkim State' was read and circulated. Its Nepalese version was read by a young graduate, C.D. Rai.

The leaflet contained the grievances of the downtrodden ryots (subjects) of Sikkim state, including the 'Sikkim Gurkhas, Bhutias and Lepchas who have suffered untold miseries in the hands of corrupt administration'. It described Sikkim 'as a small Indian state tucked away in the corners of the Himalayas'. It talked about the prevailing evils of landlordism, the exploitation of poor farmers by the absentee Kazis and thikadars (contract holders on behalf of Kazis) and the forced labour to which the ryots were subjected, both by the landlords and the state. Further, it referred to several unsuccessful attempts by the ryots in the latter half of 1946 to seek redressal from the authorities concerned. Referring to the alleged communal problems in Sikkim, the pamphlet mentioned that 'the ryots, who consist of Hindus and Buddhists, live in complete amity. The number of Muslims scattered all over Sikkim is one hundred at most. The only communal question the authorities could have in view is probably that existing between the oppressors and the oppressed, "the landlords and the ryots".'

In a petition to the maharaja dated 9 December 1947— signed and submitted by Tshering in his capacity as president of the SSC[4]—the party referred to the mass meeting of the people of Sikkim in Gangtok on 7 December, and repeated the three demands made in the party's 5 December resolutions. The maharaja was requested to reply to this petition by 24 December so that an interim government could be installed by the new year. A copy of this petition was sent to the GoI through the PO. Thondup met the delegation and promised to consider the first two demands, but was non-committal on the third, i.e., accession to India.

Here it would be relevant to explain the true logic behind, and the real meaning of, the SSC's demand for Sikkim's accession to India, as this had been misconstrued by some interested or even ignorant persons as falling short of a demand for an outright merger. As mentioned in the previous chapter, as late as 5 July 1947, Sardar Patel had asked the Indian princely states to enter into a bilateral instrument of accession only. This route was mainly adopted because Patel did not want to scare these states by using the words 'merger' or 'integration', as these states were worried about their future in a country ruled by the left-of-centre Congress. But it was well known that once the instrument of accession was signed, the merger or integration of these states into the Union of India, and later the Republic of India, would be the natural consequence. It would, therefore, be obvious that accession was the cause or means and that merger was the ultimate effect. For their merger, all states of India had to pass through the process of accession and Sikkim was no exception. Nobody had used the word 'merger' till then, but everyone knew the implications of accession.

Tucked away in a corner of India and cut off from the centre of political activities, i.e., New Delhi, credit must be given to the Sikkimese people and their leaders for following the correct protocol with regard to seeking a merger, which was unfortunately left out due to previously stated reasons. Therefore, the word 'accession' served Tshering's purpose equally well. He considered accession as the thin end of the wedge, as once it was accepted Sikkim would have also been merged or integrated into the Union of India in due course, as was the case with the other princely states who had signed the instrument of accession. Also, the very name of the party—SSC—was on the lines of the names of the INC's branches in states like West Bengal.

In fact, Tshering started raising these demands only after Sikkim was not asked to sign the instrument of accession with India. He vigorously continued to demand Sikkim's accession to India, in the hope that the previous mistake would one day be corrected by India. Tshering never used the word 'merger' even though his intentions were clear. But it was the pro-durbar elements and the GoI officials concerned who, in their enthusiasm to protect India's so-called security interests, started sabotaging each of Tshering's moves to bring Sikkim closer to India through accession.

It was now time to finalize the standstill agreement which would legitimize the continuation of Sikkim's relations with the British imperialists till a new treaty was worked out by independent India. The draft of this agreement was handed over to the Sikkimese delegation after the 3 June 1947 meeting in Secretary V.P. Menon's room in the states department. Deliberations on this agreement were mainly conducted in the states department. A background note was prepared by the undersecretary of the home and states department for the benefit of the senior officers involved in finalizing the agreement.[5] The contents of paragraph six of this note, reproduced below, were rather interesting:

> Constitutionally, Sikkim is an Indian state. His highness is a member of Chamber of Princes and used to take part in its proceedings. It is treated in all respects as an Indian state but in view of its position, relations with the state are conducted through external affairs department with an agent of the crown posted in Gangtok. Its status as an Indian state did not really matter very much since it allowed Sikkim separate existence and development on lines suited to local traditions and circumstances.

From the above, it would appear that everyone concerned in India, down to the undersecretary whose duty it was to put up background notes on the file, was in awe of Nehru and wanted to do his bit to justify Nehru's decision to treat Sikkim as a special case.

The standstill agreement was finally signed on 27 February 1948.[6] It was signed by Thondup on behalf of Sikkim and P.A. Menon, joint secretary, MEA and Commonwealth relations. Its main provisions are listed below:

> It is agreed between the Sikkim state and the dominion of India that until new agreements in this behalf are made, all agreements and administrative arrangements relating to the subjects specified in the attached schedule existing between the crown and the Sikkim Durbar on August 14, 1947, shall in so far as may be appropriate, continue as between the dominion of India, or, as the case may be, as part thereof, and the Sikkim Durbar.

The schedule contained eleven subjects—arms and equipment, control of commodities, currency and coinage, Customs, extradition, service of summons and execution of civil decrees, the existing arrangements of the Central Public Works Department (CPWD), post, telegraphs and telephones, external affairs, defence, motor vehicles, refund of duty on excisable articles, and opium and ganja.

Meanwhile, the SSC leadership got suspicious about the true intentions of the maharaja and his son Thondup, as they had not acted on any of the three demands made in their petition dated

9 December 1947. On the contrary, Thondup quietly told the leaders of his captive SNP to issue a declaration opposing the accession of Sikkim to India. This was followed by a statement in which they mentioned that the party would make every effort to maintain the special character of Sikkim as well as its integrity.

To build real pressure on the maharaja, the SSC started rallies and demonstrations in south and west Sikkim. A large rally was taken out in Namche in October 1948. In December 1948, an SSC delegation comprising Tashi Tshering, L.D. Kazi and C.D. Rai went to New Delhi to put their three demands before Nehru. They were welcomed as the heroes of the revolution. Regarding their demands, he was sympathetic to the first two, but on the request of accession, Nehru told the delegation not to insist on it as that could lead to India being accused of coercion. He also suggested that Sikkim, like Bhutan and Nepal, should be allowed to grow according to its own genius.

Seeing the SSC leaders' restive mood on their return from New Delhi, Thondup tried to appease them by appointing three of the party's nominees—Sonam Tshering (a Bhutia), Captain Dimik Singh Lepcha (a Lepcha) and Raghubir Singh Basnet (a Nepalese)—as secretaries to the government of Sikkim. Very soon, Thondup won over all three of them.

With no help coming from India, the SSC leaders held the party's annual session at Rangpo in the first week of February 1949. The party once again passed a resolution demanding the abolition of landlordism and Sikkim's accession to India. Meanwhile, the party had already launched a low-level agitation against discriminatory rents to be charged from cultivators of land. That led to the arrest of some party workers. On its part, the hard-line pro-Nepalese party—SRPS—at its meeting on 3 January 1949 had already passed a resolution (a copy of which was handed over to the PO on 18 February), wherein they resolved to approach the GoI through the PO with the request that Sikkim be declared a centrally administered area and that the administration thereof be taken over by New Delhi as soon as possible.

While Sikkim was in turmoil, in New Delhi, Ari Bahadur Gurung, a member of the Constituent Assembly (Legislative) raised a starred question (D No. 42) which was slated for 9 March 1949.[7] The question read as follows: 'Will the Hon'ble PM be pleased to state whether people of Sikkim have approached the Government of India with a proposal to merge their state with India?' Replying to this question, Dr B.V. Keskar, deputy minister for external affairs, said: 'One of the political parties in Sikkim, namely Sikkim Rajya Praja Sammelan, has sent to the Government of India a copy of the resolution passed by the party in January 1949, suggesting the merger of Sikkim with India and its governance as centrally administered area.'

In a supplementary question, Tajamul Hussain asked: 'Is it the position that Sikkim has acceded to the Indian Union?' Replying to this question, Prime Minister Nehru said: 'The question in that shape has not arisen. All these matters are pending and under consideration. The present position is that the old relations with Sikkim and Bhutan with the Government of India continue. What exactly the future relations will be is a matter for consultation between Sikkim, Bhutan and the Government of India.' It will be interesting to note that, in his answer, Nehru linked Bhutan with Sikkim, though the status of Bhutan had not been included in the question.

A note prepared by the MEA for answering supplementary questions, if any, drew attention to the policies of two parties— SSC and SRPS. In this note, it was specifically mentioned that the SRPS's demands were closely in line with the demands of the Gurkha League which deserved no encouragement. It was also felt that the starred question was raised by Gurung at their behest.

Following this debate, in his letter dated 14 March 1949 to
the MEA, PO Hareshwar Dayal took pains to explain that the
people arrested in February 1949 during the ongoing agitation,
were actually from the SSC that favoured Sikkim's accession to
India and not its merger.[8] The arrests were made not because
they expressed certain views with regard to Sikkim's relationship
with India but because they had launched a 'no-rent' campaign
in defiance of a certain notification issued by the durbar. Further,
the demand for the merger came from the SRPS, an organization
of the Nepalese whose demands are closely in line with those of
the Gurkha League.

With hardly any progress on the implementation of their demands
in Sikkim, and no tangible support from New Delhi in sight,
the SSC had escalated the party's agitation into a full-fledged,
statewide 'no-rent', 'no-tax' campaign, to protest the continued
exploitation of the tillers of the land. This led to the arrest of
some of their leaders. Provoked by this, the SSC followers started
moving towards Gangtok and finally, on 1 May 1949, over 5000
demonstrators laid siege to the palace. The durbar panicked and
requested PO Hareshwar Dayal to intervene and help restore
normality in the state in general and in Gangtok in particular.
Pursuant to this request by the maharaja, the arrested SSC leaders
were released and the army deployed to restore peace and order.

As a mark of concession to the agitating SSC leaders—on the
suggestion of PO Dayal—on 9 May the maharaja agreed to form
a five-member interim popular government to run the affairs of
the state, with the overall control remaining with the durbar.
The cabinet comprised three SSC members and two appointees

recommended by the durbar. The five members of the council, headed by Tashi Tshering as chief minister, included Rishi Prasad Alley, Chander Das Rai, Captain Dimik Singh Lepcha and Kazi Dorji Dhadul. The so-called popular ministry, however, could not take off because of internal squabbles.

The SSC raised demands for a broad-based and more representative government. With hardly any chance of the SSC's demands being met, Tshering threatened to launch a satyagraha. This led to PO Dayal requesting the minister of state for external affairs, Dr B.V. Keskar, to visit Gangtok in the last week of May 1949, assess the situation and help work out a compromise.

Keskar failed to work out an amicable solution during his four-day stay in Gangtok and left on 27 May. With the administration paralysed, in the interest of maintaining stability and on the recommendation of the PO, the maharaja dismissed the newly established cabinet on 6 June—within twenty-seven days of its formation. A former Indian Civil Services (ICS) officer from India, John S. Lall, was appointed as the diwan to help run the affairs of the state. Till Lall's arrival on 11 August, PO Dayal was appointed as the interim administrator. This was the first and last attempt during the maharaja/chogyal's rule to establish a popular government comprising opposing political and ethnic interests.

To register his protest before the Indian leaders and brief them about the circumstances leading to the dismissal of his ministry, a disheartened Tshering again led his party's delegation to New Delhi in July 1949. During the course of these meetings with Indian leaders and senior MEA officials, the SSC delegation was informed that the GoI's main interest in Sikkim was to avoid instability and chaos.[9] They were, however, assured of support for creating better understanding between the Sikkimese people and the government of Sikkim, for which an Indian diwan had especially been appointed. While the SSC returned from New

Delhi empty-handed, the pro-durbar SNP was obviously pleased with the outcome of the negotiations. The SRPS did not know how to react to the unfolding developments.

With Tshering's return from New Delhi, it became clear that India was not really interested in the establishment of a truly popular and representative government in Sikkim. One interesting thing which emerged from India's intervention to restore peace in Sikkim at this time was that neither Thondup nor Tshering were happy with the outcome. Tshering and the SSC party leaders obviously felt that India had betrayed the cause of the democratic aspirations of the Sikkimese people. That resulted in India losing the trust of the pro-democratic forces in the state, which comprised the majority of the population for a long time to come. Ripple effects of this betrayal were evident when I took over as OSD (P) Gangtok. We had to make repeated efforts to dispel doubts in the minds of the Sikkim Congress leaders that this time India would not let them down as it had in 1949. On the other hand, Thondup felt that India's intervention was stage-managed by PO Dayal to force an Indian-appointed diwan on him. That was the reason Thondup did not fully trust any diwan, except his friend Nari Rustomji, who succeeded Lall.

On Diwan Lall's arrival on 11 August 1949, an advisory committee was set up under his charge to run the affairs of the state. The members of this committee included Tashi Tshering, Kashi Raj Pradhan, Captain Dimik Singh Lepcha, Gyaltsen Tshering and Sonam Tshering. Although the SSC and SNP were both represented, the SRPS declined to join on the grounds that this committee did not truly represent all the regions and communities in the state. Soon after its formation, the advisory committee started working on establishing panchayats, holding of council (Assembly) elections and forming an executive council (cabinet). In this connection, the committee specially applied itself on the question of equitable (but disproportionate to the actual Nepalese population on one side and the combined group of Bhutia–Lepchas on the other) distribution of seats for the Assembly elections and recruitment for government jobs, from the Nepalese and Bhutia–Lepcha segments of the population.[10] According to this principle, which soon became known as the 'parity formula', interests of 25 per cent of Sikkim's population, comprising the Bhutia–Lepchas were to be equated with the 75 per cent Nepalese population.

In March 1950, representatives of different political parties from Sikkim had detailed discussions with Indian government officials and political leaders in New Delhi about the future relationship of their state with India and the role of the parties in that arrangement. This meeting coincided with the final stages of negotiations with the Sikkimese delegation led by Thondup on the Indo-Sikkim Treaty, which was later signed in Gangtok in December 1950. The outcome of both, the political talks and the treaty negotiations, was explained in a press release dated 20 March 1950 issued by the MEA.[11] According to it, the status of Sikkim 'will continue to be a protectorate of India. The Government of India will continue to be responsible for its external relations, defence and communication . . . As regards internal government, the state will continue to enjoy autonomy subject to the ultimate responsibility of the Government of India for the maintenance of good administration and law and order.' It also said that:

> For the present an officer of the Government of India will continue to be the Diwan of the State. But the Government of

India's policy is one of progressive association of the people of the State with its Government, a policy with which, happily, His Highness the Maharaja is in full agreement. It is proposed, as a first step, that an Advisory Council representative of all the interests should be associated with the Diwan. Steps will also be taken immediately to institute a village panchayat system on an elective basis within the State. This is an essential and effective process of education in the art of popular government and it is the intention that these panchayats should, in due course, elect a Council for the State whose functions and area of responsibility will be progressively enlarged.

It is obvious from this press statement that while various facets of the GoI's relationship with Sikkim had been taken care of through the signing of the Indo-Sikkim Treaty on 5 December 1950, the only concession that Tashi Tshering and the pro-democratic forces got was a promise for the establishment of directly elected panchayats. The members of the council were still to be indirectly elected by the members of the various panchayats.

With no option but to depend upon the continuing goodwill of the GoI in their fight against the durbar to secure political and economic reforms in Sikkim, on their return from New Delhi, in April 1950, the SSC leaders issued a pamphlet[12] which read as follows:

Our demand that Sikkim should accede to India has in principle been accepted because the administration will remain in the hands of the government of India official. The responsibility to maintain peace and see to the proper administration has also remained in the hands of the government of India . . . Although a responsible government could not be immediately established, every effort should be made to see to the immediate formation

of panchayats on elective system as well as to the establishment
of a constituent assembly through election within a year.

The Indo-Sikkim Treaty was signed on 5 December 1953 at the
palace monastery between PO Hareshwar Dayal and Maharaja
Tashi Namgyal. The crucial clause II of this treaty mentioned that
'Sikkim shall continue to be a protectorate of India and, subject
to the provisions of this Treaty, shall enjoy autonomy in regard to
its internal affairs'.

India remained responsible for the defence and territorial
integrity of Sikkim, and external relations whether political,
economic or financial. Sikkim agreed not to levy any import
and transit duty on goods brought into or in transit through
Sikkim. India got exclusive rights of constructing, maintaining
and regulating the use of railways; aerodromes, landing grounds
and air navigation facilities; and posts, telegraphs and wireless
installations in Sikkim. People from Sikkim travelling to foreign
countries were to be treated as Indian protected persons for holding
Indian passports. They were to have every right of entry into and
free movement within India, and Indian nationals were to have
the same rights with respect to Sikkim. The GoI had retained the
right to appoint a representative to reside in Sikkim. In case of
any dispute over the interpretation of the provisions of this treaty,
the same were to be referred to the chief justice of India, whose
decision would be treated as final.

Thondup, though pleased that he had been able to maintain
a separate identity for Sikkim outside Sardar Patel's grips, still felt
that they were being led by the GoI.[13] That same night, after the
treaty was signed, the palace hosted a banquet which was boycotted
by the SSC to indicate their disapproval. According to them, the
treaty did not provide for the establishment of a representative
government. Soon after, a Tashi Tshering-led SSC delegation

visited New Delhi again. They complained that the durbar had been sabotaging their efforts and delaying the establishment of a representative government. On his return, Tshering, in December 1950, described the proceedings of the advisory committee set up by the diwan as a proverbial fish market.

The treaty of 1950 was followed by a 'letter of exchange' dated 25 February 1951, signed by PO Hareshwar Dayal and accepted by the maharaja. It had ten clauses in which certain aspects of India's relationship with Sikkim were explained. Three of these clauses pertained to India's assistance in the economic, technical, educational and fiscal areas. The tenth clause gave India overriding powers—in case of any serious law-and-order problem, or threat to internal security, the GoI would not have to wait for a request from the maharaja to come to his assistance, 'but independently of such a request, the GoI will be entitled in such a situation to give such advice as they may consider necessary and appropriate for dealing with the situation and the maharaja shall be bound to act in accordance with such advice'. It was this clause which was invoked by PO Bajpai to induce the Chogyal to hand over the administration of Sikkim on 8 April 1973, when law and order had completely broken down in the state.

Due to the mounting demand from the political parties in Sikkim, especially the SSC, Thondup started working on setting up political institutions that were tailored to serve his own interests. His moves towards devising a system most suited to serve his dynasty's interests were motivated by the nature of the population mix in the state. When India attained independence in 1947, Sikkim's total population (as per the Census of 1941) was

1,37,000. The Nepalese population was 1,05,000 (77 per cent of the total), the Bhutias were 17,000 and the Lepchas 15,000. According to the 1971 census figures, the total population of Sikkim had risen to 2,10,000, with a proportionate growth in the Nepalese population in the crucial south and west districts.

It was, therefore, obvious that if free and fair elections were held, on the basis of universal franchise and the 'one man, one vote' principle, and without any reservation based on ethnic affiliation, the maharaja would lose his hold over the administration to the Nepalese-dominated council or assembly. It was mainly for this reason that during the course of negotiations leading up to the Royal Proclamation of 1953, Thondup insisted on maintaining a parity of seats in the council between the Nepalese on one side and the Bhutia–Lepcha segment on the other. Thondup was finally able to secure the consent of the SSC leaders, including Tashi Tshering and Kashi Raj Pradhan, to apply the parity formula through an agreement signed on 15 May 1952. According to this, 23 per cent of Sikkim's population comprising the Bhutia–Lepcha population would have the same number of seats in the council as the remaining 77 per cent of the Sikkimese population, which comprised the Nepalese segment. Even this parity formula, which was in itself discriminatory in nature, was sabotaged by Thondup by converting, through underhand means, five additional seats in the council originally agreed to by the two above-mentioned SSC leaders to accommodate various interest groups in the Assembly into a personal 'gift' to the maharaja to be filled at his own discretion.

Following prolonged negotiation between the political parties and Thondup, which lasted over two years, the maharaja finally issued a proclamation which was published in the 23 March 1953 issue of *Durbar Gazette*. It stated the composition and powers of the state council and the executive council. The state council, subject to the maharaja's final approval, was empowered to enact laws on 'transferred subjects'. Certain subjects could only be taken up with the approval of the maharaja. These included state enterprises, police, land revenue and ecclesiastical matters. Some other subjects, known as 'reserved subjects', such as the constitutional position of the maharaja and treaty relations with India, were excluded from discussion by the state council. Theoretically, the executive council assisted the maharaja in running the affairs of the state but in actual practice its powers were greatly limited. In most matters, the maharaja made the final decision. The diwan acted as the principal adviser to the maharaja and was also head of the executive council. That was the reason why the SSC described the contents of this proclamation as reactionary which curtailed people's rights.

Before the proclamation was issued, a couple of reports sent by the IB to the MEA make for interesting reading. In the first report, based on a field report dated 21 January 1953,[14] it was mentioned that the SSC had decided to boycott the elections, as and when held, if satisfactory action was not taken by the state authorities against one Baladas Rai who had stopped the Bhutias and Lepchas from attending the annual session of the SSC party at Dikchu on 8 December 1952. It also mentioned that Maharaj Kumar Thondup had persuaded the National Party leaders to welcome the proclamation as soon as it was made public.

The elections were held from March to May 1953, including primary elections at the local level. There were 50,000 eligible voters. The minimum age for the candidates was thirty years and the voters had to be at least twenty-one years old. Due to the initial reluctance of the SSC to contest these elections, there was not much enthusiasm amongst the large cross section of Sikkimese population. As a result, less than 30 per cent of the eligible voters, i.e. 15,000, actually exercised their franchise. When the results were declared, all six Nepalese seats were won by the SSC and all six Bhutia–Lepcha seats by the SNP. The third party, the SRPS, drew a blank.[15] Out of the nomination quota of five seats, the maharaja filled only four seats. The fifth vacancy was kept vacant as the maharaja did not want to fill it with a businessman of Indian origin, despite a suggestion to this effect by the MEA. Therefore, out of the total of sixteen members in the newly constituted council, Thondup had the support of ten members against the SSC's six. Thus, the pro-durbar group in the council still fell short of the two-thirds majority by one vote.

The new council held its first meeting in November 1953. An executive council of three members—comprising the diwan and councillors Kashi Raj Pradhan (SSC) and Sonam Tshering (SNP)—was set up. The term of the council, which was originally for three years, was later extended to 1957 through a royal proclamation. But the SSC soon discovered that Thondup had managed to convert five nomination quota seats, originally meant for the representation of various interest groups, as seats to be filled as per the maharaja's will or discretion. In this context, the contents of a letter dated 28 August 1953,[16] written by Diwan J.S. Lall to then PO B.K. Kapur, are rather interesting.

> I understand that when the 15 May 1951 agreement was reached, Tashi Tshering had told the Maharaj Kumar that the right to nominate the five members, which his party had conceded, would be the 'crucial test' of his good faith. Originally, the State Congress was prepared to agree to only two nominations but finally agreed to five nominations in

order to provide the representations of special interests. The State Congress representatives maintain that it was understood that overall parity would be maintained. Both Tashi Tshering and Kashi Raj Pradhan have hinted on various occasions that they did not know how the words 'without special interests' appearing at the end of May 15 1951 agreement were added.

Such an act of commission could not have escaped the notice of the GoI officials concerned. However, taking advantage of this subterfuge, the maharaja filled four of these five seats with his loyalists.

The actual impact of the addition of these four nominated seats on the proceedings of the council can be judged from the following extracts from a note dated 4 December 1953, prepared by Diwan Lall for Thondup's meeting with Nehru.[17] The note also indicates the kid-glove treatment being meted out to Thondup:

Twelve elected seats shared half and half between pro-Chogyal National Party and Sikkim State Congress. Normally this should have ensured balance and stability. But on a contentious issue in the council, the nominated (four—the fifth seat was not filled as there was a demand from the Marwari community to nominate one Indian in the council) members en-block voted with the pro-maharaja National Party. This has completely shifted the balance of political power. In view of the intense feeling on certain issues, chiefly communal, this factor is fraught with dangerous possibilities. Very careful and firm handling of maharaj kumar and pro-maharaja elements is necessary, and this, I consider can best be achieved by retaining the confidence of the young maharaj kumar himself.

What happened during Thondup's meeting with Nehru is not recorded in the MEA file that this letter was sourced from.

Not to be satisfied by this self-created 'gift' of five nominated members, Thondup started lobbying for the addition of two monastery seats to the council soon after its formation. His insistence on the monastery seats was based on the fact that the two pro-Chogyal monastery members would further increase the number of his supporters in the council. In August 1953, an SNP member of the council had already tabled a resolution advocating the creation of two monastery seats. This was still pending discussion. The proposal could only be carried through if the decision was taken on the basis of a simple majority in the council. Thondup was not convinced that such a proposal needed the support of two-thirds (eleven out of the sixteen members) of the council membership, which was anyway not possible as he had the support of only ten members.

In a note dated 22 November 1953, prepared by Deputy Secretary (MEA) V.V.M. Nair for Prime Minister Nehru,[18] it was mentioned that as the MEA could not frankly say no to Thondup about his demand for the two monastery seats, the prime minister might consider advising him about the desirability of maintaining impartiality over this issue and continue taking the advice of the diwan in such matters. Further, since the proclamation regarding the creation of the council was made as recently as March 1953, it would not be desirable to amend it so soon to accommodate two additional monastery seats. According to the note:

> If Maharaj Kumar insisted, we could say that there would be no objection if the resolution was passed in the council with two thirds majority.

This issue was not taken up at the prime-ministerial level, but was finally decided at a meeting on 13 February 1954 held in Joint

Secretary Hareshwar Dayal's room.[19] The meeting was attended
by Thondup, the PO and the diwan. After the meeting, the
following decision was noted by the joint secretary:

a) The constitution has to be preserved from changes as far as
   possible.
b) A monastery seat could be created by a person, selected by the
   monastery, being nominated by monasteries, or by one of the
   nominated seats being surrendered and set up as monastery
   seat to be filled up by monasteries.

With this, Thondup's urge to secure two monastery seats was
parried, at least for the time being.

The 1953 proclamation did not grant adequate powers to the
political representatives in the council and to the executive
councillors. Thondup's misuse of nominated quota had further
left the SSC with very little scope of using the state council as a
platform to further the cause of their pro-democratic and pro-
reform ideology. The matter was discussed by senior SSC leaders
at a meeting held on 6 August 1953[20] at senior party leader
Kashi Raj Pradhan's house in Gangtok. The SSC president,
Tashi Tshering, strongly opposed the six elected Congress
members taking part in the inaugural ceremony of the council on
7 August. However, Pradhan and the Kazi group were in support
of their six members taking part in the inaugural ceremony.
Heated discussions ensued. As a result, Tshering, along with two
of his associates, walked out of the meeting and later sent a letter
recommending a boycott of the inaugural session. As the majority
of the members, including Pradhan and Kazi, were in favour of

the party members attending the inaugural session, Tshering's suggestion was not accepted. The next morning, that is 7 August, Pradhan invited Kazi to his house again and requested him to accept the post of president of the SSC, in place of Tshering, which Kazi accepted. As attempts to strike a last-minute compromise with Tshering failed, all six members took oath on 7 August. Kazi's name had been recommended to Pradhan by one Raghubir Singh, a Sikh contractor in Rangpo, who was also a member of the INC committee from West Bengal.

With Kazi replacing Tshering as president of the SSC, the party was sharply divided into two groups—one led by Tshering and the other led by Pradhan and Kazi. They started drifting into so-called communal factions with Tshering leading the hard-line anti-parity faction.[21] He had not liked the dismissal of his ministry in 1949 and had started exhibiting anti-India sentiments after that.

The word 'communal' here denotes that Tshering started openly supporting the cause of the majority Nepalese population by demanding the abolition of parity, which obviously did not fit into India's policy of providing protective cover to the maharaja. On the other hand, Kashi Raj and Kazi, though still dependent on their Nepalese followers in south and west Sikkim, did not challenge the continuity of parity. In view of this, the Kashi Raj/Kazi group was considered non-communal and progressive

But Tshering being described as communal defies logic. How can a Bhutia leader championing the cause of democracy in Sikkim be dubbed as communal, even though his efforts were aimed at benefiting the majority of the population of Sikkim, which happened to be Nepalese?

That the SSC was falling apart on 'communal lines' was taken note of by Diwan J.S. Lall in his letter dated 26 April 1954, addressed to PO B.K. Kapur. Lall mentioned that:[22]

The predominant hard-line faction of State Congress wants
to do away with communal reservations in order to establish
majority rule. The Himalayan States are now our buffers. It
is in our interest to maintain and strengthen them and thus
denying the pan Nepalese movement's opportunities to grow.
Maintenance of established governments implies support for
progressive forces.

It is obvious that Lall had described Tshering's faction as hard-
line, and the Kazi and Pradhan faction of the SSC as 'progressive'.
But his definition of progressive had a very limited and narrow
meaning. To qualify as a progressive force, these leaders were to
carry out their activities within the narrow confines of India's by
now well-defined security interests in Sikkim, at the cost of their
own democratic aspirations, failing which they also ran the risk of
being classified as hardliners, non-progressive or even communal,
thereby losing India's sympathy and even the limited support that
was so essential for their survival.

Tshering, meanwhile, started keeping unwell since his ouster
as president of the SSC. He died on 9 May 1954 of an overdose
of sleeping pills.[23] In view of his past political standing and the
respect that he enjoyed amongst the general public, his funeral was
well attended by people across party lines and political affiliations.

Thus ended the life of an enlightened Bhutia leader who
wanted the emancipation of the downtrodden. He had wanted
to secure democratic rights and privileges for the Sikkimese
population, irrespective of their ethnic background, through
democratic means and accession of his state to independent
India. Unfortunately, he could not realize his dream, mainly due
to carefully calculated and well-planned decisions taken at the
highest political levels in India to protect the country's security
interests. His dream of Sikkim's accession to India was sacrificed

at the altar of its security interests, which as per India's perception, could only be served by the stable and strong institution of the maharaja. This perception was ultimately belied when Sikkim became a part of India in 1975.

Chapter IV

Kazi's Political Ascendance (1953–66)

The change of guard at the helm of the SSC led to some rethinking within the party about its approach towards India. Having gained experience from Tashi Tshering's dealings with Indian officials and leadership, the new SSC leaders, especially L.D. Kazi and Kashi Raj Pradhan, had realized that there was no sense in pointlessly confronting the GoI by raising demands that had not been granted through the proclamation of 1953. Even there, Thondup had been able to dilute the impact of the political reforms already carried out. Given this background, the two leaders thought that it would help in securing concessions from Thondup if they could somehow convince the Indian leaders to establish party-to-party relations with the ruling INC. It was against this background that a Kazi-led SSC delegation visited New Delhi in November 1953 and met senior All India Congress Committee (AICC) functionaries, top MEA officials and political leaders, including Nehru.[1]

Before the departure of this delegation to New Delhi, a meeting was held at Pradhan's house in Gangtok. One of the matters which came up for discussion was that Sikkim should be made a centrally administered area.[2]

It is difficult to believe that the SSC leaders attending that meeting had a momentary loss of memory about the treatment meted out by the GoI to Tshering, whose similar demands were sabotaged on one pretext or the other. In view of that it is possible that the leaders, well aware that the proceedings of that meeting would be reported to the GoI by its intelligence agencies, deliberately avoided raising their demand about Sikkim being made a centrally administered area and pursued a lesser demand of party-to-party relations. In fact, by the time they met Sardar Swaran Singh,* through their experience gained in meetings with senior INC leaders, who were in touch with T.N. Kaul, joint secretary (north), they had already lost hope of even securing party-to-party relations, and hence their ambivalence on this issue in their meeting with Singh.

---

* Sardar Swaran Singh joined Khizar Hayat's cabinet and was the minister for development and supplies in undivided Panjab. Following India's independence, he became home minister in Gopi Chand Bhargava's government on the Indian side of Punjab. When Nehru decided to bring him to New Delhi in May 1952, as a member of his cabinet, Swaran Singh was minister for capital projects and electricity in Bhim Sen Sachar's cabinet. His first assignment in Nehru's cabinet was works, housing and supplies minister (1952–57). Nehru was his own foreign minister and, therefore, wanted someone at the political level to assist him in discharging some of his MEA-related functions. Because of Singh's well-known negotiating skills, Nehru started using him for some external affairs ministry-related assignments, including negotiations with China and Pakistan. The meeting with the SSC delegation was one such assignment. Lal Bahadur Shastri appointed him as India's first external affairs minister, a portfolio he handled in two spells interspersed by two spells as defence minister. He finally had to resign in November 1975 due to his opposition to the promulgation of the Emergency by Indira Gandhi in June 1975. Unfortunately, his role as unofficial and official foreign minister of India, and also his handling of other ministries in the Nehru, Shastri and Indira Gandhi cabinets for twenty-three years, is yet to be documented and fully appreciated.

In this context, a note dated 11 November 1953, prepared by the MEA's deputy secretary for the benefit of his senior officers and political bosses who were to meet the SSC delegation, becomes relevant. According to this note:

> Maharaj Kumar and [the] National Party were anxious to gain control of the National Council in breach of the original understanding, that there would be parity between Nepalese on the one side and Bhutia–Lepcha on the other side. Further, the SSC was increasingly conscious of its political weakness in the present council and has been seeking some kind of affiliation with [the] Indian National Congress. If state Congress feels frustrated, they can then go into opposition and they can ally with pro-Nepalese Gurkha League. The revival of this movement would tend to create a solid Nepalese block in the northeastern frontiers. But in doing so we have also to ensure that the Bhutia–Lepcha are not swamped by the majority. If this happens, there may be discontent which could conceivably be worked upon by the Chinese in case they wish to create support for themselves in the border state.

Diwan J.S. Lall had already reached New Delhi to be available for consultations on this matter. A short note dated 30 November 1953 prepared by him, and put up to Kaul, reads as follows:

> During the recent council session, all the four nominated members voted en-block with six members of the National Party on a resolution of considerable national importance. It was a revelation for Sikkim State Congress leaders, especially Kashi Raj Pradhan. Pradhan even hinted at the possibility of leaving the council, but was advised against it. Understood that Kashi Raj Pradhan is trying to revive the party demand for

the affiliation of his party with All India Congress Committee (AICC), which was earlier not entertained. Kashi Raj Pradhan has raised the matter with Sardar Swaran Singh during his visit to Gangtok in early November. The main purpose of the Sikkim State Congress's delegation is this.

On receipt of the above note, Kaul added the following remarks for Prime Minister Nehru's perusal.

Maharaj Kumar has also met me and spoken on this issue. He was not happy at this demand. Kashi Raj Pradhan also spoke to me on this issue. However, Pradhan was told that the real strength of the state congress would be judged if they could develop support amongst Bhutia–Lepcha also. I would therefore suggest that while All India Congress Committee may advise State Congress from time to time, it should not send any representative to Sikkim or affiliate the Sikkim State Congress with itself at the present juncture.

Kaul took the file with his note personally to Nehru and returned it to his deputy secretary with the remark that the prime minister had seen it.

The same day—30 November 1953—the SSC delegation comprising its president L.D. Kazi, vice president and executive council member Kashi Raj Pradhan, and working committee member Ram Jiwan Prasad met Sardar Swaran Singh, the then minister for works, housing and supplies, at Nehru's instance. Following is the gist of the note recorded for the prime minister by Sardar Swaran Singh about this meeting:

The SSC delegation had already met Balwant Rai Mehta, AICC general secretary, with the request for the affiliation of their party with AICC. They were a bit confused on this issue. They looked up to the INC for help without asking for formal affiliation. Further, some Congress leaders should attend their party session in January or February 1954 and advise them with respect to problems they faced, even unofficially. They also wanted some financial help and guidance for party's organizational work. In addition to this they made the following demands:

a) Extension of India's five-year plans to Sikkim with their consequential benefits for Sikkim,

b) For starting of community development centres, P.N. Thapar of Planning Commission was invited at a lunch at my residence for Raj Kumar, where these people had some discussion on this issue,

c) On representation of Sikkim in India's parliament, they were advised to secure cooperation of other groups in Sikkim on this issue,

d) Regarding provisions relating to fundamental rights guaranteed by the Indian constitution, they were told that this desire must be expressed by the Sikkimese people at large,

e) They wanted the present limited system of 'diarchy' to be changed into a full-fledged responsible government. They were advised to create public opinion on this issue especially amongst the elected representatives of the Council. Moreover, this was seen as a domestic affair.

The SSC delegation met Nehru the next day, i.e., 1 December 1953. After the formal call, Nehru met the delegation along with PO B.K. Kapur, Diwan Lall and Joint Secretary Kaul. As per a note recorded by Kaul, Nehru spoke briefly on the following points:

(a) Sikkim State Congress must build upon its strength internally among the entire people of Sikkim including Bhutia–Lepchas, and not only among the Nepalese population, (b) It would not be proper for Sikkim Congress to affiliate to Indian National Congress at the present juncture, as it might give a handle to Bhutia–Lepchas minority to look up to Tibet, (c) The request about representation in Indian parliament could not be considered unless the demand comes from all the people of Sikkim, (d) As far as 'diarchy' in Sikkim was concerned, constitutional reforms could not be introduced overnight—though they were bound to come, (e) The state Congress could seek guidance from the Indian National Congress, who might send an observer to meet the representatives of not only the state Congress but of other parties as well, (f) Regarding establishment of extension services at the village level, the diwan has been asked to contact Mr S.K. Dey (minister) and examine this matter.

Even before the SSC delegation had met T.N. Kaul on 30 November 1953, Kaul had already met Ms Mukherjee, foreign secretary of the AICC, who came to see him on the morning of 28 November, to discuss the demand of the SSC. Kaul advised her not to encourage its affiliation with the AICC and she agreed. She, however, wanted a note on this subject to be sent to her. She also said that Balwant Rai Mehta, the AICC general secretary, would like to meet the PO and diwan. Kaul then asked the PO and diwan to fix a meeting with Mehta in consultation with Ms Mukherjee.

Kaul's advice to the SSC delegation, to develop support for the party amongst the Bhutia–Lepcha segment in Sikkim, which was reiterated by Sardar Swaran Singh and Nehru, reminds one of an old Indian proverb: *Na nau mann tel ikatha hoga, na Radha nachegi*. It means that if you don't want to concede to someone's demand, link its grant to the completion of an impossible task. By making this suggestion, the Indian leadership wanted the SSC to go on a wild goose chase. Thondup had total control over the Bhutia–Lepcha segment and had created the SNP for the purpose of opposing anti-Chogyal and progressive forces in Sikkim, especially those which did not conform to India's policy of appeasement towards him. Indian leaders and T.N. Kaul did not realize that if the SSC won the support of the SNP or pro-Thondup elements, they would not need to come to New Delhi for help. In fact, such an understating between the two opposing forces would have made Thondup's ambition of securing independence for Sikkim much easier. But he was not willing to make any concessions to the Nepalese-dominated SSC or its successor—the SNC—to build such an understanding. The SSC delegation returned empty-handed but convinced that while they could not avoid keeping India in good humour, they had to fight their battle for political reforms against Thondup on their own.

Not to be deterred by the cool and calculated, but courteous, response that Kazi and his group had received in New Delhi in November 1953, the SSC held a well-attended annual session at Rangpo on 22 April 1954.[3] In addition to reposing full faith in Kazi as its president, the party elected some other office-bearers too. The party also passed resolutions on the abolition of private and monastery estates, abolition of certain taxes, extension of settlement operations to certain excluded areas and educational facilities to backward areas. Obviously, the party did not want to embarrass India by harping on its demand of accession, which by that time had been put in the cold storage.

Interesting information, which threw light on the way Chinese guards at the Sikkim-Tibet border in Chumbi Valley treated Thondup, appeared in the PO's monthly report to the MEA for June 1954. According to it, Maharaj Kumar P.T. Thondup and his wife left Gangtok for Tibet on 27 June. This was his first visit to his parents-in-laws' house in Lhasa after his marriage. At the Chinese checkpoint at Chumbi, he was asked to give his particulars and deposit his weapons. The party stayed at Yatung and was presented the guard of honour by the Indian military contingent attached to the Indian trade agent there.[4]

Following the elections in 1953, three more polls were held in Sikkim in 1958, 1967 and 1970. The fifth and the last election, as per the 1953 and subsequent royal proclamations, was held in January 1973. After prolonged discussions between the durbar and the political parties, the total number of seats in the state council for the 1958 election was increased from seventeen to twenty, inclusive of the nomination quota of six. Three additional seats were created—one for the monasteries, one general seat meant for the entire electorate without communal and other considerations, and one under the nomination quota. Also, the winning candidate now had to secure at least 15 per cent of the votes polled in his favour from the other ethnic group. Although it was introduced to bring about greater integration of the three ethnic main groups, this could also be used by Thondup to ensure the defeat of the Nepalese candidates that he didn't favour by telling his Bhutia–Lepcha followers not to vote for them. The addition of these three seats further tilted the balance of power in Thondup's favour. The monastery and the nomination quota seat were supposed to be filled by pro-Thondup candidates but the general seat would naturally be captured by the Nepalese-dominated parties.

In the election that followed for fourteen seats, the SSC won eight seats, including the general and one Bhutia–Lepcha seat. The pro-durbar SNP got six seats, including the monastery seat. With his six nominated members, Thondup had a solid block of twelve loyal candidates in the new council. Despite the SSC having won the majority of elected seats, its senior leader Kashi Raj Pradhan, going against the advice of party president Kazi, did not lay claim to the formation of the executive council. That led to Kazi leaving the SSC and forming his own party—the Sikkim Swatantra Dal (SSD)—with the help of Namgay Tshering. Friction also developed within the SNP, which led to the ouster of its president Sonam Tshering and the election of Martam Topden (Karma Topden's father) in his place. Karma Topden was the protocol and intelligence chief to the Chogyal when I went to Gangtok. Soon after, an election petition against Kashi Raj Pradhan was accepted. In the re-election that followed, he lost his seat to C.D. Rai who had left his government job to re-enter politics. But unlike Pradhan, Rai was not given the post of an executive councillor in the five-member executive council.

In September 1959, three leaders—Kazi from the SSD, Rai from the SSC and Sonam Tshering from the SNP—met at Melli and decided to form a new party that was launched at Singtam in May 1960 under the name of the SNC. The Singtam declaration of the SNC demanded establishment of a responsible government, framing of a new constitution, universal adult franchise on the basis of 'one man, one vote' and a joint electorate. With the formation of a new party, Kazi attacked the undemocratic way in which the government in Sikkim was running, based on proclamations only. He even threatened to launch a satyagraha if his party's demands were not met by the maharaja.

A copy of the Singtam declaration was sent to Prime Minister Nehru. Given the threat of satyagraha, a prompt invitation came for the SNC leaders to visit New Delhi. The SNC delegation comprising Kazi, C.D. Rai, Sonam Tshering and a few others reached the national capital and finally met Nehru on 26 August 1960. Nehru read the contents of the declaration sympathetically and told the SNC delegates that the MEA, in consultation with the PO, would try to help them resolve their differences with the maharaja. But as was the case in November 1953, when a Kazi-led delegation of the SSC visited New Delhi in connection with their demand for party-to-party relations, nothing significant came out of the visit. But by inviting Kazi to New Delhi, India was able to ward off the threat of satyagraha.

Thereafter, the new government, obviously under the guidance of Thondup, took two controversial decisions. The first was the Sikkim Subjects Regulation of 1961, which was published in the *Sikkim Darbar Gazette, Extraordinary*, dated 3 July 1961. It laid down stringent requirements for securing the status of a subject of Sikkim (a citizenship of sorts). According to these provisions, a large number of Nepalese people in the south and west of Sikkim became ineligible for this status. According to one clause, even subjects could be dispossessed of this status if they criticized the maharaja in public. The second decision pertained to the increase in the strength of the Sikkim Guards to act as some sort of indigenous militia. While the SSC and the Kazi-led SNC opposed this, all four parties, including the SSC and the SNC were opposed to the newly published regulation. They also criticized the GoI for having approved such a discriminatory measure. The Kazi-led SNC, in their demonstration, raised slogans like 'India practices democracy at home and imperialism abroad.' Kazi also criticized the proposed increase in the strength of Sikkim Guards on the grounds that it could be used to crush political opposition in the state. All four political parties agreed to call off their agitation only in February 1962, after the durbar agreed to make suggested changes in the regulation. No action was taken on the decision to increase the strength of the Sikkim Guards. It was postponed.

The durbar, meanwhile, planned to hold early elections in 1962, but the Sino-Indian war of October 1962 led to a change of plans. The third general election was finally held in March 1967. Before that, based on the discussion between the durbar and the political parties, it was decided to further increase the overall strength of the state council from twenty to twenty-four. As per this agreement, the number of Nepalese and Bhutia–Lepcha councillors was raised by one to make it seven each. In addition, one seat each for the scheduled castes and Tsongs were added for the first time. The SNC won eight out of the eighteen seats it contested. The SNP and SSC got five and two seats, respectively. The three seats belonging to the Tsongs, scheduled castes and monasteries did not belong to any party. Out of the six members nominated by the maharaja, three were government servants. An interesting outcome of this election was that though the SNC won the largest number of seats amongst the political parties, Thondup ignored Kazi's claim to the post of an executive councillor, which naturally attracted bitter criticism from Kazi, and his wife, Elisa-Maria, of Chakung (Kazi's estate), also called the Kazini.

Elections were held for the fourth time in April 1970, in a highly polarized and tense atmosphere in which two factions of the pro-Thondup SNP, a faction of the SNC led by the ever shifty B.B. Gurung, and even the remnants of the old SSC party, made the revision of the Indo-Sikkim Treaty of 1950 a major election issue. It was only Kazi, supported by the Kazini, who stood his ground and insisted that the call for revision of the treaty was ill-timed, futile and not in the overall interest of the general public who needed urgent political, economic and land reforms. When the results were declared, the pro-Thondup SNP won seven seats, SSC got four, and despite the anti-Thondup votes being divided by the SSC and the B.B. Gurung faction of the SNC, Kazi's SNC got five seats.

Kazi was somehow able to convince his arch-rival Netuk Tshering, leader of the pro-Thondup SNP, to form a two-party coalition government comprising the SNP and the SNC, rather than leaving it to the discretion of Thondup to choose members of the executive council. A clever move, indicating the privilege of elected representatives to exercise their right to form their own government. It was obviously not to the liking of Thondup, but unlike 1967, this time Kazi was included in the executive council.

This makes it clear that the election system in Sikkim, introduced by Thondup for the first time through the Royal Proclamation of 1953, and thereafter amended from time to time, was so devised as to ensure complete control of the durbar over deliberations in the council and actions of the members of the executive council (cabinet). Though some powers were vested in the executive council, all its decisions were subject to royal approval. Cabinet posts were not a right of the parties even with the largest number of seats in the council. The maharaja used that as his prerogative to cause defections from the pro-democratic parties by doling out cabinet posts to persons of his choice. The extent of the status accorded to the executive councillors could be judged from the fact that while secretaries holding the charge of the non-transferred and reserved subjects under the direct charge of the maharaja were allowed to fly state flags on their jeeps, the executive councillors (ministers) were not allowed to do so. Also, sometimes two executive councillors were asked to share one jeep as their official vehicle.[5] Without flags, they had to park their vehicles at the nearby Nor-khill Hotel and walk to their respective seats at the Paljor stadium as and when there were public functions there. On the other hand, all flag-bearing cars, including army vehicles of and above the rank of colonels, were allowed to go till the entry gate of the stadium.

The table below* will make it clear that due to the manipulating tactics used by Thondup, with each successive election, the number of seats won by the pro-Thondup SNP continued to increase while the number of seats secured by pro-reform parties decreased. Efforts were also made to create a split in the pro-reform parties' votes by encouraging more than one party to contest against the SNP. Further, members of Kazi's party—first the SSC and later the SNC—continued to be persecuted by lodging one case or another against them. Its general secretaries, namely C.D. Rai, L.B. Basnet, B.B. Gurung, S.K. Rai, C.S. Rai and Nand Lal Thapa, were successively targeted and even compelled to leave the party. The latest victims of this policy were Kazi and Khatiwada who had to tender apologies to the Chogyal for an article critical of the durbar, which had appeared in the *SNC Bulletin* in 1972, to be allowed to contest the January 1973 elections.

	Political Party	1953	1958	1967	1970	1973	Total
1.	Sikkim State Congress	6	8	2	4	2	22
2.	Sikkim National Party	6	6	5	7	9	33
3.	Sikkim National Congress	-	-	8	5	5	18
4	Unattached Independents	-	-	3	2	2	7
5.	Total Elective Seats in the Council	12	14	18	18	18	80

*   IDE/JETRO-funded study, 'Sub-Regional Relations in the Eastern South Asia: With Special Focus on India's North Eastern Region: Chapter 8', A.C. Sinha, 2005, http://www.ide.go.jp/English/Publish/Download/Jrp/133.html.

The powers of the diwan appointed after the 1949 demonstrations were gradually curtailed. After the first two diwans—Lall and Rustomji—their utility mainly depended upon their capacity to neutralize the Indian PO's anti-Chogyal moves. The last of the diwans, by then called 'sidlon' (a Tibetan term for the head of administration), I.S. Chopra, a retired IFS officer who came on special recommendation by T.N. Kaul, was so deferential in his attitude towards the Chogyal that he lost all credibility with the PO and the Prime Minister's Office (PMO). This is evident from a paragraph in a note dated 14 March 1972, recorded by P.N. Haksar for the prime minister's perusal:[6]

> We have placed in the durbar of Sikkim a most unscrupulous adventurer I have ever come across in the shape and form of Shri I.S. Chopra. He has no loyalties to anything and least of all to his own country. But he was a friend of the foreign secretary and has always been a smooth operator. Having become the diwan of Sikkim, he could not care less what happened to Indo-Sikkimese relations.

Chopra left Sikkim in August 1972 and the Chogyal kept this position vacant thereafter, although he did drop a hint that it may be filled by a competent Sikkimese. However, when the time came to use the services of a competent sidlon as a buffer between him and the demonstrators marching on the streets of Gangtok in April 1973, the Chogyal found himself in direct confrontation with the pro-democratic forces. Actually, the need to compel the Chogyal to accept an India-appointed sidlon/diwan, by building pressure on him through the anti-Chogyal demonstration was the main subject of discussion at the meeting held on 14 March 1973 in Foreign Secretary Kewal Singh's room. This has been discussed in Chapter VII.

During the period reviewed in this chapter, some important developments took place in Sikkim, which require a special mention. These were Kazi's marriage to Eliza-Maria Langford-Rae in 1958, Thondup's marriage to Hope Cooke in 1963 and Thondup's coronation on 4 April 1965.

Kazi met Eliza-Maria through a common Nepalese friend in New Delhi in 1957. Born in Edinburgh, Scotland, she spent some time in Belgium before moving to Burma in the 1920s with her husband, an Anglo-Burmese named Langford-Rae. After their divorce, she was briefly married to a Dr Khan, about whom little is known. She finally surfaced in New Delhi in the 1950s and soon became a well-known face in the city's social and political circles. To earn a living, she undertook jobs and assignments, including teaching French at a local school and to some individuals. After a few meetings, Kazi and Eliza-Maria developed a liking for each other, which led to their marriage in 1958 at the ages of fifty and fifty-three, respectively. Eliza-Maria, accompanied by her husband, came to Kalimpong and started living in Chakung House. Being an exuberant European, she soon came to be known as Kazini Sahiba of Chakung in the social and political circles of Kalimpong and Sikkim.

In addition to being a well-known centre for Indo-Tibet trade via Sikkim's Nathu La and Jalep La, before these were closed by the Chinese in 1962, Kalimpong was notorious for its intelligence-gathering activities. In view of this, the Kazini took to the town like a fish to water. The town had an SIB (subsidiary intelligence bureau) office located in an imposing and well-located building, which looked like a small castle on top of a hillock. It had a local newspaper called *Himalayan Observer*, which came in handy for her to plant pro-Kazi and anti-Chogyal news reports.

Much has been said and written about the Kazini and her role in the political developments in Sikkim, and also about her ambitions. Most of it was negative. I would, therefore, like to present my opinion on her activities based on personal observation and knowledge. Kazi was shy and spoke little English. The Kazini more than made up on both these counts. She could draft party letters, manifestos and resolutions in English. She could write pro-party and anti-Chogyal articles for the local press. She was a good sounding board for Kazi to know what was happening in the party behind his back as a number of younger party leaders would meet her and convey what they would not have told Kazi because of their respect for his political stature and age.

By marrying the Kazini, Kazi suddenly went from being a comparatively obscure person to being noticed in New Delhi's social and political circles, owing to his wife's previous access. So did the cause for which he was fighting. The Kazini was a very shrewd and intelligent but often manipulative person with a talent for back-room politics. As a foreigner, she could attack Thondup and Hope in a manner that would have been difficult for Kazi as he was a Sikkim subject and could have invited the Chogyal's wrath resulting in his losing the right to contest elections. The Kazini, by her highly critical references, both in private and public, about the Chogyal, his family members and his autocratic regime, wanted to convey to the Sikkimese people, especially Kazi's partymen, that the Chogyal had feet of clay and could easily be pushed over. By doing so, she also wanted to take the fear of the Chogyal and his system out of the minds of the less-privileged section of the Sikkimese population. If cornered by the Chogyal, Kazi could always distance himself from the Kazini's activities by taking refuge behind her well-publicized, uncontrollable and independent style of functioning. She could pick up her phone and talk to anybody, including PO Bajpai (in French), to convey her views on developments of current interests. Though mostly exaggerated, she thought that at least some of that would stick on to the listeners.

She knew about Kazi's contacts with the R&AW, and before that with the IB. Although Kazi would not tell her the real content of our conversation, being shrewd and highly perceptive, she could judge the motive behind our meetings. For me, she was a compulsive supplier of unsolicited and subjective, if not doctored, 'intelligence' reports sent through Myngma. Almost all these reports used to contain information against persons who, for one reason or the other, had fallen foul of her at some point. It was not important to her whether such persons still enjoyed Kazi's trust. It would be relevant to mention here that she did not send a single report to me against Khatiwada (her estranged adopted son), although their rift had become public knowledge. She knew that Khatiwada continued to be relevant to Kazi's cause and she would not be able to poison our minds against him.

While pursuing her little games, the Kazini was fully conscious of her limitations insofar as the GoI's interests in Sikkim were concerned. As and when I met Kazi at his home, she would leave us alone after a few minutes. But during those few minutes she would continue with her diatribe against one person or the other. In our very first meeting at Kalimpong, after she had left us alone, Kazi told me not to take serious note of what she was saying and suggested that it would be better if I listened to her from one ear and let it pass through the other. In another meeting, he told me that the Kazini was fond of playing her little games (*apne khel khelti rehti hai*) and we need not be concerned with what she was saying or doing. It soon became obvious to me that Kazi was selectively using her to further his interests, allowing her the flexibility of indulging in her little games as long as these did not go against his party's long-term interests.

Regarding her alleged dream of becoming the queen of independent Sikkim, the Kazini was shrewd enough to know the limits to which it could be realized. She knew that India would not like to replace the Chogyal with another independent body, entity or institution. What she wanted to become was the modern-day equivalent of a queen, i.e., the chief minister's wife, with all the pomp and show that came with it. But unfortunately for her, B.B. Lal, first as chief executive and later as governor, stood in her way of fully enjoying that status. At the cost of becoming rather unpopular with the members of a friendly political party and its leaders, Lal tried to keep Kazi and his cabinet, formed after Sikkim became an associate state in 1974, on a short leash, thereby giving the Kazini very little chance to play the role of the queen. Her relations with Lal soured, and in private conversation, she started calling him 'father-in-law'. She did try to teach him a lesson on 10 March 1975, when she arranged a meeting between Prince Tenzing and Kazi. But that did not work to her satisfaction as she had bitten off more than she could chew. However, her antics gave Lal, PO Gurbachan Singh, their officers and me one sleepless night, resulting in a late-night emergency meeting at India House.

Unfortunately, the Kazini's dreams were shattered with her husband's ignominious defeat in the 1979 elections. Thereafter, she moved back to her husband's home in Kalimpong. Totally ignored and neglected by those who used to cool their heels outside her house when Kazi was at the height of political power, the Kazini retreated into a shell and developed mild dementia. Longing to go back to her place of birth in Scotland, she died in 1989 at the age of eighty-five.

Thondup's first wife, Sangey Deki, whom he had married in 1951, died on 17 June 1957, leaving behind two sons and a daughter. Feeling lonely, he started spending time at his favourite hotel, Windamere, in Darjeeling. He met Hope Cooke there for the first time in the summer of 1959. Her mother had died during divorce proceedings with Hope's father, a pilot instructor. Hope was less than two years old at that time. Her elder stepsister and she were brought up by their maternal grandparents in New York. One of Hope's uncles, Selden Chapin, was a respected US diplomat and was posted as the ambassador to Iran during that period. Thondup and Hope started to get to know each other better during subsequent meetings. Smitten by her youthful charm and suitably impressed by her American descent, Thondup proposed to her. The courtship continued for almost four years. They finally got married on 20 March 1963. Thondup was forty years old at that time and Hope was twenty-three.

Thondup's marriage to Hope brought about a sea change in the situation in Gangtok, which had a direct impact on the already-floundering relations of Thondup with the POs, especially Bajpai, and with the GoI. Sikkim started attracting international attention, both in the media and social and political circles, especially in the US. To attract such attention, or the other way around, Hope started behaving like the future queen of an independent Sikkim. According to an article which appeared in the 2 July 1973 issue of *Newsweek*, 'Hope set out to be more of an Oriental queen that ever existed this side of Siam. In speaking of herself (which she invariably did) in a Jackie Kennedy whisper, she effected the regal "we" and demanded to be treated with deference due to royalty.'

In the palace, she created her circle of close friends. She also started taking an interest in the activities of the newly created Study Forum that comprised over 100 so-called intellectuals from Sikkim, whose main task was to locate or create avenues to internationalize its separate identity. She started attracting a steady stream of foreign guests, including some distinguished ones like the US ambassador to India Kenneth Keating and Senator Charles Percy. Close scrutiny of their background for grant of visas and delay, and sometimes denial of inner line permits, for visits to strategically sensitive areas of north Sikkim became a major area of friction between the PO and the durbar. Some of these guests on their return carried stories of the alleged ill treatment meted out to Thondup and Hope by the GoI. Influenced by some of these visitors, India started getting adverse publicity in the West, indicating that, somehow, it was standing in the way of Sikkim's much-deserved independence. It must be said that while it was Thondup who was the driving force behind this campaign to build pressure on India to revise the treaty of 1950, it was actually Hope who helped him internationalize the issue. It was against this background that the coronation ceremony of Thondup, which was held on 4 April 1965, attracted international attention with the *Washington Post* writing: 'Americans are well aware that Monaco is touched with Grace; now Sikkim is radiant with Hope.'

It was Hope's article titled 'Sikkim's theory of Land Holdings and the Darjeeling Grant', which appeared in the 1966 issue of a magazine published by the government-funded local Institute of Tibetology (established in 1950), that created a stir in India House in Gangtok, as well as in New Delhi. In this article, she disputed India's right to hold Darjeeling on the plea that no Sikkimese maharaja had the right to alienate Sikkimese territory to any other power. Further, the grant was made in 1835 in the nature of a gift involving the transfer of only tenancy rights for a particular purpose and for a particular period, and it did not involve transfer of sovereign rights. In fact, that article was a reiteration of the request for retrocession of the Darjeeling area contained in a thirty-page memo prepared by a well-known

legal brain of his time, Sirdar D.K. Sen, which Maharaja Tashi
Namgyal had submitted to the British Viceroy on 1 August 1947,
only fifteen days before India's independence.[7] However, Hope's
article created a lot of commotion in India, and Indira Gandhi
had to explain in parliament that there was no demand from
any responsible quarter in Sikkim laying claim to Darjeeling. To
soothe India's ruffled feathers, Thondup later dismissed Hope's
article as a purely academic exercise.

With regard to Hope's alleged connection with the Central
Intelligence Agency (CIA), I had not seen any report or paper
that could throw light on this subject. As counter-intelligence
was in the charter of the IB, it was not our job to look for such
evidence. If the IB had any such evidence, they did not share it
with me. Hope had already left Gangtok for good on 15 August
1973, about twelve days before I arrived. On that fateful day, she
came to India House, all packed and accompanied by her children
to attend the Indian Independence Day celebrations and left for
Bagdogra, on her way to New York.

We actually did not believe that she was a CIA agent placed
in Gangtok to further US interests in that strategic region. If
the CIA really wanted to use Hope Cooke to work towards the
independence of Sikkim, the operation could have been better
planned. In that case, Hope should have been moving around
in south and west Sikkim, looking after the interests of the
estranged Nepalese population by opening hospitals, dispensaries,
schools and carrying out other welfare activities to win over their
sympathies and allegiance to the Chogyal. Further, she would
have asked Thondup to somewhat loosen his vice-like grip on
Sikkim's administration by sharing some real power with the
elected representatives of the people. On the contrary, she further
alienated Thondup from his people, especially from the Nepalese
community and their leaders, when she started behaving like a

thoroughbred Tibetan queen in the making, with all the matching mannerisms, social etiquettes and apparel.

With due apologies to my CIA friends, some of our Indian friends with whom we had discussed this matter felt we were giving too much credit to the agency's operational planners. They were of the view that how could the CIA operators lose sight of such an opportunity offered by the lonely maharaja of a strategically located state, yearning to find a suitable match in the romantic atmosphere of a colonial-era hotel in Darjeeling. But we would still like to give the benefit of the doubt to the CIA. At best, Hope's accidental positioning as Thondup's wife provided additional access to the CIA, on the American citizen network, to information of interest in this area. At worst, she was handled by an ill-informed, or even incompetent operator, which is hard to believe.

Our benefit of the doubt emanates from the fact that the CIA did not require additional access to information of crucial interest from Sikkim, as Thondup and his intelligence chief Karma Topden were already known to the CIA officials in Calcutta. In the 1950s, Thondup, as maharaj kumar, had visited Lhasa twice. He first visited his in-laws in Lhasa with his wife on a customary visit after the birth of their first child. During his second visit, he had carried an invitation for the Dalai Lama to a function organized by the Maha Bodhi Society of India. On his return, on both occasions, he was debriefed by the CIA operators posted at the US Consulate in Calcutta. Thondup used to visit London and New York once or twice a year, especially after his marriage to Hope. He also used to stay in Calcutta, where a US Consulate was located. During those visits, he was easily available for debriefing to the CIA or MI6 operatives.

It was also not difficult for a technically advanced agency, such as the CIA, to continue getting information of interest through their existing contacts without creating a high-level and visible contact such as Hope. Also, the CIA did not require an undercover agent to obtain information which was so openly and easily available. Some sort of weekly (news) letter, religiously sent every week to their respective 'parents' by two Scottish headmistresses of the local Paljor Namgyal Girls' School, Martha Hamilton (1959–66) and her successor Isabel Ritchie (1966–96), could have served their purpose equally well.

But unlike Thondup, Hope was intelligent enough to have realized the true implications of the 8 May 1973 agreement rather soon, and left Sikkim in August that year. By doing so, she avoided the agony of being a witness to her husband's ultimate downfall. She soon sought divorce from Thondup and it took some time and effort on her part to regain her US citizenship which she had renounced after her marriage. She presently lives in New York.

Before we move ahead, it would be relevant to examine as to how far the Kazini and Hope Cooke had been useful in furthering the agenda of their respective husbands. Both these ladies had their own reasons for entering into their marriages in 1958 and 1963, respectively. In our opinion, for the Kazini it was possibly the role of her lifetime which she had been longing to play for a long time. Kazi gave her sufficient leeway to perform that role and allowed her enough scope to display her histrionic talent and manipulative skills. She helped Kazi run his party. Her target was, of course, Thondup and his family, and later Hope Cooke or some others who came in her way. Whenever Thondup or his protégés raised the issue of treaty revision, she stood like a rock behind Kazi to oppose such a move on the plea that political and administrative reforms in Sikkim were more important than treaty revision. In short, in our view, she proved to be an asset to Kazi.

On the other hand, it seems to us that Hope entered into her marriage with Thondup with a dream of playing the role of a queen in a dreamland tucked away in the far corners of the Himalayas. But unlike the Kazini, Hope had married a man who had a predetermined and fixed agenda which did not leave much scope for her to do whatever she liked. We think that she did help her husband to some extent in articulating his thoughts and moves towards securing independent status for Sikkim. She also helped in projecting the image and 'problems' of the tiny state of Sikkim at an international level.

About Hope's utility to Thondup in furthering his pro-independence agenda, the following incident would be a good indicator. During my first meeting with the Chogyal on 15 September 1973, less than a month after my arrival in Gangtok, he told me that he would be going to New Delhi the next day and would meet Prime Minister Indira Gandhi to present his case before her. It was during this period that my predecessor Sayali, who had moved back to the headquarters only in August, got a call from the Chogyal's secretary, Jigdal Densapa, conveying the Chogyal's desire to see him at his Ashoka Hotel suite. With Kao's approval, Sayali called on the Chogyal around 5 p.m.[8] After initial courtesies were exchanged, the Chogyal did not say much. There was an uneasy calm in the room. Sayali felt that the Chogyal wanted to say something but was hesitating. After about thirty minutes, Sayali sought the Chogyal's approval to leave. The Chogyal came up to the main entrance of his suite to see him off. He stood there for some time without uttering a word. Finally, he significantly remarked that 'things would not have been that bad if he had married an Indian woman'. This information was promptly passed on by Sayali to Kao.

Looking back, we feel the Chogyal's remarks were open to various interpretations. Obviously, he wanted to convey that information to the prime minister, whom he was to meet, perhaps the next day. His relations with Hope till then had not soured, as he told me on 15 September that he would be going to New York soon after his visit to New Delhi to meet her and the children. He was expecting Hope to return to Gangtok with the children soon thereafter. He also knew that nobody, least of all Indira Gandhi, would believe that it was only Hope who was responsible for all that had happened in Sikkim. Perhaps the main reason why he had said so was to convey to the prime minister that had he not married Hope, his demands for treaty revision, etc., would not have attracted so much international attention. Also, it was that international attention or limelight, which led him to believe that he could ignore India's offer of permanent association in the hope that continued international pressure would finally compel India to give him what he wanted.

Thondup's father, Maharaja Tashi Namgyal, whose reign lasted almost fifty years, died of cancer on 2 December 1963. Due to his elder son and heir apparent Paljor's death in 1941, Tashi Namgyal had left the work of the state entirely in Thondup's hands and started living an almost-reclusive life. In that context, Thondup's coronation was a mere formality. Much after the customary period of one year of mourning, the coronation ceremony was held on 4 April 1965. After repeated attempts by Thondup, the GoI had finally agreed to bestow the titles of Chogyal and Gyalmo (Dharamaraja and Dharamarani, which had gone into disuse since the British rule) on Thondup and Hope, only a few days before the coronation. This further added to the glamour of the ceremony. At the coronation, the Indian government was represented by minister of state for external affairs, Lakshmi Menon. Indira Gandhi, who was included in Shastri's cabinet as minister of information and broadcasting after her father's death, attended in a personal capacity as Thondup's guest and stayed in a specially decorated suite of the palace guest house.

The coronation speech prepared by Thondup's friend Nari Rustomji, who was at that time adviser to the King of Bhutan, contained some interesting remarks about Sikkim's separate identity and its desire to gain a status like that of Bhutan or Nepal.[9] This is evident from the following:

> Our good neighbours, Bhutan and Nepal, are also much in our thoughts today and we shall continue to cherish their friendship . . . Ours is a small country, but we have pride in our institutions, our way of life and cultural heritage. It is for this that we are resolved to maintain our national identity and so direct our affairs that our land may develop according to its own genius.

The above contents of the coronation speech were loaded with references to Sikkim's desire to project and secure independent identity, and hence could not have been allowed to go uncontested by Menon. In her reply, Menon reminded Thondup that 'India has had long and historic relations with Sikkim, which go far beyond the terms which Your Highness's late distinguished father concluded with India.' The implications were clear. Menon wanted to remind Thondup, now as Chogyal, that the status of 'protectorate' that Sikkim enjoyed through the signing of the treaty of 1950, was nothing new but in fact a continuation of the relationship since the British days.

Chapter V

Demands for the Revision of the 1950 Treaty (1967–72)

When the Indo-Sikkim Treaty of 1950 was signed, which granted Sikkim protectorate status, the two sides had entered into this relationship willingly and in good faith. The provisions of this treaty had drawn a *lakshman rekha* that neither of the two signatories was expected to transgress. There were no legal grounds for Sikkim to be treated as a special case. It was plain and simple Nehru's gesture. Had Nehru not helped Sikkim, it would have been merged with India along with the other princely states without any protest. In view of that, it was felt Thondup would be grateful to Nehru and his daughter, Indira Gandhi, as prime ministers and would not do any anything that would counter the letter and spirit of that treaty.

But Thondup had never reconciled to the fact that as per clause II of the treaty, Sikkim was still a protectorate of India, as was the case during the British rule. He craved for a status similar to that of Bhutan. To this end, he appeared to have devised a two-pronged strategy. Initially, he asked for the removal of the word 'protectorate' through an amendment to the clause. Thereafter, having sufficiently softened India through his old tricks, as well as domestic and international pressure, he upgraded his demand by insisting on a new treaty relationship to be signed between two 'sovereign' states, permitting India only to defend the Sikkim-Tibet border that was crucial to India's strategic interests in this region.

To initiate his plan of action, he started looking for a suitable opportunity. China's occupation of Tibet in 1950, the Dalai Lama's flight to India in 1959 and the reverses suffered by India in the Sino-Indian war of 1962 further strengthened his resolve in the pursuit of his ultimate goal. Karma Topden came to see me on 29 October 2017 during one of his consultation visits to a New Delhi Hospital (unfortunately he died of cancer on 8 August 2018).[1] I asked him why Thondup did not apply pressure on India following the debacle in the 1962 war. Topden remarked that some of the Chogyal's friends in the media from the UK advised him to take advantage of India's weakness at that stage and press for a revision of the treaty. But Thondup preferred to wait for some more time till India was more comfortable in handling his request. Maybe it was his gratitude towards Nehru, who was still alive, which held him back from pursuing his ambition at that time.

Nehru died in May 1964. When his successor Lal Bahadur Shastri was settling down into the job, India got embroiled in a war with Pakistan in 1965. In Tashkent to attend a Soviet-brokered meeting with Pakistani President Yahya Khan, Shastri succumbed to a massive heart attack the same day that he signed the Tashkent Agreement—10 January 1966. Thondup had had a courtesy-call meeting with Shastri before that, but nothing significant was discussed. Thondup knew the new prime minister, Indira Gandhi, well. He had spent a few months as Nehru's guest at Teen Murti House, when his father had requested Nehru 'to help his son to grow up to shoulder the responsibilities that would fall to his lot in future'.[2] He had also met her when she had accompanied her father to Sikkim in 1952 and then in 1958. Later, she attended Thondup's coronation in 1965 in her personal capacity. So, he might have thought that Indira Gandhi, like her father, would also be sympathetic to his demands.

Within a year of Gandhi taking over as prime minister, Thondup realized that it was time to implement the second stage of his strategy. He came up with a three-pronged approach this time. First, he increased the pace of anti-India propaganda in Sikkim and used his trusted media contacts, both from India and abroad, to give more publicity to such activities in Sikkim. Second, he started projecting a separate identity for Sikkim. Lastly, he started using the pro-Sikkim lobbies in India that he had very carefully cultivated over the years to help further his cause. This included senior army officers—both locally posted and visiting—some GoI civil servants—both retired and serving, working on long-term deputation in Sikkim and visiting senior civil servants—and also political figures whom he had wined and dined, and who would return to India loaded with gifts purchased out of GoI-provided aid. All these people came in rather handy in projecting a favourable view of Thondup in the decision-making circles in India.

It was in this setting that Hope's article on the return of the Darjeeling areas by India was published in 1966 in the bulletin of the government-funded Institute of Tibetology. By then, Hope had already convinced the Asia Society in New York to establish a Sikkim Council, a move that was scuttled due to the intervention of the Indian Embassy in Washington DC. In 1967, Coo Coo La sent two Sikkimese women representatives to attend the Associated Country Women of the World (ACWW) Conference to display Sikkim's artefacts, including the Sikkimese flag. The next year, two artisans represented Sikkim at the World Crafts Council meeting in Peru.

Thondup, accompanied by Hope, used their visits to London and New York to build and nurse their contacts in diplomatic and other influential circles. They liked being addressed as 'Your Majesty' and 'Queen' by the obliging press and at social and private parties. A.C. Sinha, in his book *Politics of Sikkim* (Thomson Press, 1975), notes that a 2 July 1973 article published in *Newsweek*, said:[3]

> The Chogyal and Hope seemed to be dashing off to Europe and the United States almost constantly. On each return, the palace-controlled *Sikkim Herald* would make a big thing of announcing just which king and queen had entertained the Sikkim ruler—a not-so subtle attempt to imply parity between the royal houses of Europe and the rustic court of Gangtok.

However, while Thondup and others were harping on their demand for a revision of the treaty, Kazi and the Kazini did not lose any opportunity to oppose such moves, describing the need for political and economic reforms in Sikkim as more important.

Thondup also caught hold of over 100 so-called intellectuals from Sikkim and created a Study Forum to advise him on issues concerning Sikkim's national interests. Three of the suggestions of the forum were that Sikkim should join the Colombo Plan, print its own stamps to earn foreign exchange, as Bhutan was doing, and refuse aid from India if it was not extended with grace.

Meanwhile, Thondup got a news report published in the Kolkata-based newspaper *Statesman*, which most of the SNC leaders believed to be pro-Chogyal, that described the treaty as a 'hopelessly outdated straightjacket'. In May 1967, Thondup called a press conference at the palace and told the reporters that his 'country' wanted political freedom, but he was willing to wait for the convenience of the GoI. On 6 June, he elaborated on his demand further by saying that he wanted India to look after the defence of Sikkim only, leaving the rest to him to handle. He also questioned the justification for continuing with an Indian-appointed diwan (a title that was later changed to its Tibetan equivalent, sidlon). He felt that this post could be filled by a competent Sikkimese as and when available. A few days later, on 15 June, three members of Sikkim's executive council issued an unprecedented statement which said that every country had a right to seek review of its treaty obligations. Simultaneously, the government publication, *Sikkim Herald,* mentioned that if India did not start negotiations with Sikkim about the treaty revision, it would be seen as an imperialist power.[4]

While Thondup was increasing pressure on India for revising the treaty, Indira Gandhi's position had weakened considerably due to the Congress's poor performance in the fourth general elections in 1967. This had compelled her to form a coalition government. Further, the Congress government in the neighbouring Indian state of West Bengal had also lost power to a Communist-led coalition. Simultaneously, the ultra-left Naxalite movement picked up momentum in the neighbouring Naxalbari area of West Bengal. In Sikkim, on 11 September 1967, PLA troops stationed at Nathu La launched an attack on Indian positions. The clashes continued for four days. Similar clashes took place in the nearby Cho La sector on 1 October. Though the Chinese troops were pushed back with heavy losses, these clashes were a reminder for the Indian leadership of the fragility of peace in this strategic area. Irrespective of what had been mentioned in the 1950 treaty, Thondup interpreted these clashes as a harsh reminder to India of the continued need to keep him in good humour if it needed his cooperation and permission to use his territory to defend itself. But for doing that he wanted to extract a price—the independence of Sikkim.

It was in this moment of weakness that India tried its best to placate him. In September 1967, Thondup, accompanied by Hope and other members of his family, was received by Indira Gandhi and some of her cabinet colleagues at the airport, a courtesy normally extended to the head of state of a friendly country. A government aircraft was placed at his party's disposal to take them around south India, to see places of tourist and religious interest.

Whether by accident or design, Thondup had timed the escalation of his demands with the expected return of his old friend T.N. Kaul to the Indian Foreign Office, as secretary (east) to finally take over as foreign secretary in November 1968, a post he continued to occupy till 3 December 1972. It was perhaps in this context that P.N. Dhar, who was Indira Gandhi's principal secretary, mentioned that Thondup 'was encouraged by several Indian officials whom he pampered. Some of them are believed to have held out prospects of a United Nations (UN) membership for Sikkim, and the Chogyal thus believed that Delhi was too weak to resist his demands'.[5]

It was in this setting that India's Deputy Prime Minister Morarji Desai visited Gangtok in March 1968. Desai agreed with Thondup's suggestion that the excise duty levied by New Delhi on items imported to and exported out of Sikkim, could be returned to Sikkim. As excise duty was a central government (federal) tax, it was an indirect admission of Sikkim's separate status.

Thereafter Indira Gandhi, accompanied by Kaul, visited Gangtok in May. During the course of discussions with Thondup, she did informally agree that the treaty needed to be revised to accommodate some of his demands, but expressed her inability to do so due to her politically weak position at home. This was followed by a scathing article in a local fortnightly, *Sikkim*, which said that the treaty must be revised and registered with the UN. It threatened that the Sikkimese would go to any length to get their rights, failing which they would be compelled to repeat the underground Naga story (referring to the then prevailing insurgency in India's north-eastern state of Nagaland). On 15 August, when India's Independence Day was being celebrated at India House, a bunch of schoolchildren took out an anti-India procession in the nearby roads of Gangtok, carrying placards bearing slogans such as 'India Get Out of Sikkim',[6] 'We are Buffer Not Duffer' and 'We Want Independence'. This led to members of parliament (MPs) in India raising questions about this so-called 'Quit Sikkim Movement' that sounded similar to the Quit India Movement during India's independence struggle against the British. Gandhi, however, dismissed the incident as minor and assured the MPs that the matter had been taken up strongly with the Chogyal. Later that year, when Kaul visited Gangtok, he warned Thondup that if such activities were not stopped he could forget about India's support for membership of the UN or other international bodies.

During this period, the influential *Time* magazine also came out with an article titled 'Sikkim: A Queen Revisited', describing Hope's daily routine as the lifestyle of 'America's only working Queen'.

To keep the dialogue going with Thondup, India's External Affairs Minister Dinesh Singh (he held that post from 14 February 1969 to 27 June 1970) visited Gangtok in May 1969. Singh agreed that Sikkim had a special status and compared its position to that of Monaco, which had an observer status in the UN. Thondup, on the other hand, felt that Sikkim was more akin to Luxembourg, a landlocked independent state in Europe.

Singh also mentioned that Sikkim may soon be able to issue its own postal stamps, which Thondup saw as Singh's personal opinion.

Soon after Singh's visit, the mercurial K.C. Pradhan, along with Namgyal Tshering (formerly close to Kazi), formed a group called the United Front which published leaflets and pasted posters demanding a revision of the treaty. Pradhan held a number of public meetings in which he alleged that the 1950 treaty was signed 'under duress and deception'. Further, he said that 'independence is the people's demand and not [the] King's' and that the 'Chogyal cannot go against the nation's wishes'.[7] It was obvious these activities were taking place with Thondup's encouragement, approval, or even guidance.

By September 1970, T.N. Kaul had already prepared a draft of the revised treaty through which Sikkim was to be offered a status of 'permanent association' compared to the 'protectorate' status it enjoyed through the 1950 treaty. To seek the views of some senior Indian government officials, a meeting was held in Kaul's room.[8] It was attended by the then army chief Sam Manekshaw, H.C. Sarin from the ministry of defence, home secretary L.P. Singh, R&AW chief R.N. Kao and M.M.L. Hooja, director, IB. As Kayanti Shankar Bajpai, PO-designate, was in town, he was also asked to attend this meeting. Kaul explained the contents of the draft treaty and invited comments from those present. Other than Manekshaw, no one else objected to Kaul's proposals. Manekshaw said, 'You do whatever you like, but I must have full freedom over deployment and operations of my troops in Sikkim.' As Bajpai was yet to take charge as PO at Gangtok, he said that he could give his opinion only after studying the situation on the ground for some time.

Bajpai is now ninety years old and lives in his sprawling ancestral home in New Delhi's New Friends Colony. To get an idea of what was happening at the MEA during that period, I had two long sessions with him at his residence in March and April 2018. In the second, Devare (first secretary and later second in command at the political office in Gangtok at the time I was posted there) was also present. Our discussions continued even at the dining table, where typical of him, a very delicious lunch was served. His mental faculties are as sharp as ever.

According to Bajpai, within a couple of months of his arrival in Gangtok, he informed Kaul that there was nothing so serious there that could not be managed to India's advantage. Further, taking advantage of India's ambivalent attitude towards Sikkim, the durbar had usurped most of the powers which India used to wield either directly or through the India-appointed diwan/sidlon. The situation, he said, could be reversed gradually if India exhibited clarity in its policy and dealt with the Chogyal firmly. He felt that there was no need to revise the 1950 treaty. Finding Kaul not very responsive to his suggestions, Bajpai, during his visits to New Delhi, started meeting P.N. Haksar and Kao informally to tell them what he thought of the situation in Sikkim. He even gave copies of some of his dispatches to the MEA and Kao. Though Bajpai was able to retrieve the respect and position of the PO soon, Kaul continued with his pursuit of getting a new Treaty of Permanent Association signed by the Chogyal.

According to Bajpai's own records, it was obvious that by the time he joined as PO in September 1970, the MEA was still trying to formulate a firm policy towards Sikkim. In that context, three options were being considered. These were independence, closer relations and the continuity of the 1950 relations. As a merger was still unthinkable and independence was unacceptable, the choice was between closer relations as envisaged through Kaul's offer of permanent association and the continuation of the 1950 treaty relationship. But there was no clarity as to how to convince the Chogyal to settle somewhere within the limits laid down by these two parameters. Bajpai, who believed in the utility of the institution of the Chogyal to India within the existing 1950 treaty framework, had reservations about making further concessions to the Chogyal. He had even made this clear to Kaul in his dispatches. Publicly, however, he had no choice but to follow his boss. In view of that, as far as the MEA was concerned, the only viable alternative was Foreign Secretary Kaul's offer of permanent association, which despite his persuasive skills, the Chogyal refused to accept unconditionally.

While the Indian Foreign Office headed by Kaul, in pursuit of its old policy of appeasement towards the Chogyal, was offering one concession or the other, the ever-growing ambitions of the Chogyal had started attracting the attention of the legendary P.N. Haksar. Based on his observations and a number of meetings with Kaul, Haksar put together an incisive note dated 28 November 1970 for the prime minister, which is reproduced below.[9] It appears that this note was prepared by Haksar as a backgrounder to Indira Gandhi's meeting with Thondup.

> I had suggested to [the] FS that we should carefully consider and review the underlying assumptions of our policy in Sikkim. We have had several meetings. Broadly, two points of view have crystallized themselves:

a) That our economic, social and political policies must be designed to involve the people of Sikkim, so that they feel that their destiny lies with India. Our instruments for such a policy should also be carefully chosen. The ultimate aim should be that the people of Sikkim and the people of India begin to share common aspirations, common ideals, common hopes, etc.; and

b) That having regard to our policies in the past and what we have done in Bhutan, there is really no escape from leading Sikkim to a stage where it becomes a sovereign, independent State tied up with India.

My own preference is for the first alternative. Be that as it may, we have to deal, for the time being, with the Chogyal. He is going to impress upon us the need to let Sikkim exercise greater autonomy and responsibility. He will stress as his reasons: the restiveness of his educated classes, particularly the young, under the influence of the spirit of our times and India's own anti-colonial ideals; the infectiousness of developments in Nepal and Bhutan; and the dangers of resentments growing if the natural aspirations of the Sikkimese to do more on their own is denied. He may illustrate the last point with our hesitations over his requests for entering the Colombo Plan, FAO, etc., for having his foreign exchange earnings (through copper and cardamom exports) allotted to Sikkim, for issuing his own stamps, having his own militia to give sense of participation in Sikkim Defense, etc., etc.; he may also complain of India's "broken promises", e.g. to let him have a radio station.

The pressures for change really centre around him and are sufficiently manageable without any basic concessions on our part. P.M. might take the following line with him.

The existing relationship has been as helpful to Sikkim as to India. Where we have been found insufficiently considerate or overly restrictive, we are prepared to have a fresh look and meet all genuine grievances not only sympathetically but also generously. But grievances should not be manufactured or harboured till they become disproportionate—least of all by those elements in Sikkim, the ruling hierarchy, who owe their whole position to the Indian presence. We have an impeccable record of not interfering in Sikkim's domestic politics, and we have relied scrupulously on him alone. We always wish to do this and he should look upon us as his active supporter. The pressures he feels from his educated elite are very understandable and we should like to help him meet them. They cannot be met by giving in to illusions about Sikkim becoming free, prosperous and neutral like an Asian Switzerland if only India would relax its hold. They can best be met by giving the people a realization of the benefits they get from India. They will need, above all, employment opportunities which require economic development. This we would like to increase as far as possible, and if our help can be used to lead the people to be satisfied with the Indian connection, much of what he fears can be met.

It is not correct to suppose that Nepal and Bhutan have achieved greater freedom than Sikkim as compared to their equal position in 1950. Legally, all three States remain in exactly the same position as in 1950, and as for progress, he himself says that Sikkim has done better rupee for rupee. What has changed is the way relations with India have been conducted. In this respect, Nepal is not an example to encourage us, while Bhutan whatever the future may hold, has been most cooperative. We feel we have exercised a benevolent presence in Sikkim, but have not always felt we were appreciated. We do not want gratitude, but do expect friendly cooperative functioning rather than maneuvering for advantage. We have, therefore, to look afresh at Sikkim's practical problems and if possible, increase our help. We would like to feel, however, that we and the Sikkim Government are not working at cross purposes. We admire the leadership he has provided and hope it can build up more confidence on both sides. He can count on us to act as his bulwark in facing his domestic problems; we, on our part, would like to be quite sure that no changes come about that could in any way be used to weaken our security arrangements.

For the present, therefore, we would like to see how we can meet his immediate needs. It is difficult to alter basic relationship, especially as Indian opinion is sensitive on such matters, but we would gladly give thought to possibilities and review the position after we have built up a healthier working relationship.

To sum up, we should exhort the Chogyal to create a feeling of mutual trust and confidence instead of subjecting us to one maneuver or another and to pressures of various kinds.

The note makes it obvious that the PMO, headed by Haksar, was of the opinion that there was no immediate requirement to revise the existing treaty and that India should not become a victim of the Chogyal's manoeuvres and pressure tactics. But these words of wisdom seemed to have little impact on India's policy of continued appeasement towards Sikkim.

The Chogyal continued to receive royal treatment from the Indian government. In the spring of 1971, the Chogyal expressed a wish to go on a pilgrimage to important places of Buddhist interest in India.[10] PO Bajpai made a request to the MEA which was accepted. The Indian Railways provided two luxury coaches for the trip. Bajpai and Devare, with their wives, accompanied the Chogyal, Gyalmo (Hope) and the family. The group visited Nalanda, Rajgir, Bodh Gaya, Sankisa and Sanchi. They also visited Chandigarh and New Delhi. The Chogyal was extended a warm welcome wherever he went. Governors of the states he visited hosted lunches and dinners in his honour. Indira Gandhi received him with all courtesies. It was a high watermark of Sikkim's relationship with India, despite the pinpricks the Chogyal had started giving to India on a number of matters of key importance.

Nothing happened during 1971 to the revised draft treaty prepared by Kaul, mainly due to India's preoccupation with the situation in east Pakistan. Towards the end of 1971, while Indira Gandhi was busy sorting out the problems arising out of the large-scale exodus of refugees from erstwhile east Pakistan, Thondup and Hope were concentrating on organizing fashion shows in New York, in the prestigious department store Bergdorf Goodman, inviting favourable media coverage of 'His Majesty's' activities.

Although Gandhi's position at home had considerably improved due to her success in the dismemberment of Pakistan, the resultant creation of an independent country—Bangladesh— and also due to her resounding victory in the fifth general elections that followed, she still sent Kaul to Gangtok in March 1972 to gauge the feelings of the Chogyal towards an acceptable solution to his problems. Kaul showed the draft of a new treaty relationship with the Chogyal, offering Sikkim permanent association with some accompanying benefits that were not part of the 1950 treaty.

On Kaul's return, Haksar had another discussion with him. A note dated 14 March 1972, recorded by Haksar for the prime minister, is reproduced below:[11]

I tried to keep track of the goings on in the Ministry of External Affairs. The Foreign Secretary had spoken to me about his visit to Sikkim. But I have long felt that we really have no policy in regard to Sikkim except to wait upon Chogyal's varying moods. The Foreign Secretary says that he found the Chogyal 'ready and willing' and that he found him 'in a chastened mood'. With great respect, this makes no sense to me.

There was a time in 1947 when people of Sikkim were with India. Thereafter, we developed great fondness for the Sikkim Durbar and now we wait on his frowns and on his smiles.

I tried at one stage to organize some serious thinking about our policy towards Sikkim. Nothing came out of it. The basic question is: what are the sanctions behind "Permanent Association" or "Protectorate" or anything else? In this latter half of the twentieth century, a sanction behind any political framework has to be people if that framework is to prove durable. And we have totally alienated the people of Sikkim [. . .]

[. . .] We must not delude ourselves. The Chogyal wants independence, a membership of the United Nations and is gradually eroding our will [. . .]

[. . .] My own view is that until such time as P.M. has made up her mind, she should not see the Chogyal in order to put a seal to the so called "Permanent Association". In my view, we are not so utterly helpless. We can make a new beginning. We can establish contact with the people of Sikkim, develop relationship and earn their goodwill and use that as the real lever against the vagaries of Chogyal. If we decide on such a policy, I have no doubt that in the space of two years we shall get Chogyal running to us for protection against his own people. Otherwise, he will be taking us out for a ride all the time.

Kaul again visited Gangtok after a few months and conveyed that India was ready to revise the treaty by replacing the word 'protectorate' with 'permanent association with India', with Sikkim retaining the 'right to autonomy in regard to internal affairs'. Thondup consulted British constitutional lawyer and expert on international law Sir Humphrey Waldock and Nani A. Palkhivala, an Indian jurist, on this issue.[12] Both of them were of the view that permanent association 'status makes India's case for merger of Sikkim much easier at a future date'. Thondup then told Kaul that the wording of the proposed revised treaty required an amendment to read that 'Sikkim in full sovereign rights enters into a permanent association with the government of India'. This was not acceptable to India. Offering another sop to Thondup, Kaul told him that if he agreed to the removal of the clause 'in full sovereign rights', India would allow him to take immediate control of the posts and telegraph in Sikkim followed by sponsored membership of the Colombo Plan within six months. Kaul also said that membership of the World Health Organization and the International Labour Organization could follow at suitable intervals.

Meanwhile, after spending about four years as defence minister, Sardar Swaran Singh had returned as external affairs minister in June 1970. Thondup met him in New Delhi on 5 May 1972. Singh told him that the permanent association status ranked higher than that of a protectorate, but added that he did not approve of any reference to the UN in the revised treaty. Thondup met Indira Gandhi on 8 May. She too echoed Singh's sentiments.

On his return to Gangtok, Thondup suggested that clause II of the treaty could be made to read: 'though separate, Sikkim and India shall continue to be in close association with each other.' This was obviously not acceptable to India. In September 1972,

Kaul formally repeated his earlier offer for the last time. Thondup agreed to accept the permanent association status, provided the GoI unconditionally endorsed a separate letter from the Sikkim durbar that would read: 'it is also the understanding of the government of Sikkim that Sikkim and India shall continue the association between their two countries within the framework of the purposes and principles of the charter of the UN.' Swaran Singh once again told Thondup that no reference to the UN would be acceptable. Thereafter, Kaul's repeated attempts failed to convince Thondup to accept India's offer. That marked the end of India's efforts to accommodate Thondup's sensitivity to the use of the word 'protectorate' in clause II of the 1950 treaty.[13]

It must be noted that P.N. Haksar was a man of high integrity and practical wisdom, and his advice was well respected by Indira Gandhi on most issues of national and international importance. It is, therefore, not known as to how, in the face of clear written advice from her principal secretary, Gandhi continued to follow Kaul's policy of appeasement towards the Chogyal. Kaul had no direct access to Haksar's notes quoted above, but he had numerous meetings with him on this subject. Therefore, he was fully aware of Haksar's line of approach towards Sikkim. In view of his proximity to the Chogyal, it could be presumed that Kaul, during his visits to Gangtok to discuss the permanent association status, might have had sufficient time (he stayed as a palace guest) to tell the Chogyal about Haksar's opposition to such concessions as were being offered through the permanent association. The Chogyal also knew that Kaul was about to retire in early December 1972 and was expected to be replaced by Kewal Singh, who would not be as accommodating of the Chogyal's whims and fancies as Kaul had been. There was also a danger of Singh lending his support to Haksar's line of thinking. In view of that, it is not known as to what was going on in the Chogyal's mind when he did not listen to repeated appeals from an old and trusted friend like Kaul. It is also not known as to how and when the Chogyal could have convinced the Indian leadership to agree to his demands, as put forward during the course of negotiations on the permanent association treaty.

It appears Thondup was fully convinced by his legal advisers that permanent association was as good as merger. In view of that, he avoided agreeing to Kaul's offer in the hope things might change in his favour in future. Also, till then the merger of Sikkim was not on the radar of either the MEA or the PMO. Insofar as the MEA was concerned, things changed only after Kaul was replaced by Kewal Singh, and Kewal Singh didn't share with anyone else in the MEA the possibility of India accepting Kazi's request for merger till the very end. On the other hand, Thondup had no means of knowing about this change in the GoI's policy due to the highly secretive nature of the decision-making process involved.

The Indo-Sikkim Treaty of 1950 served India's interests as long as Thondup was willing to abide by its contents and observe the sanctity of the lakshman rekha it drew. India continued to honour its contents, both in letter and spirit, and helped Thondup maintain control over Sikkim and ensure stability in the state, even at the cost of the democratic aspirations of the vast majority of Sikkimese people. But Thondup's insatiable ambition of seeing Sikkim as an independent country during his lifetime did not fit into India's heightened security perceptions in 1972. In 1947, Thondup had walked out of a crowd of over 560 Indian princely states waiting in front of Sardar Patel to sign the instrument of accession which finally led to their merger with India, holding Jawaharlal Nehru's finger. In 1972, he had tried to grab the wrist of Nehru's daughter, Indira Gandhi, to lead her in a direction that was not to her liking. She was willing to draw a new lakshman rekha to accommodate Thondup's sensitivities over the 'protectorate' status for Sikkim to a point, by offering him the more respectable status of 'permanent association', but she could not sacrifice her country's security interests by leaving them at the mercy of an assertive and unreliable Chogyal of an independent Sikkim.

India's strategic interests in Sikkim at that time were too critical to let the Chogyal dream of Sikkim's independence, thereby making it a hotbed of international tug of war, with the distinct possibility of the Chinese pulling the rope from one side. In this respect, he seemed to be playing a game of chess with Gandhi. Thondup, however, did not realize that in 1972 she was playing this game from a much stronger position and was only one move away from checkmate. Credit must be given to Gandhi for holding back her next move by offering Thondup one last escape route, through the offer of permanent association, before she took the 'king'. Unfortunately, Thondup overestimated his skills and miscalculated the real impact of his moves. He was actually playing a losing game, which he thought was going in his favour. Thondup's reaction to Gandhi's moves can aptly be described through a well-known Indian proverb: *vinash kale viprit buddhi.* It means that before you embrace destruction, your thinking process gets muddled.

He could have accepted the status of permanent association and waited for a more opportune time to revisit his plans for independence, or left it to his future generations. Maybe it was the curse of a very large majority of the politically and economically deprived Sikkimese people that was now visiting upon Thondup. Indian diplomacy had tested its outermost limits through the offer of permanent association, and it could go no further. No Indian leader, not even the idealist Morarji Desai, who made a lot of noise against the merger of Sikkim when he succeeded Gandhi as prime minister, could have granted independence to Sikkim.

With a diplomatic deadlock staring her in the face—that is, Thondup unwilling to accept anything less than sovereign status, and T.N. Kaul replaced by a non-partisan Foreign Secretary Kewal Singh—Indira Gandhi finally decided to go for a course correction in India's policy of appeasement towards the Chogyal. Having tasted success through the dismemberment of east Pakistan and the resultant emergence of Bangladesh, and fully confident of the capabilities of the buoyant R&AW under the leadership of R.N. Kao, she finally told Kao in Haksar's presence to 'do something about Sikkim'. What the R&AW did in this respect is described in the subsequent chapters.

Chapter VI

My Two and a Half Avatars

As head of the R&AW's set-up in Gangtok, my only job should have been to look after the collection of Tibet- and China-related intelligence. However, since February 1973, a totally new dimension was added to the OSD (P)'s profile. It was to do with the running of spl ops directed towards facilitating the merger of Sikkim with India. This took up more of my time than my primary responsibilities. My third job, which I would like to call half a job, was to provide cover to the (non-existent on paper but rather active) IB staff posted in Gangtok and its forward posts—dealing with internal and counter-intelligence. My role relating to these two and a half jobs is outlined below.

The office and residence of the OSD (P) were located in an area called Balwakhani, on the road leading to north Sikkim. About half a kilometre up the road was the Black Cat Mess of the 17 Mountain Division, and the residences of the General Officer Commanding (GOC) and other senior army officers. Other than the movement of army vehicles and the early morning ringing of bells strung across the necks of mules carrying black cardamom, cinnamon, raw wool, oranges, etc., from north Sikkim for sale in Gangtok, there was hardly any traffic. Located between two bends, with no immediate neighbour, Balwakhani was ideally suited for carrying out intelligence-related work. The area used to have a large concentration of clouds, which provided for added mystique. My office and residence were located a little off the road with parking available in a large open space in front of it. This office was connected to India House (the office-cum-residence of the PO) through a short but winding forest path, making it easy for me to meet him without being noticed.

Regarding my real job, the post I held in Gangtok was that of OSD (P), in which the 'p' stood for police. But police work was not even remotely connected to my work. The only connection was that my predecessors and I all belonged to the IPS. With regard to collecting cross-border intelligence on Tibet and China, I had to frequently visit our forward posts in north and east Sikkim, including Nathu La and Kupup—from where we could see the tri-junction of India, Bhutan and Tibet, and also the Doklam area. For the smooth functioning of our forward posts, I had to interact closely with senior army officers of the Gangtok-based 17 Mountain Division, the Kalimpong-based 27 Mountain Division and the visiting senior army officers, especially the commander of the Siliguri-based 33 Corps. As 17 Mountain Division was based in Gangtok, I had developed excellent relations with its senior officers, including Major General Harbhajan Singh Khullar, GOC, 17 Mountain Division; Brigadier Depinder Singh, commander of 64 Mountain Brigade; Brigadier Ashok Kumar Handoo, his successor Brigadier Naresh Kumar and Brigadier Bobby Sihota of the Artillery Regiment.

I was also expected to brief the Chogyal occasionally about intelligence related to Tibet and China. During these meetings, the Chogyal would invariably shift the conversation towards current internal political developments, which provided me with valuable insights into his state of mind at that point. On his part, the Chogyal used these meetings as a parallel or non-diplomatic direct channel to convey his views on various issues to the prime minister through Kao. My meetings with the Chogyal ended in September 1974 after Sikkim became an associate state of India, as his powers were significantly curtailed.

For the performance of our spl ops duties, my predecessor had created a dedicated three-member cell headed by the OSD (P) in February 1973 out of the total sanctioned strength of the R&AW staff in Sikkim. While the OSD (P) had a multifaceted role, the other two were totally dedicated to spl ops-related work. As far as the R&AW's China and Tibet-related cross-border work was concerned, I had a very able SFO (an official ranked on a par with a deputy superintendent of police) in M.M. Pathak, who shared most of my day-to-day work, giving me enough room to supervise Tibet-related work and also plan, supervise and execute special operations. While I had to move out of the office sometimes during the day in connection with my real work and to call on senior army officers from the 17 Mountain Division and the 27 Mountain Division, and even the Chogyal, the remaining two members of this cell seldom left the office during the day to meet their 'friends' from political parties. Such meetings normally happened at night, when most of Gangtok was sleeping. My meetings with Kazi, till he became chief minister, usually took place at his residence in Kalimpong. For urgent clandestine meetings at Gangtok with my 'friends', including Kazi, we had an ordinary-looking jeep driven by Chun Chun, that used to pick them up from predetermined places. Such meetings used to happen at my residence or at the safe house.

It was my work related to spl ops which required frequent meetings with PO K.S. Bajpai. This was, in fact, an extension of close cooperation between Foreign Secretary Kewal Singh and Kao in New Delhi. But unlike Singh, neither Bajpai nor chief executive Brijbir Saran Das were aware of India's plans of ultimately facilitating the merger of Sikkim. Singh had kept it a closely guarded secret till after the status of associate state was secured. Even at that stage, only PO Gurbachan Singh and chief executive B.B. Lal were taken into confidence about the next move, i.e., the merger. Also, neither the PO at Gangtok nor Kewal Singh in New Delhi were aware of the nature and extent of our contacts with 'friends' from pro-democratic, pro-reform and anti-Chogyal parties.

I was asked by Kao to limit my contact with chief executive B.S. Das (appointed on 10 April 1973 after the Chogyal, under pressure from the rampaging anti-Chogyal demonstrators, handed over Sikkim's administration to the PO on 8 April) to only a social level, as any official meetings with him were bound to expose my cover. Das was a part of the Sikkim administration and the Chogyal was its head. The Chogyal would have felt that if I was briefing him personally about cross-border affairs, what was so special that I was discussing with Das? It was in this context that Das, in his book *The Sikkim Saga*, had made the following interesting remarks:[1]

> For reasons unknown, the Indian intelligence agencies refused to assist me, when earlier they fed regular information to the diwans. My repeated requests for assistance were turned down. They felt they could not expose themselves. Yet, everyone knew them and they were in constant touch with all the political elements.

Das knew me and my R&AW connection well. During my very first call on Das in September 1973, I told him about my limitations in providing him the information he was interested in. I also told him that I had instructions from Kao to this effect. Subsequently, we met at various social get-togethers, including those at his house. On certain occasions, Das did share with me some useful information.

The OSD (P)'s 'half a job' was created when the IB was bifurcated in September 1968 and the R&AW was carved out of it. Before that, it was an IB office responsible for Sikkim-related internal and external intelligence. After the bifurcation, as was the case elsewhere, the majority of the staff in Sikkim was retained by the IB. But they could not officially function in Sikkim as it was not a part of India. In that context, the post of OSD (P), now under the R&AW, came in handy to provide the IB staff much-needed cover that let them perform their duties in Sikkim by posing as R&AW staff. Interestingly, the OSD (P) did not know the details of what they were doing, nor did he have any administrative or operational control over the IB's set-up. Even the activities of the OSD (P) himself were not beyond their prowling eyes. Providing cover to the IB staff, being a possible target of their counter-intelligence work but not in the know as to what they were actually doing in Sikkim, was a unique experience for me.

After the bifurcation of the IB and the creation of the R&AW, the work of the two organizations was clearly defined. They had separate, independent existences. But in Sikkim the physical impact of the bifurcation was not visible to an outsider, either in Gangtok or at the forward posts where the staff of both the departments continued to function from the same premises, with clearly understood but invisible demarcation.

Due to the very nature of the R&AW's work, this division took place only in the forward posts of north and east Sikkim, bordering Tibet. In south and west Sikkim, there was only one forward post in Uttarey on the Nepal-Sikkim border. That remained under the charge of the IB. In view of that, the R&AW had no presence in south and west Sikkim. It was mainly with a view to avoiding suspicion of being involved in merger-related spl ops that none of the three members of our team visited those parts of the state during the twenty-seven months that these operations lasted. That makes the accusation by some authors about the R&AW staff meddling in the political activities in south and west Sikkim untenable. But it is true that the IB staff from Uttarey, Gangtok and posts in north and east Sikkim, in compliance with their charter of duties, were enthusiastically collecting internal intelligence, including monitoring the actual impact of the R&AW's spl ops on the ground. With regard to the spl ops, the IB staff in Sikkim was told by their seniors from Calcutta and New Delhi to cut off their links with anti-Chogyal and pro-reform leaders during the twenty-seven-month period between February 1973 and May 1975 as the job was being handled by the three-member team headed by the OSD (P). During this period, they were left with the job of collection of intelligence and counter-intelligence only.

An interesting part of this division of work between the IB and the R&AW was that my immediate boss, P.N. Banerjee, continued to be the head of both set-ups in Calcutta as joint director. Two deputy directors, P.K. Sen and R.K. Mookerji, served as heads of the two separate offices of the R&AW and the IB, respectively, and reported to Banerjee.

This would mean that Sen would help Banerjee monitor my spl ops-related work and Mukherji would keep Banerjee posted about internal developments in Sikkim, including making progress reports on the impact of our special operations, as monitored through ground reports sent by the IB staff posted in Sikkim. Without sharing this with me, Banerjee used this information to guide me as and when required. The IB's coverage in Sikkim also included keeping a close eye on the activities of the Chogyal and his men, as well as political leaders and parties and other GoI offices, etc. Banerjee remained posted in Calcutta as head of that office even after the bifurcation of the IB due to his close involvement in the operations in Bangladesh till his sudden death after a heart attack during a clandestine visit to Dhaka in July 1974.

The IB's set-up in Sikkim after the bifurcation was headed by a JAD, a junior SP-rank officer, deliberately kept one rank below the OSD (P) to provide a hierarchical cover to the IB and R&AW staff. In fact, sitting in the same office, just a couple of rooms away from the OSD (P)'s office, the IB head had no official connection with the OSD (P).

When I reached Sikkim, the post of the IB head was vacant. The last incumbent, Tejpal Singh, had been recalled in late 1972 after the Chogyal told Indira Gandhi that he had been actively interacting with the anti-Chogyal political activists in south and west Sikkim. Tejpal's post remained vacant till after the merger of Sikkim. The work of the JAD was thereafter looked after by the IB's second in command, a DCIO (Deputy Central Intelligence Officer, a deputy SP-rank officer) rank officer named V. Vaidyalingam—a typical low-profile officer with gentle manners who could merge into any crowd without being noticed. Just to show to the local staff from both departments, every working day at 10.30 a.m. Vaidyalingam would walk into my office carrying a small folder and leave it on my table for perusal. That folder would usually contain personal information about some of the residents of Gangtok. Its only utility was that it provided a comical interlude to the otherwise serious work we did. Maybe the IB wanted to keep the OSD (P) in good humour, and hence in good health, for providing them the much-needed cover in Sikkim. One day, I asked Vaidyalingam if that was the only work that the IB did in Sikkim. Very apologetically, he said, 'No, Sir. But we are under instructions to show you this much only.'

The then director of the IB, Atma Jayaram, was in close contact with R.N. Kao on Sikkim-related affairs. This was obvious from the fact that as and when I happened to visit the headquarters, Kao always used to ask if I had called on him, which I invariably had. But these calls used to be just courtesy calls. My exposure to the intelligence world till then was very limited, and hence I did not understand the subtleties of interdepartmental relations. Had that been the case, I would have requested the Director of Intelligence Bureau (DIB) to instruct his man in Sikkim to at least share actionable intelligence with me so that we could take suitable remedial measures well in time to prevent the damage, if any, resulting from developments already known by the IB. I am sure Jayaram would have agreed to my request. Maybe he would have directed me to speak to Banerjee in Calcutta, who knew about such information. As I was not fully aware of Banerjee's access to such intelligence inputs, I never raised this issue with him—neither during his visits to Gangtok nor during my meetings with him in Calcutta. Fortunately, no damage was done due to the lack of such information. But it would have made my work easier in certain situations.

The R&AW's activity in Sikkim, right from Kao's role to his juniors, was shrouded in mystery. It was like the proverbial *chakravyuh* (maze) from the Mahabharata, in which it was easier to enter than to get out. The sophistication with which the R&AW's merger-related operations were conducted can be judged from the fact that neither the Chogyal nor his sister, Coo Coo La, ever mentioned the R&AW's name as being responsible for their problems. The Chogyal, during his meeting with Indira Gandhi in Darjeeling in October 1972, and Coo Coo La on two occasions, once in Hong Kong during a press interview on 13 April 1973 and then on 7 April 1975 at Foreign Secretary Kewal Singh's residence in New Delhi, had blamed the IB, but not said a word against the R&AW.

It may be relevant to mention here that when my predecessor, Sayali, and his wife, Birenda, were invited to an exclusive farewell dinner with the Chogyal and Gyalmo in August 1972, the Chogyal told the Sayalis that though they were in 'mourning' because of what had happened in April 1973, they could not let them go without a meal at the palace. He significantly remarked, 'I can understand what you did, but I did not like the activities of the staff from the "other department" [IB].'[2] Both the Chogyal and Coo Coo La knew me and my R&AW connection well, but they never had any complaints about my functioning. Interestingly, Karma Topden, whom I knew since my Gangtok days, told me in November 2017 that he did not know that the forward post in Uttarey was manned only by the IB.[3] He also mentioned that he had a small staff of five men and that most of the intelligence about south and west Sikkim was collected by Coo Coo La through her contacts amongst the Tibetan refugees who had settled there. That speaks volumes about the confidentiality with which the spl ops were conducted by the R&AW.

It was mainly due to the high level of secrecy observed by us that the authors of some books published on Sikkim after the merger started speculating about the R&AW's involvement in the merger-related operations without any supporting evidence. Some of these insinuations were quoted in subsequent publications by other authors, thereby granting some sort of credibility to those unsubstantiated charges. Some of these are summed up below:

a) Both chief executive B.S. Das and PO Gurbachan Singh had some sort of R&AW connection.[4]

b) The R&AW's Sikkim-related operations were conceived soon after the liberation of Bangladesh in December 1971.[5] Following that, R&AW agents were dispatched to all four district headquarters to collect operational data to plan these operations. All this was done without the knowledge of Indira Gandhi. In fact, when the time came to launch these operations, she was pleasantly surprised to learn that operations could be launched within twenty-four hours of her clearance.

c) The rhythm and accent of the 3000-strong demonstrators marching on the streets of Gangtok on 10 April 1975, when merger-related resolutions were passed by the Sikkim Assembly, gave an impression of a crowd rented by the R&AW.[6]

d) Four years after the merger, the R&AW was still tying up loose ends. Payments for the services rendered had still not been made.[7] That was perhaps the reason why N.B. Khatiwada became a strong critic of the merger and the Government of India.

My observations about these charges are:

a) Das was a directly recruited IPS officer of the 1948 batch and was allotted the Uttar Pradesh state cadre. He worked in UP for over fifteen years. His last posting was as SSP (Meerut) before he opted for deputation with the GoI. In addition to his experience of handling law-and-order situations as a police officer, he had successfully served as the first head of the newly opened Indian Mission in Bhutan. These two experiences made him eminently suitable for the job of chief executive in Sikkim. But no R&AW man would be posted as commissioner, New Delhi Municipal Corporation, which was one of the posts Das had earlier occupied. Also, had Das had any R&AW connection, he would not have criticized (in his book *The Sikkim Saga*), Indian intelligence agencies in Sikkim for not providing him with the much-needed inputs to help him run the state's administration.

Regarding Gurbachan Singh, he was briefly seconded by the MEA to the R&AW as joint secretary (JS) (liaison) before he took over as the PO in Gangtok. The post of JS (L) in the R&AW was normally filled by an IFS officer who wanted to stay in New Delhi for personal reasons but could not be accommodated in the ministry for lack of a suitable vacancy. As JS (L), Singh's job was to act as a liaison officer, follow up on the R&AW's pending cases and proposals with the MEA and try to expedite decisions. During that period, the offices of the secretary (R&AW) and his second in command, as well as some top-secret branches, were located in a highly restricted area on the first floor of the South Block. On the other hand, the JS (L)'s room was located on the ground floor, along with that of other officers from the ministry of defence. Other than Kao and R&AW officers dealing with top-secret branches, including the branch dealing with MEA-related issues (I occupied that post in the early 1980s), he had no connection with the agency. As a result, he did not know what was happening in the department. It would, therefore, be reasonable to presume that Kewal Singh's selection of Gurbachan Singh to succeed Bajpai as PO had nothing to do with his connection with the R&AW. The fact that he was readily available for a short stint at Gangtok (Kewal Singh knew that the post of PO would become redundant after Sikkim's merger with India), appeared to be the main deciding factor for Gurbachan Singh's appointment as PO.

In fact, compared to my highly productive interaction with his predecessor Bajpai, Gurbachan Singh, with his semblance of an R&AW connection, stopped consulting me on a one-to-one basis, even on very crucial issues related to the situation in Sikkim.

What the authors of the books on Sikkim have missed so far is that it was Bajpai who was in touch with both my bosses—Banerjee and Kao. In addition to our meeting in Darjeeling in 1974 where Bajpai, Banerjee and I had examined the draft Government of Sikkim Bill of 1974, to suggest improvements, Bajpai would sometimes meet Banerjee while transiting Calcutta, and Kao during his visits to New Delhi. In addition to ascertaining what was happening in New Delhi, he sometimes used his connection with Banerjee to pressurize me into helping him complete some crucial tasks assigned to him by Kewal Singh.

b) The R&AW's spl ops started only in February 1973 after the Chogyal refused to accept India's offer of permanent association. In view of that, there was no reason to start preparing for these operations two years before, by crystal-gazing the Chogyal's refusal to accept the proposal in the second half of 1972. It is absolutely unimaginable that the R&AW would start preparing for an operation of this magnitude and importance without prior knowledge, if not approval, of the prime minister. Further, the R&AW spl ops were handled by a three-member cell based in Gangtok. None of these persons ever visited south and west Sikkim. All the work was done through our 'friends' from the anti-Chogyal and pro-democracy parties.

c) All anti-Chogyal or pro-Sikkim Congress demonstrations were arranged by party workers under the overall guidance of Kazi. Participants in those demonstrations came to Gangtok willingly and with the knowledge that by doing so they would secure political, economic and administrative reforms in Sikkim. It is, however, possible that some of those demonstrators might have commandeered taxis or government or private commercial vehicles to transport them to Gangtok.

d) Regarding the non-payment of dues by the R&AW for the so-called services rendered by Sikkim Congress leaders, including Khatiwada, it may be mentioned that the R&AW's entire operation was conducted on a shoestring budget. Other than the funds that the parties required to conduct their political activities, including elections, no special demand was ever received from Kazi or any other 'friend'. Even in that case, the amount required was very small, given the size of Sikkim where each constituency comprised on an average 3000 voters only. In a couple of cases, our man Padam Bahadur's offer to provide financial help was point-blank refused by his 'friends' on the plea that they were fighting for the rights of the Sikkimese people and that they didn't need financial help from outside.

The R&AW's spl ops team never promised nor paid any money to Khatiwada. I never met him alone. All the financial assistance to the Sikkim Congress was extended directly to the party funds through Kazi, to avoid wasteful expenditure, and also to allow Kazi to maintain a hold over his partymen. In fact, once it became clear to the anti-Chogyal Sikkim Congress leaders that India would not let them down as it did to the SSC in 1949; friendship with any of the three members of the R&AW's spl ops cell became a stepping stone for some of the senior Sikkim Congress leaders to further their political prospects. They were willing to do their bit without any financial assistance as they felt they were investing in their political future. They thought that some help might possibly come from us through this friendship in securing a cabinet berth or other perks as and when the ministry was formed. In fact, after the operations ended when Sikkim merged with India, I was left with a small amount, the safe custody of which became a headache for me. To lighten my burden, I sent that money through Myngma to Kazi as a final contribution from our side to his party funds.

The R&AW's financial help to our 'friends' from the Sikkim Congress pales into insignificance compared to the astronomical sum that the Chogyal was spending on pro-Chogyal parties and also on breaking up the unity of Sikkim Congress leaders. On 4 April 1974, just a fortnight before elections were held in Sikkim, chief executive B.S. Das told me at the Whitehouse Club in Gangtok that the Chogyal, who had already withdrawn Rs 20 lakh for palace repairs and reconstruction, wanted him to sanction another Rs 35 lakh for the same purpose. Das refused to do so as there was no sign of repairs, etc., at the palace and the Chogyal was not willing to give a utilization certificate for the amount sanctioned earlier. It was obvious that the Chogyal was using that money for the two above-mentioned purposes.

The most surprising thing was that while nobody took note of what the Chogyal had been doing over the years with the funds provided by the GoI to further his own interests at the cost of pro-democratic forces in Sikkim, the minuscule financial aid given by the R&AW to the pro-democratic forces in Sikkim to provide them a somewhat level field to continue their fight against the autocratic regime of the Chogyal was blown out of proportion by such authors. Maybe it was their ignorance of the R&AW's operations in Sikkim that led them to draw their own conclusions.

Given this background, it will be easier to understand the nature, extent and outcome of the R&AW's spl ops-related work in Sikkim that is covered in the subsequent chapters.

Chapter VII

The 8 May 1973 Agreement: Chogyal Contained

In July 1973, I was asked to proceed to Calcutta and Gangtok immediately for ten-days' briefing from P.N. Banerjee, the joint director in Calcutta, and Ajit Singh Sayali, OSD (P), Gangtok. In Calcutta, I learnt from Banerjee that, as approved by the prime minister, we had already launched an operation to lend support to the anti-Chogyal and pro-democracy political parties and their leaders in Sikkim, especially Kazi Lhendup Dorji, to fulfil their long-cherished desire for political, administrative and economic reforms. This operation was to culminate in the merger of Sikkim with India. The last objective was to be achieved in stages and through constitutional means, and as far as possible, through public support for the elected leaders. He also mentioned that other than Kazi, no leader had been taken into confidence about the ultimate goal.

In Gangtok, Sayali, in addition to briefing me about the Tibet- and China-related job, introduced me to PO K.S. Bajpai with whom I interacted occasionally in connection with my spl ops work. A meeting with the Chogyal, whom I had to brief on Tibet- and China-related intelligence, was left to be arranged after I took over. Joint introductory meetings with selected party 'friends', including Kazi, were not considered desirable as that could have exposed our cover and connection with them. That job was left to me to be done through Myngma after my taking charge.

Before we move on to the R&AW's spl ops to facilitate the merger of Sikkim with India, it would be useful to understand the situation there towards the end of 1972, and how the Sikkim National Congress and Janata Congress (which finally merged on 18 April 1973 to form the Kazi-led Sikkim Congress) leaders succeeded in mobilizing the support of such a large number of anti-Chogyal demonstrators in Gangtok in April 1973, thereby forcing the Chogyal to hand over the administration to India on 8 April that year. As I reached Gangtok only in August and was not a witness to the developments of March–April 1973, I had a detailed discussion about this with the then First Secretary Sudhir Devare, OSDs Jayant Sanyal and D.K. Manavalan and the Kazini's estranged adopted son, Nar Bahadur Khatiwada, who was the main force behind the mobilization of anti-Chogyal demonstrations in Sikkim (at my Gurgaon residence). I had more than one meeting with each of them to fully grasp the genesis of the April 1973 demonstrations.

Devare was posted in Gangtok as the second and first secretary during the crucial period between June 1970 and May 1974 (four years as against the usual two years). From 1972, he was PO Bajpai's second in command. Because of his position, he was closely associated with the GoI's interaction with the Chogyal, the durbar and the political leaders in Sikkim. His proficiency in Nepalese and his interaction with a large cross section of Sikkimese people proved to be extremely useful to him in understanding the various developments of that period.

As per Devare's recollection, the period between 1970 and 1972, though it appeared peaceful, was in fact marked by growing frustration and restiveness amongst the people of Sikkim.[1] The extent of the socio-economic disparity was on the increase. The majority of the Nepalese population, and several Bhutias and Lepchas from the lower strata of society, were disgruntled. Barring a few Bhutias connected to the palace, a handful of Nepalese and very few Lepchas, the rest of the Sikkimese people eked out a poor living in the remote mountainous terrain and were becoming more and more resentful of the discriminatory attitude of the Chogyal. Farming and communications, which were badly affected by the devastating floods of 1968, had not been restored, especially in the southern and western parts. Opportunities in education and employment were very few, and were mainly available to a few privileged Bhutias. The Chogyal, on the other hand, seemed centred on and rather obsessed with projecting Sikkim's separate identity. He started showing signs of desperation after India supported Bhutan's membership at the UN in 1971. His distraction had led to severe neglect of the urgent and basic needs of the population, mainly health, communications, education, jobs, etc. His frequent foreign visits with the Gyalmo (Hope) and other family members, publicity-seeking and costly fashion shows, exhibitions on Sikkim in the US; visits of foreign journalists and politicians to the state or the Gyalmo's attempts to give an Americanized look to Sikkim's cultural persona, especially amongst its youth, appeared to be on top of the Chogyal's mind. Such matters were of little interest to the people and continued to alienate them from the ruling family.

There was a clear religious divide amongst the Sikkimese population. While the Bhutias were followers of Mahayana

Buddhism, the Lepchas were originally animists but gradually started following Buddhism. The Nepalese were largely Hindus. These religious distinctions were sharp even in the small microcosm of Sikkim and inevitably impacted the political outlook. This divide was deliberately created, and sustained, by the durbar to maintain the Chogyal's hold over the Bhutia–Lepcha segment to neutralize the impact of the ever-growing demands for political and economic reforms that emanated from the numerically stronger but politically and economically deprived Nepalese segment.

Most of the Nepalese—they constituted over 75 per cent of Sikkim's population—were without Sikkim subjecthood. With poor education and practically no employment opportunities, many of them felt compelled to leave Sikkim even as the unrest amongst them grew rapidly, leading to the formation of new political groups and parties. The resentment was not confined to the Nepalese alone. Poor Bhutia and Lepcha families were also feeling left out of the 'elitist circle' promoted by the palace. Because of that, a number of Bhutias and Lepchas had also joined the SNC, a party that opposed the Chogyal.

It was against this background that the Chogyal removed the sidlon, I.S. Chopra, a former Indian diplomat whom the Chogyal had appointed without going through the established practice of having a GoI nominee. Though Chopra hardly did anything for the welfare of the Sikkimese people, with his removal there was no cushion left between the Chogyal and the ordinary people to absorb the shocks, if any, resulting from his autocratic rule. Clearly, in 1972 the Chogyal was not the same man who used to be in touch with most of the prominent people of Sikkim— Bhutias, Lepchas and Nepalese alike—and knew the goings-on in the state. The executive council of six members, which was formed in 1972, though composed of political leaders of three communities, did not really represent the average person. The gulf between the latter and the Chogyal continued to grow, to which the Chogyal and his coterie did not seem to pay any attention.

Jayant Sanyal and D.K. Manavalan (both IAS officers of the 1965 batch from the West Bengal cadre) were two of the three officers who were brought from West Bengal as OSDs to help B.S. Das after his appointment as the chief executive on 10 April 1973, to run the affairs of the state. Sanyal was given charge of the west district with its headquarters in Gyezing.[2] When he reached Gyezing around the middle of April 1973, he saw a number of government buildings still smouldering, with the district officer and other senior officers, mostly Bhutias, having abandoned their posts. It took some time for him to restore peace with help from the local shopkeepers of Indian origin and young Sikkim Congress workers. According to him, there was a clear divide amongst the local population on the basis of the haves and have-nots. The vast majority of Nepalese did not have any right to property and other basic rights, and they were considered 'chakras', meaning servants. The rich absentee landlords—mostly Bhutias and some Lepchas—lived at higher altitudes, and their lands were cultivated by the Nepalese. Another interesting observation that he made was that these areas were closer to Darjeeling than Gangtok. Due to its proximity, a few young Nepalese boys, whose parents could afford to finance their education, used to attend schools and colleges in Darjeeling. On their return, they could hardly find any jobs as these were mostly taken up by Bhutias. Having been exposed to the environment of Darjeeling, where there was no discrimination based on ethnicity and religion, these Nepalese boys were a frustrated lot. Therefore, when the anti-Chogyal sentiment started picking up momentum towards the end of March 1973, it was these educated boys who played a significant role in motivating and mobilizing the anti-Chogyal crowd to move to Gangtok, in addition to creating law-and-order problems in their respective areas in south and west Sikkim.

Manavalan joined as OSD in charge of the south district with Namchi as its headquarters on 13 April 1973.[3] He stayed in Sikkim the longest out of the three OSDs. When he returned to his cadre on 6 May 1979, he was commissioner-in-charge of all four districts of Sikkim. On reaching Namchi, he observed that the army had been replaced by the Central Reserve Police Force (CRPF). Compared to Gyezing in the western district, there was less destruction caused by anti-Chogyal demonstrations in Namchi. Some houses, especially those belonging to pro-Chogyal elements, had, however, been burnt. Anti-Chogyal and pro-democratic reform meetings were still being organized by the Sikkim Congress youth leaders. As many as 70 to 80 per cent of the Lepchas in that area supported Kazi. Kazi was at the height of his popularity and the general masses believed that under his leadership their lot would change for the better. In view of this, a large number of people from the area had enthusiastically participated in the anti-Chogyal demonstration in Gangtok. Quite a few carried their own dry ration to help them stay there for a longer period. Some of them marched to Gangtok on foot while others hitch-hiked on whatever transport (trucks and jeeps) was available.

Khatiwada told me that there was apparent discrimination against the majority of Sikkimese Gurkhas settled in south and west Sikkim.[4] As cultivators of land, they were asked to pay exorbitant revenue. They could not purchase land belonging to the Bhutia–Lepchas. Failure to pay the rent generally led to their eviction. People were generally poor, with hardly any democratic rights. The majority of landholdings belonged to upper-class Bhutias and some Lepchas, with Burmeok Kazi (Densapas) owning the largest private estate. As a result, the general public wanted a change in the system that favoured a select few. They were ready to rebel against the 'Chogyalocracy' at the earliest suitable opportunity.

A.C. Sinha, in his book *Politics of Sikkim: A Sociological Study*, published in 1975, has described the prevailing sociopolitical scene in Sikkim up to early 1973.[5] It can be summed up as follows:

a) Some of the later Nepalese immigrants, who had come to Sikkim in search of better employment opportunities, ended up working as porters in marketplaces and as landless labourers, and even bonded farmworkers. Those who wanted to cultivate land were asked to pay higher rent than the Bhutia–Lepcha cultivators.

b) No Nepalese was allowed to settle in the private estates of the ruler, as those formed part of the 'reserved areas' for Bhutia–Lepchas. Coming under the 'reserved subjects', matters pertaining to these estates could not be discussed in the council.

c) The Sikkimese concept of property, establishment and even entrepreneurship was patterned on traditional feudalism. The economic gains were distributed on the basis of personal loyalties.

d) Owing to their long association with the affairs of the state, one-third of the top bureaucrats were of Kazi background. As many as 53 per cent of the bureaucrats were Buddhists and about two-thirds (63.11 per cent) had personal affiliation with the ruler.

e) By the end of 1972, Sikkim was facing a serious political problem. The minority Bhutia–Lepcha community, with the royal support and patronage, enjoyed political hegemony, while the numerically larger Nepalese community felt aggrieved over the denial of proportionate representation in the councils of the government. There was a glaring conflict between the past Tibetan theocracy and liberal democracy, which called for an urgent solution. On the contrary, pro-palace elements, on the eve of their success in the January 1973 elections, became more oblivious towards the Nepalese sensibility as they started warning them that they must adopt the Lamaist way of life if they wanted to stay on in Sikkim.

All of this pointed to the fact that the situation was ripe for a revolt against the outmoded, autocratic and self-serving regime of the Chogyal. But the majority that was suffering under this regime was confused and did not exactly know what should be done to bring about a change. Due to the treatment meted out by India to their popular leaders—Tashi Tshering and Kazi—in their struggle for securing political, economic and administrative reforms in Sikkim, they were conscious of the fact that unless there was a significant change in India's attitude, nothing much could be achieved to improve the lot of the Sikkimese people. In view of this, the assurances that the R&AW's spl ops team gave to the pro-reform leaders in February and March 1973—that India would no longer be protective of the Chogyal's position and would not stand in their way as they demanded political, economic and administrative reforms from the Chogyal—acted like a spark. In a sense, the R&AW's special cell in Gangtok acted as a catalyst, first to cause and then to hasten the political reaction between the two pre-existing but opposing forces to finally produce a totally new, rejuvenated and democratic twenty-second state of India, i.e., Sikkim.

From February 1973, when the R&AW launched the merger-related spl ops in Sikkim, till May 1975, when Sikkim became the twenty-second state of India, the local IB staff was asked to cut off operational links with the anti-Chogyal and pro-democracy leadership in Sikkim, and limit itself to the collection of intelligence and counter-intelligence only. In October 1972, the Chogyal met Indira Gandhi during her visit to Darjeeling to attend a function at the Himalayan Mountaineering Institute. Among other things, he informed her that he was certain that the IB in Calcutta was planning something against him, possibly without her knowledge. According to him, such an action was fraught with danger, both to India and Sikkim, because of its likely impact on Darjeeling's Nepalese population, which was already witnessing pro-Gorkhaland demonstrations. The Chogyal's complaint to Gandhi resulted in the withdrawal of Tejpal Singh, head of the SIB in Sikkim. His position remained vacant till after the merger. In view of that, the R&AW's three-man spl ops team and the IB staff in Sikkim had to carry out their work with extreme caution.

By the time I went to Calcutta and Gangtok in July 1973, the first part of the spl ops was already over with the signing of the 8 May 1973 tripartite agreement between the Chogyal, representatives of the Sikkim Congress (Kazi and K.C. Pradhan) and the Sikkim National Party (Netuk Tshering), and Indian Foreign Secretary Kewal Singh. From the information gathered during my briefing from Banerjee and Sayali, and recent discussions with the latter, Padam Bahadur Pradhan,[6] other friends from the IAS and IFS posted in Gangtok during that period, and also Nar Bahadur Khatiwada, the developments leading to the Chogyal's handing over of administration of Sikkim to the PO on 8 April and finally signing the tripartite agreement are summed up in the subsequent paragraphs.

The fifth and last general elections, as per the 1953 proclamation amended from time to time, were held in January 1973. Out of a total of twenty-four seats, elections were to be held

only for eighteen. The remaining six were to be nominated by
the Chogyal. Fourteen of the eighteen elective seats were equally
split into seven for the Nepalese and seven for the Bhutia–Lepcha
segments of the population. Out of the remaining four, one each
was meant for the scheduled castes, Tsongs, state-recognized
monasteries, and the fourth was a general seat covering the whole
of Sikkim. With the nomination quota of six seats in the Chogyal's
hand, it was obvious that irrespective of the actual outcome of
these elections, the composition of the state council (Assembly)
was bound to be in favour of the Chogyal.

Results of the above-mentioned elections were expected
by 15 February. While the counting of votes was in progress,
buoyed by the performance of his party as indicated through
the votes counted by then, the leader of the pro-Chogyal SNP
Netuk Tshering, issued a statement on 9 February in which he
criticized some unnamed leaders (obviously Kazi and his friends)
of impeding Sikkim's constitutional advance.[7] He also accused
them of working towards the 'country's' (Sikkim) disintegration.
Further, while thanking India for its generous assistance in the
developmental activities in Sikkim, he mentioned that they were
confident that the GoI would help the people of Sikkim fulfil
their ambition of securing a status like that of Nepal and Bhutan.

This was not the first time that Tshering had expressed his
views in favour of Sikkim's independent status. In 1972, it was
decided by the ministry of external affairs, in consultation with
PO Bajpai, that a group of six executive councillors—namely
Netuk Tshering, Kunzung Dorji, Nima Tshering, Man Bahadur
Basnet, Ashok Tshering and Rinzing Lepcha—from the pro-
Thondup SNP and SNC be given an opportunity to visit New
Delhi and a few other cities in north India. First Secretary Devare
was deputed to escort this group on a week-long familiarization
tour.[8] The visit was to end in New Delhi with a possible call

on the foreign minister and/or Prime Minister Indira Gandhi. During the train journey, Devare was surprised to find that the executive councillors from the pro-Chogyal SNP, including Netuk Tshering, continued to discuss the need for raising their demand for Sikkim's independent status with the Indian leaders when they met them in the national capital. It appeared that before their departure from Gangtok they had been suitably briefed by someone on behalf of the Chogyal that when they met the foreign minister or/and the prime minister, they should mention directly or indirectly the need for granting independence to Sikkim. Taken aback, Devare told them that their plan of raising that issue was not acceptable. Further, if they showed any intention of bringing up this subject before them, he would request the MEA to think if the proposed call on the Indian leaders should go ahead. Though some authors have mentioned that Tshering did raise this issue in their meeting with Gandhi, Devare, who was present in that meeting was not sure of that.

It was, therefore, obvious that the statement of 9 February 1973 was issued by Tshering with the prior knowledge and approval of the Chogyal. It was also a fair indication that, with a large majority of pro-Chogyal members (including six nominated by him) in the council, the Chogyal was most likely to use it to get pro-independence demands raised and even get related resolutions passed. This could also be the reason why the Chogyal refused to accept the offer of permanent association with India in September 1972. Did he want to play this last card to improve his negotiating position?

It looked like that. But little did the Chogyal and SNP leaders know that due to friendly and repeated assurances given by the R&AW's spl ops team to the Sikkim National Congress and Janata Congress leaders, the very people whom Tshering was quoting in support of his demand for the independence of Sikkim, would soon converge in Gangtok in the form of an anti-Chogyal tsunami and shake the very foundations of his autocratic regime, something he would not be able to recover from. Also, Tshering did not realize that the same political platform, i.e., the state council, which he might have been planning to use for providing political legitimacy to the Chogyal's demand for independence, would pass unanimous resolutions, first demanding an associate state status and thereafter a complete merger with India.

The excuse that the leaders of the Kazi-led SNC and K.C. Pradhan's Janata Congress were looking for to start their anti-Chogyal protests came in the form of irregularities committed by the presiding officers of polling booths of two constituencies. These irregularities were discovered at the time of counting the votes at Gangtok. The SNC and Janata Congress polling agents and their leaders present at the counting centre walked out of the hall levelling charges of rigging. However, as the SNC and Janata Congress weren't sure of India's reaction to their protests till then, no serious follow-up action was taken. But the simmering discontent against the outmoded system of elections in Sikkim continued. As per the election results declared on 15 February 1973, out of the eighteen seats for which elections were held, the pro-Chogyal SNP got nine seats and the divided opposition comprising the Kazi-led SNC, the K.C. Pradhan-led Janata Congress and unattached independents won five, two and two, respectively. As usual, six members were nominated by the Chogyal.

Meanwhile, approval for launching the R&AW's spl ops was given by the prime minister in early January 1973. However, it took some time for Sayali to organize a three-man spl ops cell to render suitable help and guidance to the two pro-reform parties. By early February, the team was functional and Banerjee informed Kao about the same.

Based on information I could gather during my visits to Calcutta and Gangtok in July 1973 and recent confirmation of the same from Padam Bahadur Pradhan, who is now settled in Kalimpong, the strategy adopted by the R&AW team for the successful completion of the first part of this operation can be summed up as follows:

a) Take SNC leader Kazi and Janata Congress General Secretary S.K. Rai—and through him the president of his party K.C. Pradhan—into confidence by telling them that there had been a change in the GoI's policy towards the Chogyal, and in view of that it would not stand in their way when they launched their struggle for democratic, economic and administrative reforms. In fact, in its own way, the R&AW would be supportive of their efforts in that direction.

b) Using simmering discontent amongst the rank and file against the outmoded system of elections, encourage pro-democracy forces to gradually escalate their protests against irregularities committed during the January 1973 elections.

c) Each suitable occasion should be used by the anti-Chogyal leaders to motivate their followers to rally behind their leaders in their fight against the durbar.

d) The level of anti-Chogyal demonstrations be escalated gradually to peak around his fiftieth birthday on 4 April 1973.

e) Make concerted efforts to forge unity between the two anti-Chogyal parties (SNC and Janata Congress) with the ultimate objective of uniting them into one party under Kazi's leadership.

f) Leaders of the anti-Chogyal parties should be prepared to maintain this pressure for a longer period with the threat of escalation to build pressure on the Chogyal, so that as had happened in the case of his father in 1949, the Chogyal would be compelled to seek India's assistance to restore law and order.

g) Make concerted efforts to reassure the SNC and Janata Congress leaders that unlike 1949, India would not do anything to sabotage their efforts.

While the R&AW's operational team in Gangtok was planning its operations to build pressure on the Chogyal and had already established contacts with the SNC and Janata Congress leaders in that context, a meeting was held in Foreign Secretary Kewal Singh's room on 14 March 1973.[9] It was attended by the home secretary, defence secretary, PO Bajpai and the director (north) of the MEA. The R&AW's regional head in Calcutta, P.N. Banerjee, was also present. The main purpose of the meeting was to devise ways to restore India's position in Sikkim, which had been seriously eroded by the Chogyal over the years. It was essential that the Chogyal be made to agree to the appointment of a sidlon (diwan) on the recommendation of the GoI. The Chogyal had been resisting that since Sidlon I.S. Chopra left in August 1972 without a successor. In fact, the Chogyal was of the view that the post of sidlon could only be filled by a competent Sikkimese, as and when available. It was finally decided that in order to achieve that objective, political opposition to the Chogyal had to be raised significantly so that he was forced to recognize the need for an Indian sidlon.

From the date of the above meeting, it is likely that Kewal Singh had called it after hearing from the PMO and the foreign minister about the prime minister's approval of the R&AW's operations in Sikkim and from Kao about the operational team's preparedness to implement any decision taken by New Delhi in that respect. As Singh was the man who was to take decisions on how and when the Chogyal could be made to agree to India's line of action, this was his first meeting to ascertain the views of the senior Indian government officials concerned as to how to proceed further to regain lost ground in Sikkim. Interestingly, out of the members who attended that meeting only two, namely Singh and Banerjee, knew that the meeting marked the official beginning of the R&AW's spl ops in Sikkim. Banerjee was present to assess the mood at the meeting and to see if anything could be carried back for the benefit of the R&AW's operational team in Sikkim which had already started contacting pro-democracy leaders there.

In Sikkim, by the middle of March 1973, the R&AW's spl ops team had started guiding the activities of both the anti-Chogyal parties. While the discontent against the durbar continued, the eighteen elected members and six nominated members took oath as members of the newly constituted council without much fuss. But when the time came for the members of the executive council to take oath on 20 March, two of the SNC members—Razalim and C.B. Chhetri—did not show up for the swearing-in ceremony. Razalim stayed back in Namchi and Chhetri was taken by Nar Bahadur Khatiwada's men to Kazi's house in Kalimpong, where he remained holed up for about a week.

An important challenge that the R&AW's spl ops team had to face at that point was to ensure closer coordination in the functioning of the SNC and Janata Congress, with the ultimate aim of securing their merger into a single party headed by Kazi. In this respect, one of the members of the R&AW's spl ops team, Padam Bahadur, played a significant role. He contacted his old friend S.K. Rai, general secretary of the Janata Congress, and was finally able to convince him about the virtues of the unity of approach of the two parties to build pressure on the Chogyal to get their demands fulfilled. Rai, who had already been informed about the change in the GoI's approach towards the Chogyal, understood the logic and started working on the president of his party, K.C. Pradhan, on these lines. Bahadur also briefed Rai that in case his party, joined the executive council and Kazi's SNC chose to abstain, it would be considered as a pro-Chogyal act on the part of the Janata Congress, which would harm their party's interests in the eyes of their Nepalese supporters at that juncture. Further, even otherwise, their party's performance in the election had not been very good, and if they now towed a different line than the SNC, they would lose whatever support they had in the south and west. Bahadur further told Rai that it would be better to wait for the SNC to make their stand on this issue public, before the Janata Congress decided anything in this respect. It was mainly because of this that Bhawani Prasad Dahal, the sole representative of the party in the executive council, also did not show up for the swearing-in ceremony. Instead, a memorandum was sent to the state council office mentioning that the party reserved the right to nominate its member in the executive council and would not be able to do so before 29 March.

It was time to start building up the tempo for the planned anti-Chogyal agitation. After a couple of meetings in Gangtok, where the rigging of the 1973 elections was criticized and a demand for fresh elections was made, some of the SNC and Janata Congress leaders, including Kazi, Khatiwada, Pradhan and Rai, shifted their focus to south and west Sikkim to build anti-durbar and anti-administration sentiments through highly critical speeches. While highlighting the rigging of the elections, these leaders demanded fresh elections based on the 'one man, one vote' principle and broad-based democratic, administrative and economic reforms.

In his speeches, Pradhan attacked the Chogyal for his discriminatory policies, which led to his arrest on the evening of 26 March in Gangtok. The arrest provided further impetus to motivating the crowd to move towards Gangtok. Egged on by

Pradhan's arrest, and encouraged by Sayali and Padam Bahadur, the SNC and Janata Congress leaders finally decided on 27 March to form a ten-member Joint Action Committee (JAC) comprising five members each from both parties. They also framed a charter of demands, including democratic reforms, a written constitution, an independent judiciary and revision or replacement of the Indo-Sikkim Treaty of 1950. Some of the persons present at the meeting even demanded the Chogyal's abdication.

News of Pradhan's arrest helped the JAC galvanize anti-Chogyal sentiments amongst the Nepalese population, especially in south and west Sikkim. In Gangtok, on the morning of 27 March, when the newly elected council members were taking oath and the Chogyal was to address them, about 1000 demonstrators surrounded the council house as a token build-up of the anti-Chogyal demonstrations. At the end of the session, Kazi handed over a piece of paper to the Chogyal containing the JAC's three demands: the immediate release of K.C. Pradhan, democratic reforms and acceptance of the 'one man, one vote' principle.

Later during the day, the same crowd gathered around the palace. In order to ward off trouble, senior JAC members as well as National Party leaders advised the Chogyal to announce the much-needed concessions like holding fresh elections under a new electoral system and Pradhan's release. Not realizing that things were different this time—and that it was his personal privileges and prerogatives as a ruler built very carefully over the years which were the actual target—the Chogyal decided to personally address the crowd. In his speech, he mentioned that in Pradhan's case, the law would take its own course. About electoral reforms, he mentioned that these could not be introduced without revising the constitution.

As the target date, the Chogyal's birthday on 4 April, was still nine days away, the JAC did not press the matter further and the crowd started thinning out, giving the Chogyal and his men the impression that the people were still willing to listen to him patiently, and that he was able to address their grievances satisfactorily. However, two young leaders, R.C. Poudyal and N.K. Upreti, preferred to stay on hunger strike till their demands were met. They were finally taken to hospital on 1 April.

News started reaching Gangtok that an anti-Chogyal crowd would be marching from south and west Sikkim, and there was already lawlessness and intimidation of pro-Chogyal elements in that area. Such information naturally caused grave concern in the minds of the commissioner of police and senior pro-Chogyal government officers. The Sikkim police were ill-prepared—they didn't have enough manpower, crowd-control equipment or procedures in place to deal with such a situation. The commissioner's request for the promulgation of Section 144 of the Criminal Procedure Code (CrPC), which prohibits a gathering of five or more persons at any given time and place, was accepted by the Chogyal with reluctance only on the morning of 2 April. The same day, Pradhan was released, but it was too late to have any impact on the mobilization of the anti-Chogyal crowd in Gangtok.

Meanwhile, last-minute efforts by the durbar to work out a compromise between the different factions of the council picked up momentum. In this respect, a meeting was held at the palace monastery on the evening of 2 April. It was attended by senior JAC and National Party leaders as well as some pro-Chogyal senior bureaucrats led by Jigdal Densapa, secretary to the Chogyal. They reached an agreement on the 'one man, one vote' principle and Jigdal assured them that he would be able to convince the

Chogyal on the other two demands too. Apprehending that an amicable solution with pro-Chogyal elements at that stage would seriously jeopardize his party's ultimate aim of forcing the Chogyal to accept even bigger demands, Kazi expressed his inability to agree to the decisions taken at this meeting without consulting his party members. He went to an adjoining room to call his party members and came back with the answer that the solution offered was not acceptable to him and his party members, and he walked out of the room.

Not to be deterred by this setback, M.M. Rasaily, auditor-general and a known pro-Chogyal civil servant, accompanied by some SNP members, separately met JAC leaders like Pradhan and Khatiwada and told them that the Nepalese of Sikkim would never get such a chance again, as the Chogyal was totally demoralized and willing to accept most of their demands. Realizing that this was a clever ruse to disrupt the momentum of anti-Chogyal demonstrations, the JAC leaders refused to take the bait.

Nar Bahadur Khatiwada, a firebrand Nepalese leader, had played a major role in mobilizing anti-Chogyal demonstrators in Sikkim during that period. At my request, during one his visits to Delhi, he met me at my residence on 15 April 2018.[10] Thereafter, I talked to him a number of times on the telephone to seek certain clarifications. He told me that under Kazi's instructions, preparations for holding demonstrations at Gangtok coinciding with the Chogyal's fiftieth birthday on 4 April 1973 had started from the last week of March itself. All families from south and west Sikkim, and the poorer segment of the population from the north and east, comprising Bhutias and Lepchas, were told to send at least one person each from their families to Gangtok to participate in the proposed demonstrations at short notice.

Following this, some young demonstrators had started reaching Gangtok from the last week of March 1973 on their own. They came in handy to build some pressure on the Chogyal and his men. But as per the party's plan, Khatiwada, followed by a group of about 500 demonstrators, reached Kazi's petrol pump on the morning of 4 April. Their plan was to carry out peaceful demonstrations by shouting pro-Chogyal slogans, carrying his photographs and placards seeking land reforms, 'one man, one vote', and a written constitution. The original plan was to get the Chogyal to agree to their demands through peaceful means and keep adding to the number of demonstrators to gradually build pressure on the Chogyal if he refused to do so. But this group of demonstrators was stopped by the police near the petrol pump. The police used tear-gas shells to disperse them. Stones were thrown at them by some pro-Chogyal elements standing at a height.

Undeterred by this police action, and annoyed by the stone-throwing, the peaceful group led by Khatiwada started moving towards the palace. Soon thereafter, they were joined by the JAC-inspired demonstrators already in Gangtok and their number swelled to about 3000. The ill-equipped police warned the crowd on loudspeakers, and used tear-gas shells, but these had no effect. The demonstrators continued raining brickbats and stones on the retreating police force. The police opened fire to control the crowd, which led to some casualties and some people being injured. Due to the shortage of manpower in the police force, some Tibetan refugees were earlier temporarily recruited as special police officers and deployed to help control the crowd and maintain law and order. Kazi sent a telegram to Indira Gandhi the same day, informing her about the police firing which had resulted in the death of some demonstrators, the use of Tibetans in mercilessly beating up peaceful demonstrators and the total collapse of law and order in Sikkim.

On the afternoon of 4 April, while the anti-Chogyal demonstrators were trying to make a fresh move towards the palace, Prince Tenzing, the elder son of the Chogyal, left the palace with three others in his jonga to personally assess the situation. He did not encounter any crowd and nothing happened on his way to Singtam. But on his return journey, some demonstrators tried to stop his vehicle by putting roadblocks near Ranipool, a short distance from Gangtok. To frighten the crowd and ensure Tenzing's safety, Captain Chhetri of the Sikkim Guards, who was sitting in the jonga, opened fire with his service revolver resulting in some fatalities. This incident was taken full advantage of by Kazi and his men who accused the Chogyal and his son of murder. Due to the crowd demonstrating on the streets of Gangtok, the birthday celebrations at the palace were called off. Instead, a brief function was held at the palace monastery which was followed by lunch and was attended by less than half the usual number of guests.

At the end of the day, Khatiwada told Kazi that peaceful demonstrations by a few thousand demonstrators would have no effect on the Chogyal and his men, and that the party had to bring a larger number of demonstrators and start attacking the Chogyal and his administration with greater force. Kazi agreed and asked Khatiwada and other young leaders to increase the number of demonstrators with each passing day to build pressure on the Chogyal until he agreed to hand over administration of Sikkim to the PO. The same evening, Khatiwada, N.K. Subedi, Dugo Bhutia, Karma Gyalpo Lama, Loden Tshering Lepcha, Phigu Tshering Lepcha and Degay Bhutia left for the south and west districts, while some others left for the east and north districts, to mobilize people to reach Gangtok in larger numbers. However, on their way, on the night of 4 April, nineteen police stations and check posts were raided by pro-Janata demonstrators, and some rifles and wireless sets were seized. Police officers and men in charge of these posts were asked to take off their Sikkim Police uniforms and wear civilian clothes as they were now working for janata raj (public rule). From the morning of 5 April, demonstrators started reaching Gangtok. People living in the nearby villages or towns travelled on foot while others came in private taxis, trucks or any other way they could manage. Most of these persons carried dry ration. The maximum number of people, according to Khatiwada, at a given time in Gangtok was not more than 12,000. He also refuted the allegations that money was paid to certain people to participate in the demonstrations, or for reaching Gangtok, or that some people were brought from outside Sikkim. Further, the young leaders who were mobilizing the crowd belonged to all three segments of Sikkimese society—Gurkhas Bhutias and Lepchas—as the names of these leaders would indicate. Similarly, a fairly large segment of the poorer section of the Bhutia–Lepcha population also participated in those demonstrations. According to him, people participated enthusiastically as they saw in it a chance to improve their lot.

Devare recently told me that on 5 April, the weather was pleasant with plenty of sunshine.[11] The Kanchenjunga range, glistening majestically, was visible from India House. Avtar Singh, secretary, MEA, who had earlier served as PO in Gangtok, had come to attend the Chogyal's birthday celebrations on 4 April (but continued to stay longer due to the developing situation in Gangtok) and was enjoying the mid-morning sun on the lawn in front of India House. Five or six JAC leaders, including Kazi, B.P. Dahal, K.C. Pradhan and B.B. Gurung, came in a jeep to meet Avtar Singh and the PO. Seeing them at the chancery, which was located a couple of hundred yards before India House, Devare came out of his office. On hearing about their arrival, Bajpai had already joined Avtar

Singh. Kazi and his men started complaining bitterly about the Chogyal, accusing him of a high-handed attitude towards the JAC leaders and also the ordinary people. They also criticized him for the ruthlessness with which the Sikkim police had dealt with the peaceful demonstrators, which according to them had resulted in the death of some protesters. Saying that their lives were in danger, they put forward their demands for security, and administrative and political reforms. They also wanted their request to be sent to Prime Minister Indira Gandhi.

As they were leaving India House, they received a message that they might be detained by the Sikkim police if they went back to their office or houses. Thereafter, Kazi and the others accompanied Devare to his office and told him that they would not leave his room until they were provided adequate security. Devare sought instructions from Bajpai, who told him that they should be allowed to stay in the chancery until they felt safe enough to leave.

In Devare's office, they sat tense and fearful. They had tea and snacks, and as time went by, Devare had to make some arrangements for lunch. Meanwhile, these leaders came to know that the Sikkim police had raided the SNC's office at Kazi's petrol pump in the bazaar. This caused further concern. They conveyed to their representatives in the town to send telegrams to the prime minister, informing her of the repressive steps the Chogyal was taking and requesting immediate intervention from the GoI to save their lives.

The leaders remained in Devare's room till late afternoon. Kazi, who was already in his seventies, was quite tired by then and slept on a sofa. The others too were getting restless. Devare was beginning to think that they might not be able to leave before nightfall and started asking his staff to arrange for mattresses and blankets. Just then, he got information that on hearing about the police raid at the SNC's office, a mob of protesters had been seen at Ranipool, marching towards Gangtok. The palace seemed to fear that if they were allowed to come to Gangtok, it would aggravate the already-disturbed law-and-order situation. It was therefore agreed that Kazi and the other JAC leaders could leave the chancery and go to Ranipool to stop the mob. Meanwhile, news of the police raid disturbed the situation further in south and west Sikkim, where police stations were burnt, armouries and wireless equipment looted and a number of pro-Chogyal officials roughed up and locked in privately opened jails.

As per Kazi's plans, the number of anti-Chogyal demonstrators marching on the streets of Gangtok continued to increase with each passing day. Worried about his own and his family's safety, the Chogyal agreed to hand over the functioning of some police stations to the Indian army on 6 April. The next day, the maintenance of law and order was handed over to the PO, and finally on 8 April, the Chogyal formally handed over the charge of Sikkim government to the PO.

Lt Gen. P.N. Hoon (retd)—who later served as GOC–in–C of the Western Command—was commanding the Gangtok-based 64 Mountain Brigade at that time, before Depinder Singh, who later served as GOC–in–C of the Southern Command, took charge of it.[12] According to him, his GOC Maj. Gen. Harminder Singh Kochhar told him that during that period he had been asked by PO Bajpai to deliver a letter to the Chogyal informing him that as the law-and-order situation in Sikkim had gone out of control, he should sign that letter requesting the Indian army to take control. As desired, Maj. Gen. Kochhar went to the palace and handed the letter to the Chogyal. After reading it, the Chogyal crumpled the paper and threw it on the ground, saying, 'Over my dead body will I sign this letter.'

It appears that Maj. Gen. Kochhar met the Chogyal on 6 or 7 April, and till then he was not sufficiently scared of the deteriorating situation. A day or two after that, Kazi brought additional pro-Janata demonstrators to Gangtok. The attitude of the crowd became more menacing. On 8 April, at 5.30 p.m., PO Bajpai called Gurdip Singh Bedi, another first secretary, who was still sitting in his office.[13] By that time, the number of demonstrators in Gangtok had already swelled to over 12,000, and there were reports of police stations being looted in the countryside. Bajpai had already prepared a draft letter which he wanted Bedi to carry to the palace, to get it signed by the Chogyal on his official letterhead. According to this letter, the Chogyal was to request the PO, as per the terms of the letter of exchange dated 25 February 1951 (written by then PO Hareshwar Dayal and accepted by the maharaja), due to the complete breakdown of law and order and an imminent threat to him and his family, to take control of the administration of Sikkim. In this connection he would also like to place the Sikkim Guards and the commissioner of police under the command of the GOC, 17 Mountain Division. Bedi carried this draft to the palace, where he was asked to park his jeep just below the garden and proceed to where the Chogyal was sitting. Standing in front of him were some of his close advisers, including Jigdal Densapa, Chief Secretary Sherab Gyaltsen and intelligence chief Karma Topden, obviously discussing the situation created by the anti-Chogyal demonstrators whose slogans were clearly audible from that spot. It also appeared that the crowd was marching towards the palace.

Bedi had just paid his respects to the Chogyal and was about to hand over the draft letter when the palace bugler sounded the beating of the retreat and the guard commander started lowering the Chogyal's flag. Before joining the IFS in 1965, Bedi had received six months' training at the Central Police Training College in Mount Abu as an IPS probationer. He was aware of the sanctity of the moment and stood still till the bugler had finished. But the symbolism of this historic moment, and its relevance to the Chogyal's declining power, was not lost on Bedi. He could feel that this was the last time that the flag of the all-powerful Chogyal was being lowered.

Soon after, Bedi handed the draft letter to the Chogyal and explained the purpose of his visit. After reading the draft carefully, the Chogyal exploded: 'Never! I would never place my Sikkim Guards under the command of the GOC.' He went inside the palace without uttering a single word after that. Jigdal went after him and returned with the draft in a few moments. After consulting the other two in Sikkimese, he asked: 'Has the army been deployed?' Gurdeep replied that the army would be instructed to move only after the letter had been received by the PO. Jigdal again went in to meet the Chogyal and returned after a few minutes to tell Gurdeep that the Chogyal was ready to sign the letter, provided the Sikkim Guards were allowed to remain under his control. As the telephone lines were dead and there was no other means of contacting Bajpai, Bedi agreed to the Chogyal's demand, provided the Sikkim Guards did not move out of the palace, as that could lead to clashes with the angry mob outside. While they were discussing this, the roar of the anti-Chogyal demonstrators grew louder and louder. Everyone present there could hear them clearly. That unnerved Jigdal, who again went in to meet the Chogyal and returned to tell Gurdeep that the Chogyal was ready to sign the letter. Thereafter, the Chogyal's stenographer was summoned to type the letter. Meanwhile, fearing an attack on the palace, all the Sikkimese senior officers present there, except Jigdal ran to get their weapons. Jigdal, however, admonished them for their foolhardy behaviour.

With the letter signed by the Chogyal, Bedi returned to India House. On the way, he met a huge crowd chanting anti-Chogyal and anti-Tenzing slogans. The Sikkim Police was nowhere to be seen. He was allowed to proceed, as he was driving a jeep with an India House number plate. He reached India House around 8 p.m. and handed over the letter to Bajpai, who made no comments on the exclusion of the Sikkim Guards from the Chogyal's letter. Later, Bedi came to know that Bajpai had already called the army to bring the situation under control.

While Avtar Singh was still in Gangtok, P.N. Dhar, the then principal secretary to Prime Minister Indira Gandhi, accompanied by Kewal Singh, met Gandhi in her office on 6 April to brief her on the situation in Sikkim and seek her instructions.[14] The following excerpts from his book *Indira Gandhi, the 'Emergency' and Indian Democracy* give an indication of the performance of the R&AW spl ops cell in Sikkim:

> The meeting lasted only about half an hour. Kewal was surprised to find that she had already made up her mind before listening to what he had to say. He guessed that the leaders of the anti-Chogyal movement had kept her informed through R&AW. She was brief and told us that she would accept the Chogyal's request for help as soon as it came. Since she was leaving for Lucknow the next morning, a meeting of the political affairs committee of the cabinet was convened the same afternoon so that the decision could be endorsed in anticipation.

On 9 April, the minister of state for external affairs, Surenderpal Singh, apprised the Lok Sabha of the latest developments in Sikkim. He significantly remarked that 'India would now make every effort to ensure that the interests of the people are served and safeguarded and that Sikkim marches on the road to political stability, security and prosperity.'

In Gangtok, with New Delhi's support to his cause fully assured, and the limited objective of forcing the Chogyal to hand over Sikkim's administration to India achieved, Kazi called off his agitation on 9 April.

Soon after, 'he' received the Chogyal's request to take charge of Sikkim's administration, and even before the chief executive designate, B.S. Das, had arrived, PO Bajpai, in order to restore normality, revoked the promulgation of Section 144, and ordered the Sikkim Guards and Sikkim police back to their barracks.

On 8 April, the day India received the Chogyal's written request handing over the administration of Sikkim, Kewal Singh selected the very competent B.S. Das for the job of chief executive. Das, a 1948 batch IPS officer of the Uttar Pradesh cadre, had considerable experience of district-level administration (he had served as the senior superintendent of police in Meerut before opting out for deputation with the GoI) and later served as the first head of the Indian Mission in Bhutan.

Before Das proceeded to Gangtok, Kewal Singh called him to the MEA headquarters for a two-day briefing on 8 and 9 April. During this period, Das sought specific instructions from Singh on the extent to which democratic forces in Sikkim were to be supported, and on India's ultimate objective in Sikkim.

Das found the foreign secretary to be absolutely clear on both issues.[15] He told Das that the anti-Chogyal leaders had to be given full support, and they were to be assured of India's determination to set up a popularly elected government. In case the Chogyal refused to concede their demands, New Delhi was ready for a showdown, and Sikkim could be made a centrally administered state and that the policy had approval from the highest level.

While Das was being briefed, Avtar Singh returned from Sikkim. He informed Kewal Singh and the others present that as per his assessment, the demonstrations could not be sustained for a longer period unless New Delhi offered more support. His advice to Das was that he should take full advantage of the situation and make sure that the story of 1949 is not repeated. Kewal Singh also assured Das that the foreign office would take care of international reactions, including that of China. Further, Kewal Singh said that if Das and the PO worked effectively within the provisions of the 1950 treaty, there would be no problem in handling the Chogyal.

On arrival at the Gangtok helipad on 10 April, Das was received by Devare from the political office and some senior Sikkim government officials. As Das and these officials approached the town, they were received by Kazi and a fairly large number of JAC workers. Das, accompanied by Devare, had to walk some distance along with Kazi and his followers, who to the embarrassment of Das and the first secretary, went on shouting slogans in favour of Das and against the Chogyal's administration. The next morning, when Das called on the Chogyal at the palace, the Chogyal addressing Das sarcastically remarked that 'Sikkim was not Goa which could be taken over by the chief administrator' (the title was later changed to chief executive at the Chogyal's instance).[16]

When Das met PO Bajpai on 10 April, and shared with him the specific instructions he had received from Kewal Singh, the PO said that had the foreign office told him all this in such clear and concise terms, he could have resolved the issue on 4 April itself.

In the meantime, the Chogyal's sister, Coo Coo La, who had gone to Hong Kong on a shopping trip, in a press interview on 13 April, accused Indian intelligence personnel of financing the anti-Chogyal agitations in Sikkim, in which outside elements encouraged by low-level Indian intelligence agents were allegedly involved. She, however, mentioned that New Delhi was not aware of the activities of these SIB agents.

Soon after the Chogyal handed over the administration of Sikkim to India on 8 April, PO Bajpai received a message from Kewal Singh that New Delhi was concerned by news reports about the security situation in the countryside, and he wanted a first-hand report on the impact of the April agitations in south and east Sikkim. As instructed by Bajpai, on or around 12 April, Devare left for the Namchi and Gyezing areas in his official jeep accompanied by his driver alone. Making use of his knowledge of Nepalese, Devare talked to some shopkeepers and a number of residents, both Nepalese as well as Bhutia–Lepchas.

Devare told me that during that visit, he found that the anti-Chogyal demonstrators had caused considerable damage to a number of shops, houses and even government buildings. Some of those were burnt.[17] The houses of some of the Bhutias, especially those known to be close to the Sikkim durbar, were specifically targeted. The general atmosphere was tense, and there was a feeling of insecurity amongst those who were close to the Chogyal. At the same time, Devare observed, that a large number of residents of these areas seemed to believe that these agitations would put pressure on the Chogyal and persuade him to change the old system of favouritism and patronization which had benefited only a handful of people. They were also hoping that their elected representatives would now have greater say in the running of the government. Winds of democratic aspirations were thus seen to be blowing. Devare's impression at the end of the tour was that what these areas had witnessed was a spontaneous and popular movement, arising out of the local population's frustration with the existing administrative set-up. At the same time, at many places, the demonstrators had gone out of control and resorted to arson and hooliganism. On his return to Gangtok, Devare submitted his report to Bajpai and later briefed Kewal Singh personally during his visit to Gangtok on 15 April.

While Das, in consultation with PO Bajpai, was working out a plan of action on the lines indicated by Kewal Singh, he arrived in Gangtok on 15 April. Kewal Singh explained that his sudden dash to Gangtok resulted from adverse reactions over the recent developments in Sikkim 'in some friendly and not so friendly countries'. He further told the PO and Das that they had to make suitable changes in their approach. Aggressiveness had to give way to conciliation with immediate effect, without of course giving up the ultimate objectives.

Kewal Singh's 'new approach' of negotiated settlement with the Chogyal embarrassed Das and Bajpai considerably in front of the political leaders. The new line was that agitation had achieved its purpose, and we should now look forward to a tripartite alliance between Delhi, the Chogyal and the political parties.

Singh met the anti-Chogyal JAC leaders led by Kazi and K.C. Pradhan. They were assured of New Delhi's full support to their demands for democratic reform. They were also told that the Chogyal was being extremely difficult, and that all efforts were being made to bring him around. The pro-Chogyal SNP leaders led by Netuk Tshering, who wanted adequate protection of the Bhutia–Lepcha interests, retention of the Chogyal as a symbol of Sikkim's unity and a separate identity under the 1950 treaty, were also assured of the protection of their interests. He assured parity between the Nepalese on one side and the Bhutia–Lepchas on the other. They were also told that New Delhi would like to see a negotiated settlement followed by elections and the formation of a truly representative elected government.

In his meeting with the Chogyal, Kewal Singh assured him of three things: continuation of the institution of the Chogyal and his dynasty with related privileges, parity between Bhutia–Lepchas and the Nepalese, and maintaining the sanctity of the 1950 treaty. Kewal Singh met the JAC leaders again. He assured them of New Delhi's continued support. He left Gangtok on 16 April, but before leaving he noted down suggestions from both Bajpai and Das and had a separate meeting with Sayali. He took note of their views and what he had gathered during his meetings with the political leaders. Based on these inputs and further discussions in New Delhi, Kewal Singh prepared a draft confidential agreement which he wanted to sign with the Chogyal during his next visit.

According to Das, Kewal Singh's sudden arrival in Gangtok was misunderstood by the Chogyal as India's weakness. Consequently, he started persuading Das to be 'reasonable'. He also thought of using him to counter the PO's anti-Chogyal moves, as was the case with some of the diwans in the post-1949 era.

On 18 April, as advised by the R&AW's spl ops team, Kazi and K.C. Pradhan formally decided to wind up the JAC and merge their parties—SNC and Janata Congress—to form a new party called the Sikkim Congress under Kazi's leadership.

Foreign Secretary Kewal Singh returned to Gangtok on 22 April with a confidential agreement that he wanted to sign with the Chogyal. As per this agreement, the Chogyal's dynasty and its continuity, as well as his personal privileges, were assured. But he was to exercise his residuary powers only through the chief executive who would refer all disputes to the PO for New Delhi's arbitration. The draft agreement conceded the 'one man, one vote' principle, but restricted it to parity between the Nepalese and the combined Bhutia–Lepcha interests. This draft agreement, according to Das, was virtually a death knell to the expectations of the anti-Chogyal forces.

The above agreement was signed on 23 April. As this arrangement was not expected to be to the liking of the leaders of the newly formed Sikkim Congress, Kewal Singh told the Chogyal that this would be a strictly confidential agreement between them and that a tripartite agreement involving the political parties would soon follow.

Kewal Singh had detailed discussions with Das and Bajpai the same day about the contents of the tripartite agreement that he wanted to sign during his next visit. He was back in Gangtok on 7 May with the agreement which had transferred some of the reserved subjects (earlier in the domain of the Chogyal) to the elected government. But the chief executive still retained the real powers. The Chogyal refused to sign such an agreement, but Kewal Singh prevailed on him by saying that this agreement was only a 'public relations document' and that the real one would be the one signed with him on 23 April. The Chogyal finally agreed to that when Kewal Singh assured him that the 1950 treaty would continue to govern Indo–Sikkim relations, and all arrangements would follow out of its provisions.

The tripartite agreement was finally signed at 9 p.m. on 8 May at the palace by the Chogyal, Kewal Singh, Kazi and K.C. Pradhan on behalf of the Sikkim Congress and Netuk Tshering in his capacity as president of the SNP. Devare, who was present there and understood Nepalese, told me that before signing this agreement, the Chogyal was drunk and furious.[18] For about an hour he hurled the choicest curses at the Sikkim Congress leaders for betraying the cause of Sikkim and selling out to India.

Among other things, the 8 May agreement provided for the following:

a) A council (legislative Assembly) to be elected on the basis of adult franchise and the 'one man, one vote' principle every four years, under the supervision of the ECI. The composition of the Assembly would ensure that no single group, i.e., Nepalese and Bhutia–Lepcha, would have a dominant position.

b) It had provisions for an executive council (cabinet) responsible to the Assembly. The Assembly was given powers to legislate and pass resolutions on fourteen subjects such as finance, economic and social planning, education and agriculture, but it had no powers on four subjects, viz. the Chogyal and other members of the ruling family, matters before the courts, members of the judiciary, appointment of the chief executive and issues which were the responsibility of the Government of India.

c) The Chogyal was left with the control of the palace establishment and the Sikkim Guards only. There were significant omissions, but the fact that the power base had now shifted from the Chogyal to New Delhi was made clear.

d) The chief executive, an Indian official, also became the president (speaker) of the Assembly and a virtual chief minister, having a final say in the appointment of the ministers and the allocation of their portfolios. Any dispute between him and the Chogyal was to be referred to New Delhi through the PO, and New Delhi's decision was to be final.

The implications of this agreement for the Chogyal were obvious. On 9 May, when Das went to meet the Chogyal, he said, 'Welcome Mr Das, our new Chogyal.' This statement was a significant comedown from

the satirical remarks with which the Chogyal had received Das on
11 April, a day after his arrival in Gangtok.

At the end of this chapter, I would like to touch upon four issues
which need clarification and special comments. The first issue
relates to the misinterpretation of the actual reason behind Kewal
Singh's arrival in Gangtok on 15 April 1973, within a week of the
Chogyal handing over the administration of Sikkim to India on
8 April. Das and Bajpai were told by Kewal Singh that after the
8 April takeover of the administration by Das, there had been a
rethinking in New Delhi about the way things should proceed in
Gangtok. In this context, Kewal Singh reportedly told Das and
Bajpai that the earlier policy of aggressive confrontation towards
the Chogyal had to be replaced with a policy of conciliation.
According to him, this change had resulted from adverse reactions
in some friendly and not so friendly countries about the recent
developments in Sikkim. Both Das and Bajpai literally believed
what Kewal Singh told them.

As far as the R&AW was concerned, there was no confusion
on this issue. Things were clear from the very beginning. While
merger was the ultimate goal, this had to be achieved in stages
and through constitutional means with proper resolutions
passed by the people's representatives duly elected to the new
Assembly. While the R&AW was fully prepared to ensure the
victory of a maximum number of pro-India candidates in
the next elections, as and when held under the revised rules,
the pace and modalities of establishing closer relations between
Sikkim and India had to be worked out by Kewal Singh in close
consultation with Kao.

The April 1973 anti-Chogyal demonstrations had a limited purpose, as was evident from the minutes of the meeting held in Kewal Singh's room on 14 March 1973. The main purpose of that meeting was to make the Chogyal agree to the appointment of an Indian sidlon or diwan to run the administration. It is not known as to what more could have been achieved at this stage. An Indian chief executive (a sidlon or diwan of sorts with more powers) had already been appointed on 10 April. Further, the 8 May agreement had curtailed the Chogyal's powers significantly. The Assembly, which had been elected in January 1973 by means of an outmoded system weighted heavily in the Chogyal's favour, was automatically dissolved and the new election rules and regulations were to be worked out by the chief election commissioner of India.

Kewal Singh was fully aware of the requirements of his policy (the appointment of an Indian as diwan, as decided in a meeting in his room on 14 March 1973) at that stage. In fact, he was the man who was to work out the modalities for the fulfilment of the final goal to be achieved in stages through democratic process. It appears that while briefing Das in New Delhi on 8–9 April 1973, he had inadvertently let out the closely guarded secret that India was planning 'Sikkim's takeover as a centrally administered territory of India' to a newcomer like Das, and that too at an early stage. This was the final goal but there was no urgency in doing that. If there was some urgency for Sikkim's takeover, PO Bajpai, through whom such decisions were to be implemented on the ground, would surely have been taken into confidence at the time the demonstrators started pouring into Gangtok. On the contrary, Bajpai was surprised to know about Kewal Singh's briefing Das on this subject.

On 15 April 1973, while interacting with Das and Bajpai, Kewal Singh tried to undo the damage he had done by covering it up by saying that there was a need for a change in policy, thereby confusing the whole situation and keeping Das, Bajpai and also the Chogyal guessing about India's goal. Kewal Singh wanted the Chogyal to keep his hopes of some sort of settlement with India alive as long as possible, thereby containing the impact of his manipulating activities.

Secondly, regarding Avtar Singh's impression that the anti-Chogyal demonstrations could not be sustained longer as the crowd in Gangtok had started thinning out after 7 April, and which Das thought was one of the reasons for the so-called change in policy, it may be mentioned that the demonstrators were motivated by JAC leaders, through their young leaders including Khatiwada, to march towards Gangtok, for a specific purpose and a limited period only. That purpose was achieved when the Chogyal handed over the administration of Sikkim to India on 8 April. With the administration passing into India's hands, Kazi withdrew the agitation the next day as no useful purpose would have been served by the crowd aimlessly loitering in the streets of Gangtok, especially at a time when the PO and Das were supposed to restore peace and order. In fact, it was in India's interest to let the crowd leave Gangtok as early as possible, as their continued presence could have led to other complications. Having tasted success, some of the younger Nepalese leaders had already started thinking of Sikkim's future as an independent state or republic with or without the Chogyal as the head.

There was also a danger of fatigue setting in with the passage of time. Preparations for building up an anti-Chogyal crowd in Gangtok had started in the last week of March 1973. By the time the Chogyal handed over the administration of Sikkim on 8 April, the JAC leaders, including lower-rung party members, had been working tirelessly for over two weeks to keep up the pressure on the Chogyal to get their demands fulfilled. It was therefore felt that it was advisable to let the crowd leave, with the threat of their returning at short notice looming large over the Chogyal's head.

Thirdly, the information that a lot of money was distributed amongst the crowd, or even some of the leaders, to see the demonstrators out of Gangtok is based on rumours, hearsay, but most likely on conjectures. Das's remarks that the agitators were 'assured in unusually large doses of Delhi's full support to their demands for a democratic set up' has been misinterpreted in monetary terms rather than in political terms, as was actually the case. The assurances given were for political, administrative and democratic reforms and not monetary help. The entire operation was carried out on a shoestring budget. One doesn't have to pay money to disperse a friendly crowd. If some of them were hired, as has been alleged by some authors, such persons would not have stayed a day longer than the period for which they were paid. The fact is that the demonstrators mainly comprised the downtrodden people who saw in these demonstrations an opportunity to bring about a change in their lives. For that purpose, they were ready to come to and leave Gangtok at short notice at the request of their popular leaders. The presence of a large number of demonstrators in Gangtok, therefore, needs to be viewed from that perspective.

Lastly, a lull in political activities in Gangtok following the 8 May agreement has been interpreted differently by different authors. One of the reasons given, i.e., a sudden change in India's approach has already been discussed above. But its main reason was the impending change of guard in the post of OSD (P) Gangtok, through whom these operations were to be implemented. My predecessor Sayali had completed his normal tenure of three years in Gangtok. Unlike the PO and even his first secretaries, who continued much after their normal tenures, any extension in the tenure of the OSD (P) at that stage would have alerted the Chogyal and his men as to the real reason for such an extension, when the OSD (P) was supposed to be dealing with external intelligence only. In view of that, sufficient time had to be given to Sayali to taper off his involvement with the spl ops and some more to let his successor settle down and understand the leaders, people and situation.

On New Delhi's side, it was not that all the stages of this operation were meticulously planned to the last detail in one go. The broad outlines of the proposed action at each stage were decided by three persons—Foreign Secretary Kewal Singh, R.N. Kao and the then principal secretary to the prime minister—with the approval of the foreign minister and the prime minister, but once the political go-ahead for the same was received, the finer details of its implementation on the ground were left to Kewal Singh. Depending upon the need for expert advice from outside this group, concerned officials from other departments or ministries were also consulted from time to time. It was obvious that the next stage was the implementation of the provisions of the 8 May agreement, especially the holding of fresh elections under the aegis of the ECI. Keeping that requirement in view, in my very first meeting with Kazi at Kalimpong in the second week of October 1973 (within two months of my arrival in Gangtok), I requested him to raise his party's demand, through public meetings and memos addressed to Das and the PO, for the implementation of the provisions of this agreement. Kazi called his party's meeting within a couple of days and handed over a letter, signed by General Secretary S.K. Rai to the PO, demanding urgent implementation of the provisions of the agreement. The GoI had to take some time to react to this demand. Besides, elections could not be held in Sikkim in winter, as some parts of north and east Sikkim were covered in snow then. In view of that, elections could not be held before April 1974. That explains the long gap between the signing of the May 1973 agreement and the April 1974 elections.

Chapter VIII

March towards Democracy

Realizing the importance of my assignments, soon after my arrival in Gangtok I had started maintaining a diary to record developments of interest and action taken to further the interest of the R&AW's spl ops. Most of the contents of this and the following chapters are based on those notes. For clarity's sake, I have summarized the information contained in the diary subject-wise as far as possible, as literally following date-wise entries would have resulted in jumping from one subject to another.

With the 8 May agreement signed and the Chogyal's failure to get written assurances from Prime Minister Indira Gandhi about his own position and the separate identity of Sikkim as per the terms of the 1950 treaty, the R&AW's spl ops in Sikkim moved on to its next and most crucial phase. The main objectives were to consolidate the gains made through the 8 May agreement, render suitable help to Kazi to maintain the unity of his party—which in turn could help him get majority seats (at least two-thirds) in the Assembly as and when elections were held—and finally, get suitable resolutions passed in the council.

For the sake of clarity, this phase has been covered in four chapters: This chapter ends just before the framing of the election rules and regulations, and the next three chapters deal with the elections in April 1974, the passing of the 11 May 1974 resolution, and finally the passage of the Government of Sikkim Act, 1974, which resulted in Sikkim becoming an associate state of India.

As Kazi had not taken anybody else into confidence about his final goal of Sikkim's merger with Indian help, there was a considerable trust deficit amongst the Sikkim Congress leaders and party workers about India's true intentions. The memory of India letting the Tashi Tshering-led political movement down in 1949 was still fresh in their minds. They apprehended that India would use them once again to build pressure on the Chogyal to get some concessions from him, such as permanent association (which the Chogyal had earlier vehemently opposed) or even a new treaty, and then dump them. Also, the Chogyal's last-minute desperate efforts, made through senior civil servants led by Jigdal Densapa, at the 2 April 1973 meeting at the palace monastery could only be scuttled at the last moment due to a clever move by L.D. Kazi. The Chogyal was now willing to go many extra miles to accommodate the Sikkim Congress's popular demands. In view of that, we had to cover our flanks from all sides before making our next move.

To achieve the desired results, the following seven-point strategy-cum-action plan was devised in consultation with P.N. Banerjee, during my visit to Calcutta in July 1973:

a) Give repeated and full assurance to the anti-Chogyal and pro-India political leadership, that unlike 1949, the GoI was not going to let them down this time. Further, India had finally lifted its protective hand from the Chogyal's head and was now fully supportive of their efforts towards securing their long-cherished democratic and economic rights and other privileges.

b) Isolate and contain the activities of political elements from within the Sikkim Congress nursing pro-independence ambitions.

Kazi Lhendup Dorji, popularly called Kazi or
Kazi Sahib, devoted his life to free Sikkim from
the Chogyal's rule.

(From left to right) Governor B.B. Lal; the Kazini, Kazi's wife;
Mother Teresa and Kazi in Gangtok on 16 February 1976.

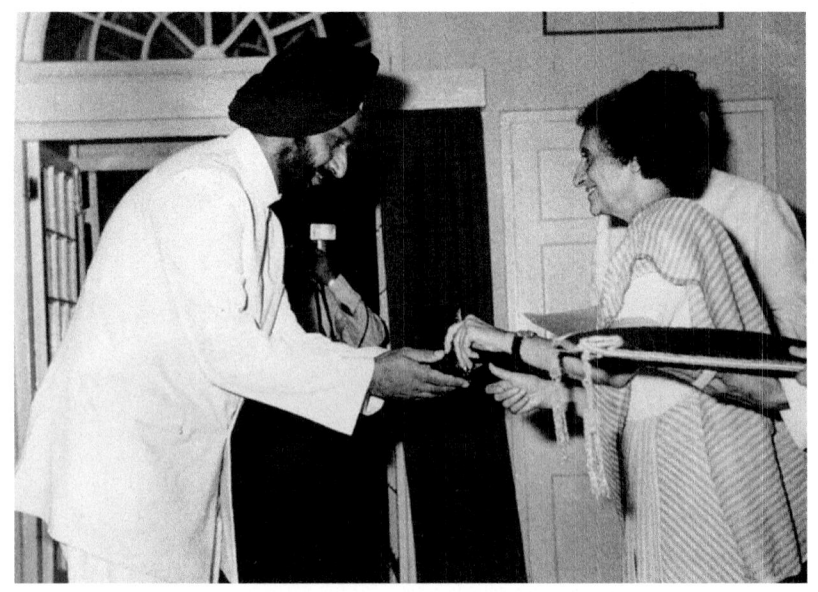

G.B.S. Sidhu, OSD (P), Gangtok, receives the Indian Police Medal for
meritorious service from Prime Minister Indira Gandhi on 6 August 1976
at 1, Akbar Road, New Delhi.

R.N. Kao, secretary (R&AW)

Padam Bahadur Pradhan, senior field officer in
the office of the OSD (P) in Gangtok

Myngma Tshering, deputy field officer in
the office of the OSD (P) in Gangtok

(From left to right) First secretary Ranjit Gupta, Political Officer K.S. Bajpai, Foreign Secretary Kewal Singh and Kazi at the palace in Gangtok on 4 July 1974, the day the Chogyal ratified the Government of Sikkim Act.

At a polling booth in west Sikkim on 15 April 1974

c) Give direction to the anti-Chogyal political movement, leading to the demand, first for greater integration with India and finally for merger. Without blowing our cover, guide L.D. Kazi and his friends and followers, in setting the desired pace for achieving their goals. Meanwhile, keep in touch with PO Bajpai to know what was happening at the foreign secretary's level and render requisite help to him, as and when required, to further our mutual interests without compromising the nature of our operations.

d) Demands for closer relations with India should, as far as possible, emanate through public speeches of and memos handed over to Das and the PO by important Sikkim Congress leaders, and finally through resolutions adopted in the Assembly, as and when constituted. All efforts be made to enlist maximum possible support for these resolutions from the Lepcha and if possible from the Bhutia segments of the Assembly members also.

e) Forge unity amongst anti-Chogyal parties, and take action to eliminate or contain dissident activities, if any, from within the Sikkim Congress. Increase the support base of the pro-India political leadership, especially Kazi Lhendup Dorji, amongst various segments of the Sikkimese population, by inducing or encouraging Lepcha and Bhutia segments of the political leadership to join forces with him. Ensure that the Kazi-led Sikkim Congress secures at least a two-thirds majority in the Assembly as and when elections were held. That would help in passing any important constitutional bill in the Assembly and also indicate the level of popular support behind such bills or resolutions.

f) Keep the anti-Chogyal pot boiling through regular public meetings and submission of memoranda and resolutions by Sikkim Congress leaders on one pretext or the other. Weaken pro-Chogyal political forces, especially their support base in north and east Sikkim.

g) In addition to the above specific directions, we were to keep close watch over unfolding developments and take corrective measures, if needed, in consultation with Banerjee and Kao.

The general atmosphere in Sikkim, following the signing of the 8 May agreement can be summed up as follows:

a) The Chogyal's position was considerably weakened, but like a wounded tiger, he was licking his wounds and planning his next move. The pro-Chogyal SNP was in disarray, confused and short of funds. The majority Nepalese population and poorer sections of the Bhutia–Lepcha segment, were upbeat. But none of them were talking about merger with India at the moment. Nor had anyone, other than Kazi, realized at that stage that India was gradually preparing the grounds for merger through public support for Kazi's moves. They were happy if the provisions of the 8 May agreement were fully implemented.

b) Unlike the R&AW, where Kao, Banerjee and the OSD (P) Gangtok were all aware of the final goal of their special operations, in the MEA, for security reasons, Kewal Singh had kept it a closely guarded secret till the very end. He followed a step-by-step approach, releasing the script for the next stage only after the previous target had been successfully achieved. After his inadvertent comment to Das in New Delhi on 9 April 1973, about the possibility of Sikkim becoming a centrally administered territory, Singh had become extremely cagey. Soon thereafter, he was able to create sufficient confusion in the minds of both Das and Bajpai about India's ultimate objectives. His changed attitude led to PO Bajpai falling back on the ministry's old policy of betting on a much weakened and chastened Chogyal to protect India's security interests in the region. In view of that, both Bajpai and Das believed that India had achieved its final objective when Sikkim became an associate state.

c) The pro-Chogyal Bhutia community in general, and the Sikkimese bureaucrats at all levels, had realized that this time the Chogyal would not be able to recover lost ground, and it was, therefore, in their own interest to secure their personal and their community's future by cosying up to the new centre of power, i.e., India, through Das and the PO. The Lepcha community, whom the ruling Bhutia class had tagged along for so long to safeguard their so-called combined minority interests by keeping the majority Nepalese in check, had also become conscious of the fact that if the Chogyal could not protect his own interests, he and his Bhutia protégés would be of little use to the Lepcha community in the face of rising Nepalese nationalism. This had led to a rethink on the part of some Lepcha leaders to open a direct line with the GoI. In that, we saw a much-needed opening to wean the Lepchas away from the Chogyal's fold, and we were finally succeeding.

As our main work in Sikkim was related to the collection of cross-border China and Tibet-related intelligence—I had to brief the Chogyal at regular intervals. In view of that, within a few days of my arrival at Gangtok, I contacted Jigdal Densapa, his secretary, to fix a meeting. Thereafter, Bali and I were invited to a cocktail party at the palace on 2 September 1973. It was a small group comprising the Chogyal, Jigdal Densapa (a confirmed bachelor), his intelligence and protocol chief Karma Topden and his wife, Cherry, police commissioner S. Dutta Chowdhury and his wife, and First Secretary Gurdip Singh Bedi (my batchmate from the IPS 64 batch who joined the IFS in 1965) and his wife, Winnie. Finding the Chogyal alone, I conveyed to him personal greetings from Kao, which he gracefully reciprocated. As he had a bad cold, the Chogyal left after about half an hour. Thereafter, Jigdal talked to me for about twenty minutes. Alluding to the recent developments in Sikkim and the perceived change in India's attitude towards the Chogyal, Jigdal said, 'We should forget about the past and start afresh. Sometimes a man acting merely on impulse says something without actually meaning that. We have been misrepresented, and even our best friends like T.N. Kaul worked against our interests.' He had a very high opinion of Police Commissioner Dutta. Pointing towards Bedi, he said that I should not be misguided by diplomats like him, an indication of the strained relations of the palace with PO Bajpai and his team.

Jigdal's remarks about Kaul were a bit surprising, as it was generally believed that he was a close family friend of the Chogyal's. Maybe Jigdal's remarks had something to do with Kaul's last visit to Gangtok in September 1972, when he unsuccessfully tried to convince the Chogyal to accept New Delhi's proposal of Sikkim's permanent association with India. Presumably, Kaul did not warn the Chogyal enough about how poorly Indira Gandhi had taken his refusal to accept the offer of permanent association. A more plausible reason appears to be that Jigdal was trying to protect the interests of an old friend, in the face of a 180-degree turnaround in the policy of appeasement which was followed by Kaul till the last day of his stay as foreign secretary. This would be evident from the fact that the Chogyal continued to meet, and possibly consult, Kaul as and when the latter came on short visit to New Delhi from Washington DC.

My first formal call on the Chogyal was fixed for 15 September. After the exchange of courtesies, I briefed him on the situation across the border. Thereafter, the conversation shifted to other issues. He told me that he would be going to New Delhi on 16 September and would meet Kaul (at that time India's ambassador to the US). He was also planning to go to New York towards the end of December after Christmas to meet his young children from Hope and bring back the Gyalmo. Hope wanted to come earlier, but he told her to stay back and return with him. He talked about his children who had been admitted to schools in New York. He also mentioned Yang Chen (his daughter from his first wife) and her kidney ailment, which was not responding to medication. If the medicines did not work, they might consider a transplant. When I asked him about his own health, he said it was all due to nervousness.

When I asked as to what would be his advice to me regarding my actual work, with folded hands he said, 'Hazur, we will talk at length after some time. We will meet, we will meet.' However, he said that now that politics had entered Sikkim, he was not very happy about it. There were people who wanted to throw the poor Tibetans out of Sikkim. He had relocated some 300 families of Tibetan origin in Namchi Estate. People did not want Commissioner Dutta to stay in Sikkim. The Chogyal said, 'He was the most efficient officer I had seen. I have great regard for this man and am really thankful to the GoI for having placed his services at the disposal of the government of Sikkim.'

Being my first meeting with the Chogyal, he kept the conversation limited to his personal and family affairs. His remarks about his wife Hope indicated that the Chogyal at that stage was still hopeful of her finally returning to Gangtok. But that was not to be, and in my future meetings with him, the Chogyal did not touch upon this subject again.

That New Delhi was extremely concerned about the Chogyal's next move was evident from a small incident that happened sometime in September.[1] The Chogyal, accompanied by two of his friends, including former diwan and his ICS coursemate (Thondup, as Maharaj Kumar, had attended part of an ICS training course with Nari Rustomji and B.B. Lal) Nari Rustomji, went on a visit to north Sikkim. Bajpai happened to be in New Delhi during that period. Devare received instructions from New Delhi that the Chogyal and two of his friends, who had gone to north Sikkim, should not be allowed to go beyond a certain point as there were apprehensions that the Chogyal might cross over to Tibet and seek political asylum with the Chinese government. First Secretary Devare was asked to be ready to move at short notice by helicopter and hand over a personal message from the PO to the Chogyal, asking him to return to Gangtok. Thereafter, a close watch was kept on his movements through the locally deployed Assam Rifles and the IB's forward posts. However, it turned out to be a false alarm, and the Chogyal and his party started returning to Gangtok before Devare could proceed to north Sikkim to deliver that message.

Having settled in my job, it was time to meet Kazi. A message was sent through Myngma Tshering to Kazi and a meeting was fixed in the second week of October at his Kalimpong residence (Chakung House). Being the first meeting, I took my wife and two children along to make it look like a social call. The meeting took place in the evening. The Kazini was also present. Most of the initial conversation was monopolized by the Kazini and was centred on the exploits of the Sikkim Congress workers during the April 1973 agitation, and the resultant retreat of the 'mighty' Chogyal's men who were 'brought down on their knees'. Kazi's only contribution was an occasional smile, sometimes in amusement at what his wife was saying. After a while the Kazini told Bali, 'Oh dear, let us move over to the other room. These men are boring and we should not be wasting our time listening to them.' This was a clever move by the Kazini, as she knew that I might have something important to discuss with Kazi. As soon as the ladies left the room, Kazi told me that I should not take the Kazini's words seriously, as she was in the habit of dramatizing everything. In the local language, his advice was that I should listen to her so that the information goes in through one ear and comes out of the other.

Operationally, our conversation was brief and centred on two subjects. Firstly, I requested him that it was time his party started demanding—through public meetings and written memos addressed to the GoI through the PO and Das—early implementation of the provisions of the 8 May agreement, especially the framing of the election rules which could pave the way for holding fresh elections on the basis of the 'one man, one vote' principle. Secondly, he should try to enlist the support of Lepcha leaders, especially Rinzing Lepcha, who had a considerable following within his community. I also sought his advice on whether he would have any objection to my contacting Rinzing Lepcha to enlist his support for the Sikkim Congress. He readily agreed and said it was a good idea.

Here, I would like to make some remarks about Kazi. While sitting in his room and talking to him, I got the impression that I was sitting in the presence of a veteran of India's freedom movement. He seemed to be one who was unfortunately let down by his own countrymen (Indians), who were in a position to help Sikkim's cause when India got its independence and even after that. Like Tashi Tshering, Kazi also had a dream—suitably tempered as per his own temperament—to free Sikkim from the autocratic and self-serving regime of the Chogyal, and hand over power to the popularly elected leaders of Sikkim. His eyes used to glisten with the hope that one day Sikkim would be a part of independent India, and there would be no discrimination there based on caste and religion. Where every hard-working young man and woman would have a chance to carve out his or her own future as per his or her desire and capability. He could visualize that being a small state Sikkim could be made to look like a model and prosperous state of India, if funds were properly utilized on its development. I always treated him with the respect that was due to an Indian freedom fighter. I considered myself a political assistant to him, appointed by India to help him realize his lifelong dream, i.e., the merger of Sikkim with India for the benefit of the Sikkimese people.

On my return from Kalimpong, I called Myngma to discuss the modalities of contacting Rinzing Lepcha (a former member of the executive council from the pro-Chogyal National Party) and somehow convincing him that his future now lay with the Kazi-led Sikkim Congress. It was decided that Myngma would carry my personal message to him and try to convince him to formally join Kazi's party. Thereafter, we would watch his public posture for some time. My meeting would be fixed only after we were sure that he was fully committed to the cause of the Sikkim Congress.

Within a couple of days, Myngma was able to establish contact with Rinzing. As discussed, Myngma informed him that keeping in view his stature within the Lepcha community he was carrying a special message on my behalf. Coming straight to the subject, Myngma told him that being the most popular leader of the Lepcha community in Sikkim, it was now his duty to safeguard his community's interests. The Chogyal and the Bhutia leaders had for long exploited the Lepchas by tagging them along with Bhutias, to neutralize the impact of the growing Nepalese population, but in practice the plight of the Lepchas had not improved over these years. Under the changed circumstances resulting from the 8 May agreement, even the Chogyal was finding it difficult to save his position. Therefore, how could the Chogyal and his loyal Bhutia friends help the Lepchas get a better deal from New Delhi? It would, therefore, be in his own interests if he joined Kazi's party. Otherwise, someone else could take the leadership position in the Lepcha community with Kazi's help, and he would be left out. To Myngma's pleasant surprise, he found that Rinzing was already thinking on these lines.

Finding Rinzing receptive to his suggestions, Myngma further told him that he would like him to meet with the OSD (P) at an appropriate time. Meanwhile, however, he should meet Das and the PO, along with some of his Lepcha followers, and demand full protection of their rights, independent of the Bhutias, keeping in view their claim of older Sikkimese ethnicity.

Our advice to Kazi appeared to be working. After a couple of days, PO Bajpai told me at a cocktail party hosted by India House that Kazi had met him and handed over a resolution passed by the party, along with a forwarding letter signed by General Secretary S.K. Rai. Through this letter the party had requested the GoI for urgent follow-up action on the promises made through the 8 May agreement, especially about the framing of election rules and holding of elections. He also mentioned that before his meeting with Kazi, he was rather apprehensive about the divisive activities of the pro-Chogyal National Party and the Youth Pioneer Movement, but now he felt confident that things were not as bad as they had appeared to be. According to him, Kazi who enjoyed the full support of the people in south and west Sikkim, had also won over the support of a sizeable section of the people in the north, especially from the Lepcha community.

One of the interesting developments within a couple of months of my arrival in Gangtok was the visit of West Bengal Chief Minister Siddhartha Shankar Ray to Gangtok, from 21–24 October. Ray was received at the local helipad by senior Indian and Sikkim government officials. He had a fairly large contingent, including some of his personal friends, with him. He and some of his close friends stayed at the palace guest house. The commissioner of Jalpaiguri Division, Monomoy Bhattacharya, who was also a part of his delegation, stayed with the PO. The Chogyal hosted a rather lavish dinner on 21 October for which some delicacies were flown in from Hong Kong. The Chogyal's sister, Coo Coo La, had also returned to Gangtok on 20 October to supervise arrangements.

The next evening, at a dinner hosted by PO Bajpai, some Sikkim Congress leaders were also invited. The Chogyal, who was present there, was in a sullen mood. But Karma Topden was seen taking an interest in introducing some of them, especially Khatiwada, to commissioner Bhattacharya. Ray and his team left on 24 October.

It was obvious that Ray had come to Gangtok at the Chogyal's invitation. The Chogyal and his family had business interests in Calcutta, and, as such, good relations with West Bengal leaders were always helpful. But Ray's arrival in Gangtok at this juncture was indicative of the following:

a) The Chogyal had not invited Ray only to further his business interests in West Bengal. Also, Ray could not have come to

Gangtok at that juncture without prior clearance from Indira
Gandhi.

b) Ray might also have been briefed by Indira Gandhi to probe
the Chogyal's mind on the developments following the signing
of the 8 May agreement. On the other hand, as indicated
by Jigdal in my last meeting with him, the Chogyal would
have conveyed a message to Gandhi seeking some sort of
forgiveness for his past mistakes and requesting the restoration
of pre-April 1973 relations based on the 1950 treaty. This was
indeed corroborated by Bajpai to me after the dinner at India
House on 22 October, when he said that he had learnt that the
Chogyal told Ray in confidence that he was ready to submit to
India's wishes, provided the Indian government was willing to
look after his interests.

What bothered me most was that the Chogyal might have played
his Pan-Nepalese (Nepalese population of Sikkim joining hands
with Gurkhas of Darjeeling and neighbouring areas in their
demand for Gorkhaland) and anti-communism cards on Ray, by
highlighting the likely impact of the anti-Chogyal demonstrations
of April 1973 on the neighbouring Darjeeling and Siliguri areas of
West Bengal. The Chogyal had been playing this card with India for
too long, and also in my subsequent meetings with him. In view of
that, in my dispatch on Ray's visit to Kao, I highlighted this issue.
I informed Kao that we should not be deterred by such propaganda
by the Chogyal, as I was confident that after the merger of Sikkim
with India, the Nepalese population of Sikkim, which might have
sympathies for their counterparts from Darjeeling, would not
like to join hands with them in their demand for Gorkhaland.
In fact, they would be highly wary of their moves from across the
border in this connection. Similarly, they would also be extremely
cautious about the spread of communism in Sikkim. Further, they

would be extremely protective of their new-found independence and would not like to share their resultant prosperity with anyone else from outside, irrespective of their ethnic, religious or ideological affinities. I requested Kao that the Chogyal's propaganda on these lines should not, in any case, have any impact on the final objective of our spl ops.

My next meeting with the Chogyal took place on 2 November 1973 and lasted for about forty-five minutes. This time, he was more relaxed and willing to talk on subjects of my interest. He started with the weather. Looking at the dark clouds towards Nathu La, he said there could be snowfall in that area soon. As a part of my briefing, I told him that the Chinese had started giving some liberty for religious worship in Tibet. To that, he said the Dalai Lama should not agree to the Chinese offer of being only a religious head. He was worried about the Tibetan refugees, in case the Dalai Lama decided to go back to Tibet on the terms presented by the Chinese.

Further, the Chogyal told me that he was going to Sarnath as some Mongolian Buddhist monk was coming to deliver a lecture there. The invitation had come to him in his capacity as president of the Maha Bodhi Society of India, and he had decided to attend. Also, the lamas had invited him to stay there for a couple of days to meditate. He would again be going to Bodhgaya on 9 December in connection with the Buddhist monastery that had just been built there with Japanese help—the monastery was to be inaugurated by the President of India. On his way back, he would stop in Calcutta to look into his business interests.

Shifting the conversation to internal developments and referring to the April 1973 agitation, the Chogyal said that the communist influence in Sikkim was on the rise, and that Ray during his recent visit had also agreed with him. Otherwise, violent activities such as the burning of government buildings and damage to places of religious worship in Gyezing area were unheard of in Sikkim. There was forcible cutting of the cardamom crop, and typical leftist slogans of peasant emancipation were shouted. He said that he could understand if a Sikkimese person had murdered someone or had run away with a woman, but otherwise he couldn't understand these actions. Therefore, something must be done before it was too late. Further, it was good to borrow socialist ideas for the betterment of the people but enforcing a purely socialist way of life, as prevalent in some of the communist countries, was not desirable. He felt that people should be allowed to have a free hand in carrying out their activities as per their belief.

By the last week of October, I had completed two months of my stay in Sikkim and had familiarized myself with the problems that needed immediate attention. It was also time for Kewal Singh to plan his next course of action. That was obviously the framing of new election rules, which could lead to elections under the supervision of the chief election commissioner of India, as envisaged in the 8 May agreement. One of the members of our spl ops team, Padam Bahadur, was regularly being asked by his political friends about the prospect of holding early elections. But Kewal Singh hadn't said anything on this issue till then. In my first meeting with Kazi at Kalimpong in the second week of October 1973, I had requested him to hand over a memo to the PO and Das requesting the GoI to take urgent follow-up action on the promises made in the May 8 agreement. He did as advised within a couple of days of that meeting. But nothing was heard from New Delhi. We, therefore, decided that there was no harm if our friends from the Sikkim Congress should hold a public meeting in Gangtok to vent their feelings on this matter and request New Delhi to expedite the election process in Sikkim. A message in this context was sent to Kazi through Myngma, requesting him to do the same urgently.

Suitably briefed, Kazi's Sikkim Congress leaders held a public meeting in Gangtok on 4 November. As per the original plan, the speakers noted the gains made through the 8 May agreement and requested the GoI and Das to make arrangements for holding early elections. Leaders criticized the Chogyal and his intelligence chief Karma Topden. It was the most bitter criticism of the Chogyal so far at a public meeting, which under previous circumstances would have led to the withdrawal of the speakers' right to Sikkim subjecthood. The Chogyal was not used to such criticism, that too at a public meeting in Gangtok. He was furious and lodged a protest with PO Bajpai through Jigdal on 7 November. Jigdal informed Bajpai that if no action was taken against some of these leaders, he would presume that the GoI was indirectly supporting the Sikkim Congress. This led to Das issuing an order prohibiting such activities on the part of political leaders. This order was also published in the official organ, *Sikkim Herald*.

Jigdal also told Bajpai that the Chogyal desperately needed a written assurance from the foreign secretary that the 23 April 1973 'confidential' bilateral agreement was the real agreement and would prevail over the 8 May agreement. Further, the Chogyal also wanted assurance that the GoI would protect his personal position and privileges as envisaged in the 1950 treaty.

With the demand for fresh elections picking up momentum, it was time for the pro-Chogyal parties to do their bit by holding public meetings to bolster the cause of the Chogyal. The National Party was rather quiet, but on 11 November 1973, a group of young pro-Chogyal Sikkim Youth Pioneer Movement (SYPM) leaders headed by Rinchen Wangdi (Coo Coo La's daughter Sodeun La's fiancé) held a meeting in Gangtok, which was attended by about 200 people. Despite their reputation, the tone of the speakers at this meeting was sober and businesslike, and they did not criticize the GoI or the PO or anyone else. It may have been due to the PO's warning to Jigdal a few days before the meeting that there should be no criticism of the GoI, otherwise it would be presumed that the Chogyal was not interested in maintaining good relations with India. As against the Sikkim Congress's demand for early elections, the SNP and SYPM were opposed to holding elections under any new rules and were still insisting on the continued relevance of the Royal Proclamation of 23 March 1953, with the principle of parity and nominated seats enshrined therein.

Meanwhile, the rift amongst senior Sikkim Congress leaders over N.B. Khatiwada's alleged links to the Communist Party of India (Marxist), was emerging. Some of the senior Sikkim Congress leaders like B.B. Gurung and K.C. Pradhan, who continued to maintain clandestine links with the Chogyal, started using Youth Congress leaders like R.C. Poudyal and N.K. Subedi to publicly criticize Khatiwada to discredit him in the eyes of the Indian government. On the other hand, the Sikkim Congress was anxiously awaiting election rules to be finalized and wanted the 'one man, one vote' principle to be institutionalized and parity removed. To broaden their popular base, which would help the party gain a stronger position in the new Assembly, the party was trying to strengthen its hold on the Lepcha community, and to some extent appeared to be succeeding in north Sikkim.

Towards the end of November 1973, Bajpai was getting worried about the reported dissensions within the Sikkim Congress, especially between Khatiwada, Subedi and Poudyal. He thought that if such persons got elected, it would be difficult to control them. He also felt that Subedi was more popular amongst the masses in south and south-west Sikkim than Khatiwada. Therefore, he preferred Subedi to Khatiwada as a member of the Assembly. I told him that it would depend on how the election rules were framed and also on the selection of suitable candidates by senior party leaders, especially Kazi.

In the last week of November 1973, a bit of a scare was created with the arrival of one deputy SP and one inspector of the Crime Investigation Department from Bihar Police. They had come to Gangtok in connection with the investigation into the Royal Nepal Airlines Corporation (RNAC) hijacking case and stayed for four to five days. In June 1973, members of the Nepalese Congress had hijacked a Royal Nepal Airlines plane to fund their cause of multiparty democracy in Nepal. The police team reportedly told the police commissioner that the hijackers had some links with Kazi and Khatiwada and, therefore, they wanted these persons to be arrested. Due to insufficient evidence against them, the commissioner expressed his inability to arrest them. It was obvious that this information was planted by the pro-Chogyal elements through the Nepal police, and it was meant to defame Kazi, Khatiwada and their party. I had received information on the afternoon of 27 November, and informed Banerjee on the phone the next morning, followed by a message. As desired by Banerjee, I requested the PO to telephone the SP in Darjeeling to stop these people from taking any action against the

Sikkim Congress leaders. As the SP was out on tour, the PO told me that he would inform the Sub-Divisional Magistrate (SDM), Kalimpong, B.R. Bajaj, on phone for further necessary action.

A high-level discussion took place at the palace on 30 November, which was attended by the Chogyal, Jigdal, Karma Topden and other trusted advisers of the Chogyal. The purpose was to work out a strategy to deal with Kewal Singh and later with India's chief election commissioner who were scheduled to visit Gangtok soon. Coo Coo La, who had specially gone to New Delhi to consult some friends and advisers on the stand the Chogyal should take during Singh's visit, returned to Gangtok on 29 November and went straight to the Sir Tashi Namgyal Memorial (STNM) Hospital where her husband was admitted. She was badly missed at the strategy session at the palace. Her husband had acute high blood pressure, which had resulted in a stroke and partial paralysis. It was later learnt that Coo Coo La's husband, who was taken to Calcutta for an emergency operation, died on 3 December. His body was brought to Gangtok on 5 December. I conveyed my condolences through Karma Topden, and presented a silk *khada* when his body was being taken from her residence for cremation on the morning of 7 December. There were about 5000 persons present, and half of them walked uphill to the cremation ground.

Kewal Singh arrived in Gangtok on 30 November. Jigdal and Karma Topden were seen in a sullen mood at the helipad, where they had come to receive him. That was perhaps due to the serious illness of Coo Coo La's husband, a former governor of Shigatse province of Tibet, and Coo Coo La's resultant absence from their strategy session at the palace. The foreign secretary had a one-to-one discussion with the Chogyal late on 30 November itself. The PO was with him. The Chogyal cried and said that his children and wife had left him, and that his future was uncertain.

The next morning, i.e., 1 December, Kewal Singh met members of the political parties. The pro-Chogyal National Party leaders pleaded that the elections should be held only when normality returned to Sikkim. Obviously their request for a delay in elections was made to help the Chogyal work on a segment of the Sikkim Congress leadership with a view to creating a rift amongst them and also to seek assurance from the prime minister about his own future. Soon thereafter, Jigdal also asked the PO as to how elections could be held in such a tense atmosphere. Further, if the elections were held, they would be compelled to enter the field, and his younger brother was also available for this purpose.

On 2 December, Kewal Singh met Das and his three OSDs at 11.30 a.m. I also met him later and apprised him of the general political situation in Sikkim, without giving details of the operational side. I assured him that the Sikkim Congress would be able to secure a comfortable two-thirds majority in the Assembly. That same evening, the PO held a reception at India House. Almost all the Sikkim Congress leaders who were absent at the palace reception were present. They looked rather happy and requested Kewal Singh for photographs.

At the PO's reception, Jigdal told me that he was rather happy about the outcome of Kewal Singh's visit as 'we have finally started seeing eye to eye with each other'. At that time, I could not understand the meaning of Jigdal's comments, as the Sikkim Congress leaders who were all present there were also grateful to Singh for helping them in furthering their cause. How these two opposing camps could be happy with the outcome of Kewal Singh's visit was bit of a surprise to Bajpai and me. Singh left on the morning of 3 December.

The same day, Bajpai called me at 11.30 a.m. and mentioned that Jigdal had told him too that the durbar was happy about the foreign secretary's visit, but as far as he knew, 'we have not lost any ground' compared to our previous stand as a result of that visit. The mystery was solved when I met the Chogyal on 9 December. The Chogyal said that the foreign secretary had told him that India had somehow put its fingers into the Sikkimese pie, and they would like to get out of that sticky situation as early as possible by holding elections. It was obvious that Kewal Singh had played a trick on the Chogyal to soften any opposition that he and the National Party might have had to the early elections.

On 7 December, the PO called me at 10 a.m. to discuss the recent resignations of Netuk Tshering, Kunzung Dorji and some other members of the pro-Chogyal Sikkim National Party. He was of the view that some of these leaders should be won over by Kazi. However, it was finally decided that such matters should be left to Kazi's political sagacity. But on return to my office, I asked Myngma to meet Kazi and tell him from my side that his party should be careful about approaches, if any, from such leaders who could act as Trojan horses.

On 8 December, I received a message from Kao that I should call on the Chogyal and Coo Coo La, and personally convey to them his condolences on the death of her husband. I fixed meetings with both of them through Karma Topden. I met them on 9 December, forenoon and afternoon, respectively, and conveyed Kao's condolences. Coo Coo La mainly talked about the weather, while the Chogyal talked about the visits of the foreign secretary and the chief election commissioner.

The Chogyal said that he had a free and frank discussion with Foreign Secretary Kewal Singh, who told him that India wanted to get out of the situation in Sikkim by holding early elections. The Chogyal also made the following significant observations on the prevailing situation in Sikkim:

a) If India was interested in Sikkim from the defence point of view, they should come out clearly with their terms and conditions. If these were agreeable to us, we will definitely abide by them.

b) No trust should be placed in the Sikkim Congress leadership because they can say 'jai' for India now and 'jai' for somebody else later.

c) He could appreciate that the general public needed to be educated about their democratic rights, privileges and duties. But, on the contrary, they were being taught to shout pro-CRPF slogans in every demonstration.

d) Officers like Bajpai and Das are not going to stay here permanently. They are going to be transferred sooner or later, and someone else will come in their place. But the Chogyal and his supporters are going to stay here, and the GoI should place more trust in them.

e) The chief election commissioner (T. Swaminathan) could not explain as to how he could hold the elections so soon. If he is going to follow the level of legal procedures laid down by the election laws of India, it would require lot of time to plan and execute everything.

The Sikkim Congress-affiliated Youth Congress held a meeting at Rangpo on 8 December. N.B. Khatiwada was elected as its president by five votes. There was some commotion over the issue of his alleged CPI(M) membership. Khatiwada did not contradict these allegations. On the contrary, he took the offensive and inquired as to what was wrong with communism. Further, it was being practised in China and Russia, and to some extent, in India also. R.C. Poudyal and others stated that the socio-economic progress achieved by the non-communist countries was much higher than in the communist countries. Therefore, they would not like communism to spread in Sikkim. There was considerable resentment amongst the Youth Congress members on this issue. Whenever asked to give his views on the subject, Kazi avoided any comments. This made other senior leaders of the party feel that Kazi was being unduly protective of Khatiwada.

Later, on 23 December, when SDM (Kalimpong) Bajaj came to see the Tibetan New Year dances at the palace, I invited him for dinner to my residence. He said that according to his information, Kazi, the Kazini and Khatiwada had no connection with the CPI(M). He did not know who was spreading these rumours. Even West Bengal Chief Minister Ray had been misinformed on this subject (obviously by the Chogyal during Ray's recent visit).

Incidentally, on 8 December, when Khatiwada was being attacked for his alleged communist connection, Bajpai told me that one of the leaders of the Sikkim Congress had learnt from Kazi that Nar Bahadur Khatiwada was an agent of the GoI, and as such, he could do nothing to stop his activities. It appeared that the concerned Sikkim Congress leader was poisoning the PO's mind against Khatiwada, as Kazi was not known to make such irresponsible remarks. Incidentally, I never met Khatiwada alone. Sometimes my written or verbal messages meant for Kazi were passed through him by Myngma.

In the second week of December 1973, we came to know that the Chogyal was planning a visit to the Nepalese-dominated areas of south and west Sikkim from 11–14 December. We also learnt that the main purpose of the visit was twofold. Firstly, he wanted to have first-hand knowledge of the extent of his popularity in these areas. Secondly, in case he faced any large-scale protests and violence, he could use that as a pretext for getting the elections postponed. He took Das with him on this tour, so that Das would appear to be a former sidlon accompanying him on the tour. Also, if there was any violence, Das could be a witness to it, which could be used as evidence to get the elections postponed.

Keeping in view the above considerations, I sent a message to Kazi through Myngma about the real purpose of the Chogyal's visit and requested him to arrange for peaceful protests, and a cold reception, through the Youth Congress leaders. However, in doing so, extreme caution had to be observed in not letting the protesters go out of control, yet making it obvious to the Chogyal that the local population, i.e., the Nepalese, hated him and wanted to get rid of his autocratic rule.

Accompanied by Das and Chief Secretary Sherab Gyaltsen, the Chogyal left Gangtok on 11 December. For two days each he stayed in Namchi and Gyezing, where he received a cold reception. Welcome arches were covered with rags and torn saris. Colourful scarves with the word 'Chogyal' written on them adorned some dogs, who in turn were tied to these arches. Men, women and children standing on the roadside turned their backs to receive them. At some places, the ladies even turned their bare bottoms towards him. Slogans such as 'Chogyal Go Back', 'Chogyal Murdabad', 'Don't Come Back', and 'Bastard Chogyal, Go Back' were shouted. The Chogyal returned from this tour a sad man. All the misgivings about his past popularity were cleared. He took his wrath out on Karma Topden and the others for not providing him adequate intelligence about the real mood of the people in this area.

According to some Sikkim Congress leaders, faced with daily unpleasant encounters with the Chogyal, Karma Topden had to finally request Das to post him to Calcutta. But some other Sikkim Congress leaders felt that as Karma Topden's family had been serving the Chogyal for years, no amount of criticism or abuse by the Chogyal could have compelled him to seek transfer to Calcutta. They were of the view that the Chogyal, who by this time had started feeling uncertain about his future, wanted Karma Topden to get himself posted to Calcutta to look after his and his close family members' business interests in Calcutta and other areas of West Bengal. Das finally posted him as head of the Sikkim Trading Corporation (STC) in Calcutta. This posting could have also provided the Chogyal, through Karma, regular access to some US diplomats posted in the consulate in Calcutta. During a recent meeting with Karma Topden, I asked him about the real reason for his posting to Calcutta.[2] He said he wanted a change, but the Chogyal was actually against it. The Chogyal, in a lighter tone, even told him that in Gangtok he had been doing the job of a 'Kissinger', carrying his messages to India House, etc., and in Calcutta he would be reduced to a mere businessman. Karma Topden, however, requested the Chogyal to allow him to go to Calcutta, and he reluctantly agreed.

Chapter IX

April 1974 Elections:
Democracy Institutionalized

Repeated demands by the Sikkim Congress leaders for holding early elections had built pressure on the ECI to finalize the rules and regulations, and make arrangements for conducting the polls in Sikkim on priority. In that context, Chief Election Commissioner T. Swaminathan had already paid a one-day visit to Gangtok on 4 December and had detailed discussions with PO Bajpai, Chief Executive Das, and the Sikkim Congress and National Party leaders to ascertain their views on the proposed elections. Swaminathan's discussions resulted in the addition of two seats, one each for the scheduled castes and monastery, to the thirty seats provided in the 8 May agreement, taking the total number of seats to thirty-two. The scheduled-caste seat was expected to go to the Sikkim Congress and the monastery seat to the pro-Chogyal SNP. That way, the parity between the Bhutia–Lepcha and the Nepalese segments was not disturbed.

While Swaminathan was still fine-tuning the rules and regulations for the smooth conduct of elections, as a first step to set the election ball rolling, R.N. Sengupta, an IAS officer of the 1956 IAS batch from the West Bengal cadre, was appointed as the election commissioner for Sikkim on 18 December. For reasons mentioned in the previous chapter, the Chogyal wanted to delay this appointment. Bajpai and Das had a tough time convincing the Chogyal to sign Sengupta's appointment letter. They told the Chogyal that there was an urgency around his appointment, as the new electoral rolls were to be prepared and published by 26 January 1974, after taking into consideration objections, if any. Sengupta's appointment led to hectic political activity in Sikkim.

Insofar as the activities of the Chogyal and the pro-Chogyal parties were concerned, as usual, the two-day New Year (Losar) celebrations took place at the palace on 22 and 23 December. On the first day, there was a small group of senior officers and other special guests. The Chogyal was seen meeting the guests and was in a jovial mood. However, the next day, he remained confined to one place and did not mix with the crowd. The Chogyal, Jigdal and Karma Topden were seen with sullen faces. It appeared that Jigdal's return from New Delhi on 22 December had changed the atmosphere, as it was learnt that after waiting for ten days there, he could meet only Kewal Singh and that too for ten minutes. The Sikkim Congress leaders boycotted this function.

On 27 December, we learnt through Padam Bahadur's contacts within the senior Sikkim Congress leadership that a disheartened Chogyal was seriously considering abdicating in favour of his son (the information was later confirmed by Bajpai). Before doing so, he wanted to consult his family in New York and London, as to whether he should commit himself to the proposed elections. At that point of time, he felt that there were only the following three options before him:

a) Contest and lose the elections, and finally lead a life of insignificance in Sikkim.
b) Abdicate in favour of his son.
c) Pack up and go either to London or New York, as some of the royalty had done in the past.

While nursing such thoughts, the Chogyal was still ready to cut short his impending visit to New York and London if he could discuss his fate with Prime Minister Indira Gandhi. As expected, the Chogyal returned from London and New York early and spent a couple of days in New Delhi, where Jigdal also joined him. On his return to Gangtok on 9 January 1974, the Chogyal told Das that he was not very happy with his recent visit to the national capital. He had started believing that the GoI was not at all interested in helping him out of the present situation, and there were indications that they had decided to merge Sikkim with India. There was a noticeable change in his attitude as compared to his earlier stance of accepting even a lesser role in Sikkim. He once again started believing that Sikkim should enjoy an independent status sooner or later. He also started thinking of abdicating in favour of his eldest son, Tenzing, in the coming summer. Further, though he may not divorce Gyalmo, she would not be coming back.

To me, it appeared that the stiffening in the Chogyal's attitude had resulted from his discussion with Hope and her friends during his visit to New York. He might have been advised that now that India had already decided to seal his fate, he should not let things slip out of his hands without putting up a fight, thereby exposing India's real intentions. But it was finally Jigdal's policy of striking a deal with India which prevailed, and the Chogyal stopped thinking on these lines. We, however, felt that irrespective of Jigdal's sobering influence, if the Chogyal and

Jigdal continued to be openly snubbed by New Delhi any longer, the Chogyal may lose his patience and start playing an active and open role in the political scene of Sikkim. He could also further intensify his efforts to create dissensions amongst the Sikkim Congress leadership by openly promising far greater powers to political parties than were granted through the 8 May agreement, or they could hope to secure through the good offices of India. In view of that, my recommendation to Banerjee was that New Delhi should keep the carrot of accommodation dangling before the Chogyal, at least till the new council was formed after the elections. At that stage, we could put the Chogyal directly in the line of fire of the newly elected Assembly members and leave it to them to decide his future.

The Chogyal, accompanied by Das and Jigdal, again went to New Delhi on 13 January 1974. Bajpai also joined them later. The Chogyal stayed there for over ten days, and accompanied by Das and the PO, returned to Gangtok on 25 January, just in time for the Republic Day celebrations at India House on 26 January. Jigdal and Karma did not show up at Gurdip Bedi's party that evening. It appeared that some sort of consultation was going on at the palace after the Chogyal's return.

At the Republic Day (26 January) function at India House, we observed that the Chogyal, who was the chief guest, appeared to be lost in thought. While addressing the gathering, Bajpai said that the previous year had been a period of stress and turmoil for everyone, and he hoped that the current year would bring about a better and more fruitful understanding between the GoI and Sikkim. At the end of the function, the Chogyal shook hands with most of the guests around him but ignored the Sikkim Congress leaders. On their part, the Sikkim Congress leaders enjoyed the disgust in the eyes of the Chogyal, and appeared to be relishing their changed equation with him, an indication of their growing confidence in facing the Chogyal. None of the SNP leaders and SYPM members turned up.

On 30 January, Murari (OSD K.M. Lal) told me at the Whitehouse Club that one Nar Bahadur Bhandari, a former teacher and known pro-Chogyal Nepalese youth, was already in possession of draft blueprints of the proposed election rules and constituency delimitation documents for the elections in Sikkim. As Bhandari had been won over by the durbar and was being groomed as the Nepalese face of pro-Chogyal political opposition to the Sikkim Congress, it was obvious that these documents had been given to him by the durbar. Murari felt that the durbar was not playing a fair game, as it wanted to convey to the Nepalese leaders that the GoI was still secretly in touch with him and was going to strike a deal with him behind their back.

Obviously, the Sikkim Congress leaders expressed their resentment on this issue to the PO, who, in turn, conveyed his anguish to Jigdal and the Chogyal, who were on the defensive. The Sikkim Congress leaders were of the opinion that the durbar should not have been taken into confidence by New Delhi on such sensitive issues, without consulting them first. However, the publication of a news item in the *Times of India* issue dated 28 January 1974, in which Swaminathan had given out some details of the elections process, provided Jigdal and Chogyal an escape route to defend themselves on the plea that if he could issue a press statement on this issue, why could they not inform their men about these developments.

As per information received from Padam Bahadur, a secret meeting of the SYPM was held in the Rongli area of Gangtok on 10 January 1974 (a few days before that meeting they had opened a new office behind Denzong Cinema, in Rongli). It was decided that the differences between the SYPM and the National Party needed to be sorted out early in view of the coming elections.

Thereafter, the SNP had a meeting in Gangtok in the last week of January 1974. With very little chance of their candidates winning from south and west Sikkim, and also due to shortage of funds, the SNP decided not to field any candidates from these districts. Instead, the party decided to support some independent candidates or the candidates having affiliations with the proposed Himalayan Congress—a new party which was expected to emerge with the help of some old Janata Congress members walking out of the Sikkim Congress, due to differences over the issue of continuation of parity. In this context, the palace had been working on K.C. Pradhan, B.B. Gurung and S.K. Rai for some time.

It appeared that the efforts of the SYPM and some other leaders to invigorate the pro-Chogyal groups and parties did not succeed. By the end of February 1974, the SNP was in a state of confusion and disarray. Sonam Gyatso, who used to finance the party, had refused any monetary help and told the prospective candidates that he would be able to give only Rs 200 each to them for filing their nomination papers. Kunzung Dorji and R. Chhopel, who met Sonam Gyatso at his residence, pleaded for more financial assistance. A meeting of the working committee of the party was also held on 14 February, which was attended by M.B. Basnet, R. Chhopel and Kunzung Dorji. Dorji even suggested that the party be dissolved, but his proposal was turned down. Finally, it was decided to put up only six candidates on the party ticket. After a failed attempt to form the Himalayan Congress with the help of some dissident Sikkim Congress members (this plan was nipped in the bud due to Padam Bahadur's influence over S.K. Rai and K.C. Pradhan), Sonam Gyatso did not want to support the SYPM.

On the morning of 25 February, the Chogyal left for Bagdogra by road on his way to Calcutta, Bombay and finally the UK and the US to meet his children from his first wife, and Hope and her children, respectively. This time, he wanted to spend about a month away from Gangtok. One of the reasons for this was that he wanted to remain in the good books of New Delhi by giving an impression that he was not interfering in the elections. Bajpai told me that the Chogyal seemed to have got some hint during his visit to Shillong that the GoI was rather worried about the Nepalese problem in Assam and Bengal. This had regenerated some hope in the Chogyal that due to the similarity of the problem faced by Sikkim, Assam and West Bengal, New Delhi might reconsider its views about his future role in Sikkim.

Insofar as the activities of the Sikkim Congress were concerned, soon after Myngma's meeting with Rinzing Lepcha, the latter's activities and those of some of his close associates from his community picked up momentum. They had already started gravitating towards the Kazi-led Sikkim Congress, but were of the view that it would be useful if they could maintain some semblance of a separate identity. In view of that, Rinzing Tongden Lepcha formally joined the Sikkim Congress and named his group Sikkim Congress (Lepcha).

A delegation of twelve Lepchas, including Rinzing and Nayan Tshering, met Chief Executive Das on 12 January for two hours. They requested Das that the Lepchas being the older ethnic group of Sikkim should be recognized as a separate entity from the Bhutias and that a separate quota of seats be earmarked for them in accordance with their population within the Bhutia–Lepcha segment. Das, however, told him that the Bhutia–Lepchas would be having common seats, and no separate seats could be allocated to the Lepchas as that could lead to requests for reservation of seats from other communities such as the Tsongs, etc.

Myngma also learnt that before Rinzing and his Lepcha friends met Das, Sikkim Congress leaders, including Kazi, had already met Das the same day. Kazi had told Das that he was facing problems from within his party over maintenance of the old parity formula. In view of that, it was absolutely essential to do away with the parity formula to save his party from disintegration. Das took note of this request but said it may not be possible for him to do anything to change the system at that stage. However, unlike the past, there would be enough scope for his party to get its own Bhutia–Lepcha candidates elected to the new Assembly.

We learnt from our forward post in Lachen in north Sikkim that in the second week of January 1974, some of the pipons (village headmen) from the north, especially the Lepcha areas, told their men not to vote solely for the pro-Chogyal SNP candidates this time, but to divide their votes between the Sikkim Congress and SNP candidates. This way they would be able to protect their interests, should either of the two parties form the government. Lachen and Lachung in the north were earlier the strongholds of the pro-Chogyal SNP. This time, there was a rethinking on the part of the local population as to whether it was worthwhile to put all their eggs in one basket. This information was passed on to Kazi for further exploitation of the changing mood of the electorates from that area.

Following that, an open meeting of the Sikkim Congress (Lepcha) attended by about 500 people was held at Djongu (in north Sikkim) on 30 January 1974. Kazi, K.C. Pradhan, B.B. Gurung, Rinzing Lepcha and Nayan Tshering Lepcha addressed this meeting. The audience, mostly comprising Lepchas from nearby areas, was asked to vote for the Sikkim Congress so that their community's interests could be safeguarded. Rinzing Lepcha and Kazi reached an informal understanding according to which out of the fifteen seats meant for the Bhutia–Lepcha segment,

Lepchas would get the lion's share of Sikkim Congress tickets for contesting elections.

The Sikkim Congress circulated a leaflet on 27 January to demand the framing of election rules on priority. According to a rumour, even Khatiwada was not happy with the maintenance of parity and had an argument with Kazi on 30 January. However, when Khatiwada, along with R.N. Dahl and senior leader C.S. Rai, met the PO, he said that he was committed to parity as envisaged in the 8 May agreement and his public utterances may not be taken seriously. But Dahl later told one of Padam Bahadur's 'friends' that he was not satisfied with Khatiwada's explanation.

Padam Bahadur also learnt that the palace had decided to use two Nepalese civil servants—C.D. Rai (head of the publication department) and M.M. Rasaily (the auditor general)—to create dissension within the Sikkim Congress leadership by taking K.C. Pradhan and S.K. Rai into confidence. Pradhan and Rai had reportedly confided in some persons that if parity was maintained in any form in the forthcoming elections, they would withdraw their support from the Sikkim Congress. There was also a rumour that they may form a separate party called the Himalayan Congress, with a view to demanding the abolition of parity. In this endeavour, some pro-Chogyal leaders were to give them a helping hand. This was a serious development and if the information were true, it could divide the Sikkim Congress votes in the council. In view of this, Padam Bahadur fixed separate meetings with Rai and Pradhan, and had a detailed discussion with them on the subject. Both of them told Padam Bahadur that they were not being given due importance in the party by Kazi, and they also did not like Khatiwada's dominance in party affairs. Padam Bahadur told them that it was not an opportune time for them to pick a fight with Kazi. On the contrary, they should have a candid talk with him, and most probably Kazi would respect their opinion, keeping in view their seniority. Padam Bahadur also told them firmly that irrespective of their seniority, without Kazi's backing at that juncture, they would lose whatever they had gained since the April 1973 agitation. It appeared that Padam Bahadur's advice worked as rumours of the formation of the Himalayan Congress died a natural death thereafter. Simultaneously, Kazi was informed about the views of these two leaders through Myngma Tshering, and Kazi did try to placate them in his own way.

Foreign Minister Sardar Swaran Singh arrived at Bagdogra airport on 3 February to take stock of the developments in Sikkim. All the senior Sikkim Congress leaders received him at the airport. Later, they met him at the Military Engineer Services (MES) inspection bungalow in Sukna-based 33 Corps near Siliguri at 7.30 p.m. and thanked him for the help that India had extended to them. They, however, protested against the retention of parity and a separate seat for the sangha (monasteries), which was usually won by pro-Chogyal men in the past. Not to be left behind or misunderstood, the Chogyal also met the foreign minister at Bagdogra airport.

The PO left with the foreign minister the next morning. But just before Bajpai left for New Delhi, he told me that he would be meeting Kao there on 7 February and Banerjee in Calcutta on 8 February. He said he might talk to them about his oft-repeated need for a political adviser for the Sikkim Congress leaders, who according to him were totally ignorant about the political game. He also told me that before he returned, I should make all efforts to ensure that the Sikkim Congress leadership veers around to accept the present election formula of parity and not make too much noise against it.

Just to forewarn Kao and Banerjee, I sent messages to both about Bajpai's plans to meet them. I also gave my views on the subjects Bajpai was to discuss with them. I was personally against giving any outside political advice to Kazi and his party for two reasons. Firstly, the elections were around the corner and the involvement of an outsider at that late a stage would have confused the issues rather than helping the party. Secondly, it would expose an outside connection and invite criticism from the Chogyal. In view of that, I had to occasionally play this role by drafting or correcting their memos, speeches, etc.

My last meeting with Kazi was in the second week of October 1973. Since then, most of my communication with him was through Myngma, either verbally or through typed notes. I felt that I should meet Kazi again to seek his views on the current developments. This time, I left my family at the Circuit House in Kalimpong and met him on 6 February at a different location as I did not want the Kazini to know about our meeting. The gist of my discussion with him is outlined below.

Kazi told me that after some initial resistance from some party members on the maintenance of parity in the coming elections, some sort of a consensus had been built around the new election formula. But the party still wanted the sangha (monastery) seat to be truly representative and not limited to monastery voters. The party was solidly behind him with one or two exceptions. Action was also being taken to keep such persons under control. Further, Kazi said that Khatiwada would be told to apologize to the PO for having given the press statement dated 2 February 1974, in which he had criticized the Chogyal. He had formed region-wise groups, comprising reliable and honest party members, to collect election funds from their respective areas. But considering the capacity of the general public to contribute, the party would still require financial assistance from our side just after the nominations were filed. (The amount he wanted from us was far less than I had expected.) A tentative list of candidates who would be contesting the elections was almost ready. Each candidate would have a dummy/cover candidate to deal with unforeseen contingencies. A copy of this list would be passed on to us in the second week of February on his arrival at Gangtok. We could then check the antecedents of these candidates and advise him if there was any objection from our side against any of them. The list of party candidates would be finalized only after hearing from us.

Meanwhile, it was learnt from our other 'friends' in the Sikkim Congress that the party was finding it difficult to decide on the candidate from Dentam constituency in the west district. B.B. Gurung and K.C. Pradhan wanted C.B. Chhetri (Katwal) or I.B. Gurung, but Rinzing Lepcha and some other younger members wanted N.B. Khatiwada as the candidate. Gurung and Pradhan were jealous of Khatiwada's growing importance within the party and wanted him out of the election process. With the party unable to take a firm decision, a total of seven candidates, including the two persons named above, filed their papers as independent candidates. Khatiwada filed his nomination with an umbrella as his symbol. Ultimately, when the election results were announced, Khatiwada won with a big majority with the remaining six candidates losing their security deposits. To make up for his insistence for contesting from Dentam as an independent candidate, after the results were announced, Khatiwada invited Kazi to Dentam, and he and his followers took Kazi through Dentam bazaar in a makeshift rath which was pulled with long ropes by party workers from the area.

The Chogyal did his best to avoid giving his approval to the newly drafted election rules. Bajpai was frustrated at the Chogyal's dilatory tactics. This became evident from what Bajpai told me at Dr (Lt Col) J.K. Talwar's (medical officer, Political Office) house on 18 December. The PO said that he could get anything signed by the Chogyal that day except the election formula to be adopted. He did not understand what we were going to gain from holding the elections. According to him, the only solution was a total merger, which we might not be able to achieve through elections. As usual, I did not say anything.

By the second week of February 1974, the political situation in Sikkim was rather fluid, with various parties thinking on different lines. The Sikkim Congress still wanted parity to be diluted, if not totally removed. The reduction in parity, even by the slightest margin, would help them tell their Nepalese voters that they had been able to secure a change in the old parity system established by the Chogyal. It would also help them counter the propaganda launched by the durbar through C.D. Rai and M.M. Rasaily to create confusion in the minds of the Nepalese voters, by saying that the Nepalese had got nothing out of the April 1973 agitation. The Sikkim Congress also did not like the allocation of a separate seat for the sangha (monastery), and there was considerable resentment over this within the party.

On the other hand, the durbar wanted parity to remain, but was cleverly inciting some Nepalese leaders to speak openly against it to embarrass New Delhi about its inability to satisfy the demands of the Sikkim Congress. While still trying to remain in the good books of New Delhi, the Chogyal was secretly resisting every move to give more power and privilege to the Nepalese, which he felt would mark the end of Bhutia–Lepcha culture and also Bhutia domination in Sikkim's politics and administration.

Meanwhile both sides spread rumours, leading to a lot of uncertainty. The Sikkim Congress leaders spread rumours that some SNP leaders had resigned. On the other hand, pro-Chogyal elements continued to spread rumours that the Sikkim Congress had split and a separate party was being formed. They also highlighted Khatiwada's alleged connections with the CPI(M).

The PO and Das were to deal with the diverse factions and viewpoints, but it would have been better if the Sikkim Congress had been taken into confidence immediately after the foreign secretary's arrival, thereby giving less time to the palace to cash in on the issue of continuation of parity in one form or the other. There was some ray of hope that the Sikkim Congress might not take a public stand on the abolition of the sangha seat, which may be difficult to abolish. If the Sikkim Congress leadership hardened their public stance on this issue, it would be difficult for them to retrace their steps without losing face with the Nepalese population. Suspicions were growing within the Sikkim Congress leadership about the real reasons behind the durbar having been taken too much into confidence by the GoI on the framing of the new election rules, etc. The durbar took full advantage of this confusion by spreading rumours that India was secretly trying to enter into a deal with the Chogyal.

The last date of filing nominations, i.e., 15 February, was approaching fast. Both the Sikkim Congress and pro-Chogyal parties were still struggling to finalize their candidates. On being approached by the Chogyal around 10 February, PO Bajpai got the last date changed to 20 February, with the date of polling remaining the same.

Meanwhile, Sikkim Congress leaders B.B. Gurung and K.C. Pradhan met Murari on 12 February and handed over a list, reportedly containing the names of sixteen Nepalese and fifteen Bhutia–Lepcha candidates who were supposed to be contesting elections as Sikkim Congress candidates. The names of some senior leaders such as C.S. Rai and S.K. Rai did not figure in it. It seemed that this group did not want both the Rais to be included in the list of candidates due to their seniority, which could block their own chances of getting ministerial berths after the elections. However, as per Padam Bahadur's information, the names of the Nepalese candidates were yet to be finalized.

Kazi was informed of this development through Myngma. Kazi was requested that while deciding the names of the candidates he should ensure that different factions or groups, especially from the Nepalese segment, should be properly balanced to reduce their potential for mischief after the elections. He informed Myngma that he was aware of this development and was already working on the suggested lines.

On 16 February, Kazi called Myngma to hand over the final list of Sikkim Congress candidates who would be contesting elections as the party's official candidates. Our three-man spl ops team went through the list carefully. As nothing objectionable was found in the list, it was returned the same day with the message that we had no objection to any of these candidates. At the end of the last day for filing nomination papers on 20 February, it was discovered that while the Sikkim Congress had filed papers for thirty-one seats (no official candidate was fielded from Dentam), the pro-Chogyal SNP had filed papers for five candidates only. For the rest of the seats, the pro-Chogyal candidates, including those from the newly raised pro-Chogyal People's Democratic Party, were contesting as independent candidates as their party could not be recognized at that late a stage.

To take stock of the prevailing political situation in Sikkim, in view of the forthcoming elections and the role that the army might have to perform during that period, a meeting was held in Gangtok in the third week of February 1974 at 64 Brigade headquarters. This was attended by approximately fifty army officers, including Maj. Gen. Harbhajan Singh Khullar. Also, PO Bajpai, Sudhir Devare, Gurdip Bedi, K.M. Lal and the CRPF's CO Mahender Prasad attended it. I was also invited, but I told Col Madhok (G-1, 17 Mountain Division) that as I was not handling internal developments, no useful purpose would be served by my attending that meeting. At the end of the meeting, it was decided that there would be no requirement for army deployment under normal circumstances. But it could be kept in reserve for deployment in emergency only.

As a result of the interaction between Chief Election Commissioner Swaminathan, Election Commissioner R.N. Sengupta, PO Bajpai and Chief Executive Das, and keeping in view the popular demand of all the political parties, it was decided to bring over 100 neutral GoI staff of various ranks to conduct the election in an impartial manner. It was also decided to use the old electoral rolls as the basis for holding the April 1974 elections by accommodating objections, if any, against the entries in these rolls. Regarding

allocation of an equal number of constituencies to the Bhutia–
Lepcha segment, the six seats of north and east Sikkim (where
the majority of Bhutia–Lepchas lived) were divided into fifteen.
The remaining fifteen were located in south and west Sikkim.
For the remaining two seats, namely the scheduled castes and the
monastery, eligible voters from the whole of Sikkim could exercise
their franchise.[1]

Swaminathan reached Gangtok around 12.30 p.m. on 5 March
and returned on 7 March. During his stay in Gangtok, he met Sikkim
Congress leaders on 5 and 7 March. To the pleasant surprise of the
Sikkim Congress leaders, Swaminathan told them that the current
election formula could be revised in future based on the experience
gained through the coming elections. They saw a ray of hope in
Swaminathan's assurance, which helped the Sikkim Congress leaders
counter durbar-sponsored propaganda that the Sikkim Congress
had not been able to achieve the abolition of parity. Swaminathan
met the SNP and independent candidates on 6 March. The main
purpose of this visit was to impress upon the Sikkimese leaders that
as the elections were being organized by the ECI, these would be free
and fair. He also held a separate meeting with the staff earmarked
for election-related duties to discuss election arrangements. Before
he left Gangtok, Swaminathan gave a press interview, in which he
mentioned the possibility of revising election rules at a future date in
case they did not find favour with the elected leaders. However, in
the 8 p.m. broadcast on All India Radio (AIR) on 7 March, the last
clause was missing.

PO Bajpai had told me a number of times that it was time
for the Sikkim Congress leaders to finalize the party's platform
(manifesto) for the elections. But it had to be carefully worded in
view of our future requirements. A day before Bajpai left for New
Delhi with Swaminathan, on the morning of 7 March, he called me
and informed me that he would be meeting Banerjee in Calcutta

and would discuss the need for framing a suitable platform for the Sikkim Congress. Further, he would also like to discuss the modalities of working out certain poll adjustments amongst different parties, so that some independent candidates might win and Sikkim Congress candidates might lose. This, he felt, would help create the requisite balance between the Sikkim Congress and independent members, which could be exploited to our advantage at an appropriate time. He also felt that the victory of some SNP candidates would make the election process look credible. I sent a message to Banerjee the same evening with my views on these subjects. About the Sikkim Congress manifesto, he was told that it was being worked on in consultation with Kazi and would be finalized soon. About political adjustments, I informed him that we should not dabble in such risky adventures, as we might end up with just a simple majority of Sikkim Congress candidates in the new House, leaving enough scope for the Chogyal to sabotage our plans. It was obvious that Bajpai was not aware of our final goal of merger, which could only be achieved if a maximum number of Sikkim Congress candidates were elected to the Assembly. In view of that, I suggested that we leave it entirely to Kazi to decide what type of legislative party he would like to have, to get important resolutions passed, when the time came for the same.

The same evening, I met Murari at the Whitehouse Club. It seemed that the PO and Das had made similar suggestions to him also. Murari told me that he had expressed his inability to do such things. Insofar as Das was concerned, he thought that the pro-Chogyal SYPM was a group of inexperienced youth and did not enjoy a good reputation even amongst the Bhutia electorate. He tried to work out an arrangement in consultation with the Chogyal, Bajpai and Kazi to put up some older, experienced and respected leaders from the Bhutia community as candidates so that 'at least eight to ten members from the opposition' could be elected to act as responsible opposition. But his efforts did not produce the desired results due to opposition from the concerned groups or individuals. Also, Kazi was not amenable to such suggestions as he had his own plans to further his agenda of ultimate merger of Sikkim with India.

Pursuant to Bajpai's remarks on the need for finalizing the Sikkim Congress's manifesto, I prepared a small note containing my suggestions on the points, which could be considered for inclusion, and passed on a copy of this note to Kazi through Myngma. We, however, left the actual finalization of the manifesto to Kazi and his men, given their experience of drafting party manifestos in the past. Also, the Kazini was there to help them draft such an open party document. My suggestions mainly centred on the party's struggle for political, economic and administrative reforms, especially those promised in the 8 May agreement. While closer relations with India—especially Sikkim's participation in political and economic institutions—was highlighted, no mention of a merger was made. Myngma was told to verbally inform Kazi not to make any mention of it in the manifesto, as that would sound alarm bells in the palace, leading the Chogyal to come out in the open to fight against them. We also requested Kazi to hold a meeting of senior party members where the manifesto could be discussed and finalized, as that would give an impression of the party taking joint decisions on such important matters. The manifesto was soon released, and it contained most of our suggestions. The word merger had not been mentioned.

As the pro-Chogyal National Party had lost credibility amongst the Sikkimese people, a new pro-durbar party called the Sikkim

Independent United Front (SIUF), also known as the People's Democratic Party, was floated with a young and energetic Nepalese N.B. Bhandari* as its president. Bhandari's selection to lead this party was a deliberate ploy to fool the electorate from south and west Sikkim about a new Nepalese party contesting against the Kazi-led Sikkim Congress. This party held its first meeting in Gangtok on

---

* Nar Bahadur Bhandari was born in October 1940 in west Sikkim. After completing his graduation from Darjeeling, he worked as a schoolteacher in south-west Sikkim. Being a young Nepalese with no past pro-Chogyal political baggage, Sonam Gyatso recognized his potential and won him over to the Chogyal's side to oppose the Kazi-led Sikkim Congress. Interestingly, in the early stages of his political career, while addressing one of his pro-Chogyal meetings at Somvarya (Monday) Bazaar in south Sikkim, he escaped being lynched by Sikkim Congress workers by jumping into the jeep of OSD Jayant Sanyal who was passing by. Showing perseverance and persistence, and with the active support from the older members of the SNP and some pro-Chogyal SYPM men, Bhandari moved up the ladder of anti-Kazi political activities and soon became the head of the SIUF. Thereafter, he started attacking Kazi as a desh bechoa and demanding the immediate withdrawal of Indian officers on deputation. He contested the April 1974 elections mainly on these two issues. In the face of a popular anti-Chogyal wave, however, his party could not win even a single seat.

In the immediate aftermath of the merger, as a frontman of the former Chogyal who wanted to settle scores with Kazi for having overthrown his regime in 1975, Bhandari formed a new party called the Sikkim Janata Parishad in 1977 and contested the 1979 elections. For various reasons (discussed in Chapter XIV), in the 1979 elections, Bhandari's anti-Kazi (seller of the country), and anti-Government of India officials campaign worked, and his party won sixteen out of thirty-two seats in the Assembly and he became chief minister with the help of a sangha member of the Assembly. Kazi's new party, i.e., the Janata Party, could not get even a single seat, and he himself lost his seat to a comparative newcomer.

10 March 1974, which happened to be the day of the weekly Sunday Haat (bazaar). It was attended by just twenty-five members of the party, but about 300–400 persons, mainly visitors to the haat, stopped by to listen to what was being said. P.S. Tsong was in the chair and others, including N.B. Bhandari, Sonam Gyatso (the Chogyal's brother-in-law, who was mainly responsible for floating this party), D.P. Razalim and Shailesh Chander Pradhan were the speakers. They did not criticize the GoI, but some speakers criticized the SIB whose men were allegedly moving on the streets of Gangtok openly. We felt that this was a beginning and more such meetings would follow. It would, therefore, be advisable for Kazi to accuse the Chogyal of funding this group before these people started criticizing him and his party for receiving funds from India. We learnt on 10 March that a majority of locals in the Chungthang area in north Sikkim, mainly comprising Bhutias, had decided to vote in favour of the Sikkim Congress and had decided to send a letter to Kazi pledging their support to his party.

Meanwhile, a news item captioned 'Uncertainty in Gangtok' appeared in the *Statesman* issue of 12 March. It highlighted the inherent contradictions between the interests of the Nepalese and Bhutia–Lepcha communities at a time when the elections were so close. The purpose was to sabotage the growing influence of the Kazi-led Sikkim Congress in the Bhutia–Lepcha areas, which were erstwhile strongholds of the pro-Chogyal National Party.

On 13 March, a group of local residents met at Lachung, north Sikkim. The meeting was attended by about 180 people and was called by the pipon, Tenzing Kazang. All those present there were administered an oath that they would vote for pro-Chogyal SNP candidates. The pipon threatened to excommunicate anyone who voted for another party—meaning that person would not be allowed to go to the Gompas for worship and no lama would visit his or her house. At the end of the meeting, the pipon distributed

Rs 1000 and one case of rum amongst them. It was obvious that this meeting was financed by the Chogyal. Pro-Chogyal independent candidate Lekpal, accompanied by Sonam Gyatso, also visited Lachung on 14 March. They gave Rs 2000 and two cases of rum, some sugar and tea, etc., to the local Bhutia community. All the persons present there vowed to vote for Lekpal.

At a lunch hosted by the PO at India House on 24 March for the Commander, 33 Corps, H.C. Rai, the PO inquired whether I had received any instructions from the headquarters about our plan of action once the elections were over. I told him that I had heard nothing about it. But he was rather emphatic that if nothing was done immediately, we would start facing some odd demands after the elections. He told me that it would be better if I could go to Calcutta and discuss the matter with Banerjee, who in turn should go to New Delhi and meet Kao. I told him that I might go to Calcutta after a week, but he was of the view that a week may be too much of a delay. I kept quiet. I did not want to tell him that such decisions were actually taken by Foreign Secretary Kewal Singh in consultation with Kao, and we would come to know of that at an appropriate time.

The Chogyal's sister, Coo Coo La, was our closest neighbour—she was staying on the lower side of the road in the Forest Guest House. She invited Bali and me to a dinner on 24 March. Her daughter, Sodeun La, and her fiancé, Rinchen Wangdi, who also headed the SYPM, were there too. It was an impressive seven-course meal. I had heard a lot about her charm and beauty, but it seemed as if age had taken a toll on her beauty. But as far as her charm, grace and mannerisms were concerned, she was her old self. We mainly discussed social and cultural issues. Rinchen took me out for some target shooting with arrows. I naturally complimented him on his proficiency. At the end of the dinner, Wangdi gifted me a five-foot-long cured bamboo bow piece, which he said had been done to increase its pulling strength.

After some time, rumours started floating again about K.C. Pradhan leaving the Sikkim Congress and forming a new party due to his differences with Kazi. In view of that, Padam Bahadur met him on 29 March to ascertain the truth. He stayed with Pradhan for about two hours. Pradhan was not happy about the CRPF permitting pro-Chogyal independent candidates to hold meetings in south and west Sikkim. He actually led some processions against the independent candidates, but the CRPF did not help him at all. During the course of his meeting, Padam Bahadur felt that Pradhan still held pro-India views, but did not like the ambivalent attitude of the GoI. He had strong suspicions that the Indian government wanted to keep its options open. Otherwise it would have openly come out in support of the Sikkim Congress at that crucial moment. He was of the opinion that the Sikkim Congress might lose the Gyezing, Dentam and Senyong seats. In that respect, it appeared that Pradhan had been influenced by B.B. Gurung. But he was also very close to S.K. Rai. Padam Bahadur felt that irrespective of his growing proximity to Gurung, who for long was suspected to be close to the durbar, it should be possible to keep Pradhan under control, but with Rai's help.

By the end of March 1974, the Chogyal's propaganda that the new Assembly members would have no real powers had started working on some Sikkim Congress leaders. Both Padam Bahadur and

Myngma Tshering, after meeting their Sikkim Congress friends, told me that they wanted to know the powers of the Assembly and executive council, whom they would be accountable to, whether there would be a speaker, whether the executive councillors would be called ministers, what would be their relations with the chief executive and what would their leader be called. Both of them, as advised, told their friends that this would all depend on the outcome of the Assembly elections, and the new constitution that they would be adopting.

On 2 April, we learnt that on the occasion of the Chogyal's birthday on 4 April, members of the SYPM would bring four truckloads of Tibetan road labourers from north and east Sikkim. They were to gather near Whitehouse Club close to the palace. On the other hand, Sikkim Congress leaders and some of their followers would also collect in the bazaar to mark the first anniversary of the April 1973 agitations. There were apprehensions that the two groups might clash.

Das was rather worried on this account and had told Murari and CO Prasad of the CRPF that any breach of peace in Gangtok on that occasion would not be taken lightly by New Delhi. He said that every possible measure had to be taken to prevent confrontation between the two sides. Murari contacted some Sikkim Congress leaders and advised them against taking out any procession towards the palace. On our part, I called Padam Bahadur and Myngma Tshering to use their influence over the party members to avoid a confrontation with the SYPM-led Tibetan labourers. The combined attempt succeeded in keeping the Sikkim Congress volunteers confined to the bazaar, petrol pump and Ranipool areas. Even the SYPM members could not bring the desired number of Tibetan labourers to Gangtok.

Meanwhile, the Chogyal's birthday (he had returned on the afternoon of 2 April to attend the celebrations) was celebrated at the palace on traditional lines, though the atmosphere was a bit muted. To personally assess the situation in the town, I took a quick round of Gangtok Bazaar after the Chogyal's birthday lunch was over. Though there was some tension in the air, it was generally peaceful. Deployment of a large contingent of CRPF and the advice given to the senior Sikkim Congress leaders appeared to have worked. After observing a two-minute silence in the memory of those who had lost their lives in the April 1973 agitation, and short speeches by the leaders, the procession started moving towards Kazi's petrol pump and thereafter to Ranipool from where they dispersed. But in the countryside, at a number of places in south and west Sikkim, the Sikkim Congress volunteers did not allow the Sikkimese flag to be hoisted and stopped the locals from celebrating the Chogyal's birthday.

On 7 April, the Sikkim Congress held a public meeting in Gangtok, which was attended by about 1000 people. Kazi, K.C. Pradhan, N.K. Subedi and some others delivered speeches. Pradhan's speech was quite impressive. In the afternoon, pro-Chogyal independents also held a meeting, which was attended by about 200 people. They criticized the GoI and the Sikkim Congress.

On 8 April, I learnt by chance that three inspector-rank IB officials—K.B. Malla, K.S. Chauhan and S.P. Bharthwal—who had been relieved from the IB on 31 January 1974, had come to Sikkim under cover. They were posing as assistant returning officers for the April elections. The PO kept the secret from me, but given the officers' background, his office sent their LPCs (last pay certificates) and service books to my office by mistake. However,

they overlooked certain letters written by the IB headquarters to N.B. Menon, joint secretary (north), MEA. Earlier, on 2 February, Murari had told me that they had got three men at their disposal who had arrived from India. He did not know their background but said they would soon be assigned some sensitive jobs. When Murari wanted to know their background from the PO, he was told that it was entirely Das's business. Had Bajpai's office not mistakenly sent the documents to me, the background of these three men would have remained a mystery to me. But it appeared that the three IB officials had come to Gangtok at Das's request to the foreign secretary during one of his visits to New Delhi.

It was, however, not known as to what additional information or intelligence these three men on a short stint could provide that was not available to Das through the three IAS officers in charge of the four districts of Sikkim, a state with a population of less than 3,00,000. These IAS officers included Gangtok-based Murari, who had arrived in Sikkim post the April 1973 agitations and was holding charge of two districts—north and east Sikkim.

The *Hindustan Standard* carried a front-page news item titled 'Sikkim Assembly to be Advisory Body' on 9 April 1974. This was obviously planted through pro-durbar elements in Calcutta. The contents of this article lent support to the durbar's propaganda to confuse the Sikkim Congress candidates by impressing upon them that even if they were elected they would have no powers, and the real power would still be vested in Das and the Chogyal. I also learnt from the PO that, on 12 April, the Chogyal had written two demi-official (DO) letters, one each to the prime minister and the foreign minister. In the letter to the foreign minister, he had expressed his desire to have the powers of the Assembly be defined early, and the letter to the prime minister was sent in a sealed cover.

During this period, the PO received a letter from the governor of Assam, L.P. Singh. This was a follow-up of his previous correspondence covering the Chogyal's visit to Shillong. According to him, Justice Sen had not given any legal advice to the Chogyal but only friendly advice. Sen thought that the Chogyal was in desperate need of some assurance about the prime minister's continued faith in him. Also, his foreign currency reserves had hit rock bottom. He was also of the view that his political eclipse had brought his relationship with Hope to a standstill, and that he might not finally abdicate.

On the afternoon of 11 April, the PO told me over the phone that a reporter had met him the previous day and told him that Panjola (the husband of the Chogyal's half-sister, Langzing La, also known as Semla), whom he had met a few days ago, told him that there would be some trouble during the forthcoming elections and that he would be photographing these events and sending these to the foreign press to earn a lot of money.

The PO's information had some relevance to the information I had got when, accompanied by my wife, I had called on Panjola and his wife on 3 April. Panjola had shown me a number of cameras and photographs he had taken. When I appreciated his photographic skills, he had said that due to his service with the Chogyal, he had not been able to devote much time to his family business (he was the son of Tshetan Tashi, a photographer) and land. He was planning to take six months' leave without pay to devote more time to his shop so that he could make a good living. Being the eldest in the family, he said he had to look after the interests of his family, and his job did not give him enough time and money. Panjola also mentioned that a reporter by the name of Chakraborty had met him recently, and showing some interest in buying his Yashica camera, had borrowed the same for a trial. It appeared that the same Chakraborty had met the PO.

Meanwhile, we had also received reports that in case the pro-Chogyal independents felt that they were not going to win, they could create a law-and-order problem during elections. One of the constituencies where such trouble was expected was Dentam, from where Khatiwada was contesting as an independent candidate. In his case, even some of his own party men would like to get him defeated by sabotaging his campaign.

Foreign Secretary Kewal Singh reached Gangtok on 13 April. It was a quiet visit and not many people knew about the reason he was there. Accompanied by Bajpai, he had a quiet lunch with the Chogyal. Later, Sikkim Congress leaders Kazi, S.K. Rai, Rinzing Lepcha, Jonathan Lepcha and Phigu Tshering Bhutia met Kewal Singh at 5 p.m. Singh told them that they should not believe the news reports published in dailies such as the *Hindustan Standard*. I also briefly met him later in the evening. Jigdal Densapa met him at 7 p.m. At the time of Singh's departure from Gangtok on 14 April, while waiting to see off Kewal Singh, Jigdal told Gurdip Bedi in my presence that very soon 'your half excellency will become full excellency'. These remarks were significant, as it appeared that Jigdal by now had started apprehending the ultimate merger of Sikkim with India. Also, these remarks could have resulted from the Chogyal's disappointment with his talks with Kewal Singh.

It appeared Kewal Singh had come to Gangtok for three reasons. Firstly, with elections only a couple of days away, he wanted to personally assess the situation in Sikkim. This was obvious from his short discussions with me. He wanted to know the election prospects of the Sikkim Congress. I reiterated my earlier stand that they should be able to get at least a two-thirds majority. Secondly, he wanted to dispel doubts in the minds of the Sikkim Congress leaders that the council members and the executive councillors would be powerless—a doubt that had been deliberately created by the Chogyal's men. Lastly, he wanted to warn the Chogyal that if any of the pro-Chogyal independent candidates and or their supporters tried to disturb the peace and create a law-and-order problem during the elections, it would be presumed that he was not interested in the smooth implementation of the terms of the 8 May agreement.

Elections were held on 15 April. It appeared that Kewal Singh's meeting with the Chogyal on 13 April had the desired effect, as the polls passed off peacefully. With the results due on 19 April, a number of reporters had come to Gangtok. They conducted interviews with the PO, Das and the Chogyal. One of the reporters told Bedi that the Chogyal had told him that India should either merge Sikkim fully or give it complete independence.

The results came as a pleasant surprise to us. Kazi's Sikkim Congress bagged thirty-one out of thirty-two seats, including Khatiwada's independent seat and the monastery seat, which had previously always gone to the pro-Chogyal SNP. Only one SNP candidate, Kalzang Gyatso, won. According to Das, even 'the Chogyal complimented Election Commissioner Sengupta on the fair conduct of elections. Not even a single election petition was filed'. Much later, the Chogyal and some of his friends alleged that the elections were rigged. The extent of the Sikkim Congress's victory was beyond our expectations. We had thought that the Sikkim Congress would win a comfortable two-thirds majority (over twenty-one seats), which was enough to get any bill passed.

The 1953 constitution of Sikkim, introduced through a royal proclamation, did not mention the minimum requirement of a two-thirds majority for passing a constitution bill or for making any amendment therein. But the April 1974 elections were held under a different set of rules, which were acceptable to all concerned. In the absence of any clarity on the subject, it was presumed that as the elections were held under the supervision of the chief election commissioner of India, the procedure followed by the Indian parliament for passing a constitution bill would be followed too. The Indian parliament required at least a two-thirds majority of its members to do so. At the time the list of party candidates for these elections was being prepared, Kazi was advised that their selection should be based on two criteria: likelihood of winning and loyalty. The magnitude of the Sikkim Congress's victory, with a margin of ten Assembly members over and above the required two-thirds majority, made the Chogyal's work of sabotaging any bill difficult, if not impossible.

With such a huge victory margin for his party in the newly elected Sikkim council (Assembly), Kazi was now ready to move beyond the provisions of the 8 May agreement and pass such resolutions in the council as were required to establish a closer relationship between Sikkim and India.

Chapter X

The Resolution of 11 May 1974:
Demand for Closer Ties with India

The landslide victory of the Sikkim Congress in the April 1974 elections came as a big jolt to the Chogyal and his protégés, who were always looking for opportunities to create dissension within the party. Given this, we had to be on our toes to ensure the unity of the party so that our next target, as and when assigned, could be achieved. The margin of the Sikkim Congress's victory had made the Chogyal's task difficult, but we could not afford to be complacent due to continued doubts about K.C. Pradhan and B.B. Gurung's commitment, who were still maintaining contact with the durbar. Being senior leaders, they could also influence the other members of the Assembly.

It was against this background that I called on the Chogyal around noon on 20 April, hoping that he would say something about the election results. The outcome of that meeting has already been covered in the first chapter. I found out that the magnitude of Kazi's victory had totally demoralized the Chogyal, and he was willing to compromise even on the contents of the 1950 treaty. He had also realized that only abject surrender to Indira Gandhi could salvage whatever was left of his power or position.

While keeping the anti-Chogyal tempo up amongst the Sikkim Congress leaders, we had to prepare the grounds for the next course of action. On 25 April, as suggested by us, Kazi, accompanied by some Sikkim Congress leaders, called on the PO and handed over a copy of the resolution passed by the party leadership, along with a letter signed by General Secretary S.K. Rai addressed to the PO. In this resolution, the Sikkim Congress thanked the GoI for the help extended to the Sikkimese people. It also requested that further steps be taken to fulfil the promises made in the 8 May 1973 agreement. In fact, on receipt of instructions from Banerjee, a copy of the typed-out resolution was passed on to Kazi through Myngma on 23 April, with a request that after the resolution was adopted at the party meeting, a signed copy of that resolution be handed over to the PO as soon as possible. The PO, who thought it would be difficult to procure such a resolution, was relieved to see it. Ultimately, this resolution became the basis of the crucial 11 May resolution passed by the Assembly.

I also learnt on 26 April that the Chogyal and the newly elected members of the Assembly might separately visit New Delhi sometime in May to know about their respective futures. This time, the Chogyal was in a much weaker position insofar as his negotiations with India were concerned. It was also expected that before he left, some pro-Chogyal elements may raise the issue of alleged rigging at the recently held polls and also about the use of force by the Sikkim Congress workers for securing votes.

On the other hand, the Sikkim Congress leaders were still not sure as to what steps were likely to be taken by the GoI for the implementation of the 8 May agreement and what would be the nature and powers of the Assembly and executive council. However, as ascertained by Padam Bahadur from senior Sikkim Congress leader C.S. Rai, in anticipation of the formation of the executive council, there was a virtual scramble for the public works department portfolio where easy money could be made through manipulating contracts.

On 3 May, the Chogyal left for Varanasi to attend a meeting of the Maha Bodhi Society of India. On his way, he was also likely to meet the chief minister of West Bengal with whom he was likely to exchange views about his own future. He returned on 7 May, accompanied by the PO and the police commissioner. The Chogyal was visibly happy at the cocktail party he hosted for the visiting commander of 33 Corps, Lt Gen. H.C. Rai.

Meanwhile, the PO had informally received an advance copy of the draft of the bill that was to be introduced in the newly elected Sikkim council as the Government of Sikkim Bill of 1974. This draft was prepared by A.K. Rajagopal, former additional secretary, ministry of law. Rajagopal was later appointed as constitutional adviser to the government of Sikkim for this purpose. The PO had received this draft from Kewal Singh for comments by a three-member team comprising PO Bajpai, P.N. Banerjee and me. He was asked to maintain strict secrecy in this matter. Bajpai, who loved to play the role of a spymaster, prepared an elaborate plan for the three of us to meet at an R&AW safe house in Darjeeling. As per this plan, I was to leave Gangtok a day in advance and stay the night in Kalimpong. The next day, I was to pick up Banerjee from Bagdogra airport and take him to the safe house where Bajpai would be waiting. When I told Banerjee about this plan, he asked me to come straight to Calcutta for a day, to brief him on the matter before all of us met at Darjeeling. I was, however, told not to tell Bajpai about my visit to Calcutta. I reached Calcutta in the afternoon on 1 May and briefed Banerjee about the general outlines of the draft bill, which Bajpai had shown me but not given a copy for security reasons.

In Darjeeling, we stayed away from prowling public eyes in the R&AW safe house. On 3 May, the three of us went through the draft thoroughly, subject and paragraph wise. Wherever we felt the need for some change, Bajpai made a note of our suggestions for his record. Our main suggestion was that the draft bill must fully and clearly address the false propaganda launched by the Chogyal about newly elected members of the council and the council of ministers having no powers, and the real power being with the Chogyal and chief executive. Further, if possible, the draft bill should go beyond what had been promised in the 8 May agreement. Having done our job to Bajpai's satisfaction, I dropped Banerjee at Bagdogra airport on 4 May and proceeded to Kalimpong where I had to meet Kazi as per a prior appointment.

As planned earlier, on my way to Gangtok I stopped at Kalimpong to meet Kazi. As that was my first meeting with him after the elections, I congratulated him on his party's success. He was still his old self; humble, unassuming and pro-India to the core. The landslide victory which his party had achieved had not had any effect on him. Here is the gist of our discussions:

a) I explained to Kazi that his party candidates' refusal to take oath at the palace monastery in the presence of the Chogyal needed to be toned down. They needed to let Das find a solution to that. In that context, they could let the younger members take the lead. Hopefully, some solution would be worked out soon.

b) He was requested to write a letter on his party's behalf or take a delegation personally to Bajpai and Das, requesting the GoI for the appointment of a constitutional adviser who could frame the new draft constitution. This was essential for ensuring more powers to the future governments and for curtailing the powers of the Chogyal. They should also ask for immediate implementation of the provisions of the 8 May agreement.

c) There was utmost need for maintaining unity amongst the party legislators till the new constitution was adopted, as they needed a two-thirds majority to pass the bill. People like B.B. Gurung and K.C. Pradhan, and some others, had to be kept in good humour till then.

d) He noted down these points and felt it would be possible to take care of these requirements. He, however, said that as his party did not have sufficient experience in handling legislative and constitutional matters, it would be better if some experienced person was placed at his disposal in Kalimpong for some time to guide him in such matters. I promised to pass on his request to the concerned, but assured him that in the meanwhile, he could always depend on me for that purpose.

Following my meeting with Kazi in Kalimpong, the Sikkim Congress legislative party had a two-day meeting at a temple in Gangtok on 5 and 6 May. Kazi was elected as the leader of the legislative party in the newly elected Assembly. Secondly, it was decided that the party should request the PO and B.S. Das to convene the Assembly session on priority. A copy of these resolutions (which were finally seen and suitably amended by me earlier during the day) was handed over to the PO on 6 May itself. Though obviously happy with its contents, Bajpai wondered as to who had drafted this innocuous-looking resolution.

On the evening of 8 May, Myngma brought a message from Kazi that despite his best efforts, the majority of his party's legislators were still opposed to taking oath as members of the new Assembly in the presence of the Chogyal. He wanted me to draft a protest letter addressed to Das conveying his party's objection. As desired by Kazi, a letter of protest addressed to Das was given to Myngma on 9 May to be passed on to Kazi the same night. Kazi was also requested that in case Das was not able to find some solution to this problem, he and his partymen should go by Das's decision. But Myngma could not find a suitable opportunity to hand over this letter to Kazi or Khatiwada that day. Khatiwada collected this letter from Myngma early on 10 May. This letter was delivered by Kazi to Das a few hours before the oath-taking ceremony.

Das was, however, able to solve the oath-taking issue to the satisfaction of the Sikkim Congress leaders by convincing the Chogyal that he would personally take the oath at the palace monastery in the presence of the Chogyal as the president of the Assembly on the morning of 10 May, and thereafter he would administer the oath to the newly elected members of the House the same day.[1] The Sikkim Congress members' refusal to attend the Assembly session in case the Chogyal tried to address it was resolved by Das by convincing the former to leave the hall immediately after the inauguration of the new session, and to let him read his address on his behalf. Banerjee, who wanted the oath-taking and the related issue of the Chogyal's address to be resolved amicably, was informed of the outcome of our team's efforts the same day.

The Assembly was inaugurated by the Chogyal. After ten minutes, he left the hall and the proceedings were taken over by Das. Das read the Chogyal's address in his absence, and the Assembly was adjourned for the next day. The Sikkim Congress legislators boycotted the, palace lunch on 10 May but attended the cocktail party at India House the same evening.

The PO called me early on 9 May and asked me to meet him at India House at 11.15 a.m. He had a list of all the elected members of the Sikkim Assembly. He had already prepared a plan of action as to how each one of the newly elected Sikkim Congress members could be dealt with in order to get some important resolutions passed in the Assembly. In that respect, he made some suggestions, especially about N.K. Subedi, Rinzing Lepcha, Nim Tshering Lepcha, Adar Singh and Tashi Tenzing. I told Bajpai that we did not know any of them, and even if we did, we would not like to risk exposing ourselves by dabbling in the internal matters of Kazi's party so openly, and that too without his knowledge and behind his back.

I then asked the PO as to who would be dealing with the Sikkim Congress leaders, as the time had come for getting the desired resolution passed in the Assembly. Further, as that would require hectic lobbying with some selected Sikkim Congress leaders, it was time for him to plan a strategy. He told me that he would tell me at an appropriate time. To my surprise, after a while, the PO handed a piece of paper to me. It contained two resolutions which had to be successfully moved by Kazi in the current session of the Assembly. He said that this work had to be done by us. I told him that I would not do that as I had not received any such instructions from my bosses—Banerjee or Kao.

Anticipating that the PO would call Banerjee, on returning to my office I contacted him myself and briefed him about my discussion with Bajpai. As expected, soon thereafter the PO also called Banerjee. Banerjee told me that according to the PO, these were very important resolutions and he would need our assistance in getting these moved successfully in the Assembly. In view of that, Banerjee wanted me to render all possible help to Bajpai and complete the task to his satisfaction. The next day, i.e., 10 May, at 3 p.m., a revised draft was received from the PO. The documents containing the draft resolutions were passed on to Kazi the same day. In this respect, Kazi's attention was drawn to our discussion of 4 May at Kalimpong in which I had requested him to move such a resolution in the Assembly as soon as it was received by him from us. Myngma told him that the documents were drafted by a GoI legal expert and contained two resolutions which needed to be passed in the House on 11 May, before the end of the session. He was also requested not to make any changes in this document. Members of our spl ops team held meetings with their respective friends one by one throughout the night to convince them to lend a helping hand to Kazi for the passage of these resolutions. As planned, the resolutions were passed unanimously on 11 May. Much to the annoyance of the Chogyal, even the lone opposition member of the National Party, Kalzang Gyatso, voted in its favour. Myngma had somehow convinced Gyatso that open defiance of Kazi's moves would not be in his long-term interests.

Das, in his book *The Sikkim Saga*, especially takes note of this when he says, 'While moving the motion on the vote of thanks, he (Kazi) made two far-reaching points which have had a major bearing on the future events in Sikkim.' The resolution, quoted by him in the book is reproduced below:[2]

> The Assembly accordingly resolves and hereby requests the Government of India to depute immediately a Constitutional Advisor for (i) giving a legal and constitutional framework for the objectives of this Resolution; (ii) defining the powers of the Chogyal, the Chief Executive, the Executive Council and the Assembly; and (iii) recommending to the Government of India specific proposals for further strengthening Indo-Sikkim

relationship and for Sikkim's participation in the political and economic institutions of India, as defined by this Resolution.

B.S. Das, in his capacity as chief executive, sent a copy of the above resolution to the Chogyal, who protested its 'illegality', as according to him it went much beyond the 8 May agreement. Later on, a copy of the resolution, along with the Chogyal's comments, was sent by Das to New Delhi through the PO.

Soon after, some pro-durbar elements held a meeting at Nor-khill Hotel on 17 May. It was decided to form a new party named the Sikkim Prajatantra Party. Over 100 villagers from north and east Sikkim, and twenty active pro-Chogyal members, including N.B. Bhandari, attended it. About Rs 5000 was spent on lunch and drinks. The party held its first public meeting on 19 May in Gangtok bazaar. The meeting was attended by as many as 200–300 people. The leaders criticized Sikkim Congress leaders, especially Kazi, for having sold Sikkim to India and also for letting down the Sikkimese people by not forming a government (cabinet) yet. They also criticized the GoI by saying that the 'pioneers of Panchsheel observe its principles'.

A couple of days after this meeting, Padam Bahadur learnt from his Sikkim Congress 'friends' that the palace had assigned duties to some secretaries of the government of Sikkim to win over certain members of the Sikkim Congress legislative party. This was to block the adoption of the new constitution as and when moved in the council. But these friends were also of the view that if K.C. Pradhan and B.B. Gurung, and some Lepchas, could be kept in good humour by Kazi, there should be no difficulty in getting the constitution bill passed. There was also some criticism, especially amongst the pro-durbar elements, of Das's appointment as president (speaker) of the Assembly as he was neither a Sikkimese nor an elected member of the Assembly. All these activities took place during the absence of the Chogyal, so that the GoI might not think that the Chogyal was behind all those moves.

After spending four years in Sikkim as first secretary, Sudhir Devare was transferred, and he hosted a farewell dinner at his residence on 21 May. The Chogyal accompanied by Jigdal Densapa and the PO had returned from New Delhi the previous evening. All three were present in this party. The Chogyal and Jigdal looked unhappy about the outcome of their visit to the capital. Jigdal told Bali as to how fit her father, Foreign Minister Sardar Swaran Singh, had looked. Further, although he was extremely busy, he did not show any signs of fatigue. While Bali was talking to Jigdal in my presence, the Chogyal joined us. After talking to Bali for a while, he said, 'Incidentally, Jigdal has turned anti-India.' Jigdal blushed and said, 'La', in respectful surprise at what the Chogyal was saying. The Chogyal's remarks, however, indicated that even a person like Jigdal, who had advised him to adopt a conciliatory approach towards India, had been disappointed with the outcome of their recent visit to New Delhi.

Finally, on 22 May, the newly appointed Constitutional Adviser A.K. Rajagopal—senior advocate in the Supreme Court, retired additional secretary in the ministry of law and former member of the Law Commission—arrived in Gangtok with a copy of the draft constitution. He called on the Chogyal the same evening.

The next day, the newly elected Sikkim Congress members of the Assembly also met the adviser at India House. Rajagopal discussed with them the implications of the 8 May agreement. He said that it was a preliminary and probing session, and gave them a copy of the draft constitution. He asked them to study it and come back with suggestions when they met him again on 25 May.

The National Party members, including M.B. Basnet and the lone Assembly member, Kalzang Gyatso, met Rajagopal on 24 May and told him that they would like to have complete independence. They later softened their stance and came down to a constitution which could preserve the rights of the Bhutias and Lepchas and the position of the Chogyal as enshrined in the treaty of 1950. They were also given a copy of the draft constitution to elicit suggestions.

As the Sikkim Congress leaders were to meet Rajagopal on 25 May with their suggestions for improving the proposed constitution, I discussed the matter with the PO on 24 May. I requested him to ask Rajagopal to prepare a draft of a suitable response that he was expecting from the Sikkim Congress leaders in this context. I wanted to pass that on to Kazi so that he could discuss its contents with other Sikkim Congress leaders and submit the same with additional suggestions, if any, to the constitutional adviser during their meeting with him. A copy of this draft was later received from Rajagopal through the PO at 6 p.m., and was passed on to Kazi the same night through Myngma and Khatiwada for further necessary action.

A dedicated group of Sikkim Congress legislative committee members deliberated over the draft constitution bill, and their draft response which was passed on to Kazi by us, throughout the night of 24 May. After studying the contents of these two documents in detail, some party members made suggestions and amendments.

The next morning, i.e., at 7 a.m. on 25 May, Myngma brought a typed note from Khatiwada containing his party's comments on the memo and also the contents of the draft constitution. I went to India House to show it to Bajpai. He had some objections to it. I said that we should give some credit to the party members who had worked overnight and let these suggestions remain as such. It should be left to the constitutional adviser to accept or reject any of them. We made a couple of changes, and the PO finally agreed.

We requested Kazi and Khatiwada, through Myngma, to go ahead and deliver their party's response to the constitutional adviser. Later, we learnt that the party members once again had a detailed discussion on this document, and had minor differences, but generally, it was a healthy discussion. Thereafter, Kazi and his men met the adviser at 12.40 p.m. for about one and a half hours. The memo and its annexures, as seen by us (PO and me), were handed over to the constitutional adviser by twenty-odd Sikkim Congress leaders who were in Gangtok. Rajagopal left Gangtok on 26 May.

With important developments relating to the framing of a new constitution taking place, it was time to meet the Chogyal again to ascertain his reaction to the recent developments. The call was fixed through Jigdal at short notice. I met him at 5 p.m. on 25 May.

On my arrival, I saw him checking some registers under a tent pitched outside in the lawns. An unusual sight compared to my previous visits. Following is the gist of my discussions with him:
a) He was happy about the assurances he received during his last visit to New Delhi, and hoped that New Delhi would take further steps to give practical shape to these commitments.

b) However, Das's letter of date had created some doubts in his mind as to what the real intentions of the GoI were. (He did not mention the contents, but it seemed like Das had written to him on the proposed powers, etc., of the new Assembly members and the executive council.)

c) He wanted the three OSDs (Murari, Sanyal and Manavalan—IAS officers on deputation from West Bengal) and the CRPF battalion to be withdrawn. He said that Sikkim being smaller than a subdivision of an Indian district, it did not require such a top-heavy administration. If the CRPF had to stay in Sikkim, it should work under the operational control of the police commissioner, whom he described as an extremely efficient and a professional officer (the PO later showed me copies of the two letters the Chogyal had written to the prime minister and foreign minister on these lines). It appeared that the Chogyal was trying to feed the same information through me.

d) He did not understand the real purpose of the Sikkim Congress leader's proposed visit to New Delhi.

The Chogyal's remarks on the above subjects were on known lines. He felt that the OSDs were acting against his interests. His old loyal senior Sikkim government officials had also started feeling that the OSDs were encroaching on their domain. Regarding the CRPF, his reaction was understandable. Over a period, he had realized that it was the CRPF that was standing in the way of his followers organizing any anti-Sikkim Congress demonstrations. He felt that as long as the CRPF was under Das's charge, he and his men would not have a free hand to destabilize the situation.

At a farewell dinner hosted by Gurdip Bedi for Devare on 26 May, the PO told me that he would be going to New Delhi the next morning and wanted me to talk to him before that. When I called, he told me that he was going to meet Kewal Singh who had just returned from London. On 26 May he had also spoken to Joint Secretary N.B. Menon. He had told him that they wanted the Sikkim Congress legislative party members to come to New Delhi immediately. But both the PO and I agreed that the visit should take place only after the date for the Assembly session was fixed. This was essential to deny the Chogyal and his men sufficient time to brainwash the Sikkim Congress legislative party members and create doubts in their minds. As decided in consultation with the PO, I also sent a message to New Delhi on these lines. Under such circumstances, our suggestions were always accepted by New Delhi, and that too, promptly.

At this stage, I would like to provide the readers with a bit of a deviation from the hectic political activities and give them an insight into what was going on in the minds of some of the pro-Chogyal elements at that time. In the previous chapter, I had mentioned my meeting with Paljor Tashi, alias Panjola (the husband of Langzing La, the Chogyal's half-sister) on 3 April, when he showed me his cameras and some photographs and I had appreciated his photographical skills.

At the farewell dinner hosted by Gurdip Bedi for Devare on 26 May 1974 (where the Chogyal and Jigdal were also present), Panjola, who was in charge of the Chogyal's security and protocol affairs, was having an animated discussion with one of the Indian guests at the party, and I happened to be a part of that group.

We were standing at a distance from the Chogyal and Jigdal. Panjola said that the people of Sikkim had been cheated by the GoI. The Sikkimese had placed a lot of faith in India, but India had stabbed them in the back. Sikkim got aid from India, but most of it came out of the Colombo Plan funds, etc. Even if that money came from GoI funds, they would not bother about such aid. People thought that now Karma Topden had been shunted out of the palace, they could have a free run. 'But I can tell you that as Karma's replacement as chief of protocol, I can be worse than Karma. We have been clean-bowled by the GoI, and we have been facing full tosses, beamers and bouncers, but let me tell you that when our turn to bowl comes, India will not fare any better.' Further, he said that India had given all sorts of aid and other facilities to Nepal, but Nepal's attitude towards India had changed. India's overbearing attitude was responsible for this.

Till then, Panjola's tone was normal but when host Gurdip Bedi came to us, he started shouting at the top of his voice. Pointing his finger towards Bedi, Panjola said, 'He was one of the troublemakers in Sikkim.' Finding a suitable opportunity, I left the place quietly to let Gurdip face the music. Panjola continued talking to Bedi for about five minutes more. Thereafter, Bedi dashed towards the PO and took him out, ostensibly to tell him what Panjola had been shouting about. Later, Rinchin, his sister, was seen talking to Panjola outside the house. The PO and Das were of the view that Panjola had lost his mind, but to me he looked reasonably sensible, albeit a little high.

On 3 June 1974, Panjola met Atish Sinha, the third secretary at India House, and told him that he was a much-misunderstood man, and that he was not anti-India. According to him, the real people who were anti-India were Rai Bahadur Densapa (Athingla), his son, Jigdal Densapa, and the Chogyal's sister, Coo Coo La. Further, the GoI had favoured a number of people and had even offered the post of ambassador/high commissioner to Jigdal Densapa in some Indian mission abroad, but nobody had bothered about him so far. He also told Atish that an anti-India conspiracy was being hatched in the palace to misguide Kazi— they were misinforming him that as long as the chief executive was there, his own powers would be curtailed. Therefore, Kazi should ask for the removal of the chief executive from the scene. Panjola said they were also trying to win over some members of the Sikkim Congress who were close to Kazi, so that if the proposed constitutional bill did not suit them, the same could be blocked in the Assembly (both these things were true). While revealing these designs of some pro-Chogyal elements, Panjola, however, did not tell Atish about his own contact with Rinzing Lepcha. Rinzing later told me that, on 6 June, Panjola had tried to mislead him by telling him that the GoI had entered into a secret agreement with the Chogyal and it would, therefore, be in his own interests if he shifted his loyalties back to the Chogyal.

Meanwhile, the PO consulted Kazi about Panjola. Kazi mentioned that Panjola's family did not enjoy good relations with Jigdal and Coo Coo La, and they might have been indirectly working on him to incite him against the GoI, so that he might lose his job with the Chogyal. Out of curiosity, we made our own inquiries from some friends close to Panjola's family. It was learnt that Panjola had some sort of bipolar disorder, which compelled him to behave irrationally sometimes, and he was being treated for that.

It was now time to work towards the implementation of the crucial 11 May 1974 resolution, which had been unanimously passed by the Assembly, and which had also demanded that the GoI take suitable action for strengthening the Indo–Sikkim relationship, and for Sikkim's participation in the political and economic institutions of India. For this, Constitutional Adviser Rajagopal was already finalizing the draft Government of Sikkim Bill of 1974.

Chapter XI

Halfway House: Sikkim as an Associate State

The Assembly session to take up the newly drafted constitution bill was to start sometime in June 1974. It was felt I should meet B.B. Gurung* and Rinzing Lepcha to assess the support the Assembly would extend to the proposed bill—a bill that could also

---

* Born in 1929, B.B. Gurung, after graduating from a Calcutta college, worked for some time as a schoolteacher and also as a reporter with a Calcutta-based paper. He joined the Sikkim Congress in 1947, and later worked as its general secretary for a brief period. Thereafter, he kept changing parties and was a member of the Sikkim council a couple of times. Because of his shifting loyalties and pro-Chogyal inclinations, Kazi did not include him in his cabinet formed after the April 1974 elections. He was, however, appointed as speaker of the Sikkim Assembly in 1977 after the death of the incumbent, C.S. Rai. Finding Kazi's fortunes dwindling, he joined the R.C. Poudyal-led Sikkim Congress (Revolutionary). He contested the 1979 elections but did not get any post as the N.B. Bhandari-led Sikkim Janata Parishad was able to cobble up a majority and formed the government. He got his chance when Governor Homi J.H. Taleyarkhan dismissed Bhandari's government and appointed Gurung as chief minister on 11 May 1984. However, his tenure lasted only thirteen days, as he could not prove his majority and lost the vote of confidence in the House.

take care of the demands raised through the 11 May resolution. According to some reports, Gurung, whose loyalty to Kazi had always been suspect, was trying to form a separate group with the support of R.C. Poudyal and K.C. Pradhan. On the other hand, as per Padam Bahadur's information, Rinzing Lepcha, by that time, had become quite close to Kazi.

Fortunately, I met Gurung at a cocktail party on 27 May. He told me that he and Poudyal were feeling neglected, and that Kazi was not paying attention to them. Finding the place not very congenial for further discussion, I told him to come to my residence at 8.30 p.m. As decided, he was picked up by my driver Chun Chun from a predetermined place. While talking to him, I was conscious of the fact that whatever I told him would be conveyed to the palace. In view of that, most of the time, I listened to him and conveyed the impression that the GoI may not go to the extent of totally removing the Chogyal from the scene, and some compromise could be worked out between the democratic aspirations of the people and the Chogyal's own interests. That was also done to confuse the Chogyal about the GoI's true intentions. During the course of my earlier meetings with him, I got the impression that he was actually conscious of the fact that most of the Sikkim Congress leaders knew that he was secretly in touch with the durbar. Given this, whenever he met me—there were not many occasions, though—he would always express his unstinted support for Kazi and the Sikkim Congress by way of clearing any doubts, if any, in my mind.

During this meeting, Gurung said that the Sikkim Congress was one solid block. Regarding the likely visit of Sikkim Congress legislative party members to New Delhi, he said that everyone should go to the national capital and not just nine or ten persons as was being suggested by some other leaders. He thought it would be good exposure for some people who had not even crossed Siliguri.

According to him, he and his friends 'are not bothered about what the recently formed pro-Chogyal Sikkim Prajatantra Party leaders would say about this visit. We do not want to waste any time on refuting such baseless and useless allegations, as we are busy with much more important work of framing the constitution and meeting knowledgeable persons like Rajagopal.' There was some sort of pride in his eyes about the importance of the work that he and the others in the party were doing. It also showed that Kazi was keeping the party leaders busy and involved in discussing the pros and cons of framing the new constitution, so that when it was finally adopted, credit could be given to those people.

Gurung described the allegations of Pradhan being won over by the palace as incorrect and motivated. He described Pradhan as a heavy drinker and an indiscreet person, who regularly played mahjong with some pro-Chogyal individuals. In their company, 'he says a lot of irresponsible things which ultimately reach the ears of the Sikkim Congress leaders and create doubts in their minds about his loyalty to Kazi'. Gurung was of the view that Pradhan's marriage to a Gurung girl on 26 May might help him win over Pradhan and bring them politically closer. Further, 'Das has given us a place in the MLAs hostel where eight to ten MLAs, including R.C. Poudyal, N.K. Subedi and B.P. Dahal, are staying. Now we have more time at our disposal, which has helped us hold joint discussions on subjects of common interest at short notice. A committee of nine members, including all these men, has been formed to discuss matters of constitutional importance which will help us articulate the party's views when they meet the constitution adviser.'

Gurung wanted me to believe that as a senior party leader, he was making every effort to ensure that it stayed committed to the passing of the constitution bill in the Assembly. Further, as was the case with some other Sikkim Congress leaders whom

I met during this period, Gurung was also trying to impress me with his loyalty to India and also to Kazi, so that it could help him get some position of responsibility such as the post of a cabinet minister or even a member of the Indian parliament, when Kazi formed his government after the new constitution was promulgated. As Gurung had left no scope for me to say much, I only said that with senior and committed leaders like him around, I was convinced that the Sikkim Congress would have no problem in passing the proposed constitution bill.

On 4 June, at 12.30 p.m., I met the PO in his office. He sought my views on the most suitable dates for convening the Assembly. In view of the postponement of the visit of the Sikkim Congress leaders to New Delhi, I felt that it was essential that the constitutional adviser come to Gangtok immediately, so that the Sikkim Congress leaders could explain to their followers why they could not visit New Delhi so far. As discussed, the PO sent a message to New Delhi on these lines. I learnt on 5 June that Rajagopal was coming to Gangtok on 7 June for three days, for further discussions with the concerned parties.

During this meeting with the PO, it was also agreed that Kazi should formally request Das to convene the Assembly session soon so that some important matters could be discussed. On returning to the office, I prepared a draft letter on these lines and sent it to Kazi through Myngma. Through a separate note, we requested Kazi not to tell anyone else that the reason this session was being convened was the passing of the constitution bill. We presumed that an alerted Chogyal would oppose the convening of the session on one pretext or another. He could also redouble his efforts to create a rift amongst the members of the Sikkim Congress legislative party. A few days later, Kazi handed over his request to Das. The Assembly was summoned on 20 June.

I learnt from PO Bajpai the next day (5 June) that Kazi had come to him earlier during the day and was rather unhappy about the delay in convening the Assembly. He had told Bajpai that he would write to Das requesting him to call the session soon.

So far, I had been using Myngma to carry our messages to Rinzing Lepcha. A personal meeting with him was postponed to a later date. With the Assembly expected to meet soon, I met Rinzing on 6 June. As he was fair, tall and always dressed in traditional Lepcha attire, including headgear, he could be spotted from a distance. Incidentally, Rinzing was a good singer. Our meeting had been fixed at an out-of-the-way safe house. It lasted more than an hour. The gist of what Rinzing told me is outlined below:

a) The Lepchas continued to be one solid block and there was no possibility of any rift amongst them.

b) The Chogyal's intelligence inspector, Dawa Gyalpo, had recently fixed a secret meeting between him and the Chogyal at Sonam Gyatso's house. Although the Chogyal reached Gyatso's house in disguise, Rinzing did not go there on the advice of Kazi, who had told him that such a meeting would tarnish his image and make the people think that he was trying to strike a deal with the Chogyal behind their backs.

c) A senior Sikkim government official had told him that the Chogyal had received some assurance from New Delhi regarding his position. They suggested that it was high time he returned to the Chogyal's fold so that he could continue enjoying power. He was also briefed by Panjola on similar lines. Rinzing said that Panjola was not insane. This had been corroborated to him in confidence by Sonam Gyatso. During his recent conversation with Panjola, Rinzing found him to be very logical. Rinzing did not like Langzing La (Panjola's wife and the Chogyal's half-sister).

d) Rinzing, as leader of the Lepcha legislative group in the Assembly, and some other Lepchas were going to submit a memorandum to the constitutional adviser, requesting him to make special provisions in the proposed constitution for the betterment of the underprivileged and downtrodden communities, including the Lepchas. He wanted me to help them with this. They had already prepared a memo, a copy of which was given to me.

e) B.B. Gurung was a very shrewd man. On the day Das hosted the lunch for the newly elected Assembly members at Nor-khill Hotel, Gurung had confessed to Rinzing and Khatiwada that he was also in touch with the Chogyal and his men, and had recently received Rs 2000 from the Chogyal. Rinzing thought Gurung had actually got more money than that. He also mentioned that the Chogyal was feeling helpless and ignored as most of his men had lost the elections. Despite that, Rinzing felt that people like Gurung, Pradhan and others were secretly in touch with him.

f) Sonam Gyatso and N.B. Bhandari had told him recently that the Sikkim Congress leaders were going to New Delhi to sell Sikkim, and that they might sign a new constitution during this trip. Rinzing told both of them that if that was a goodwill visit at the expense of the GoI, why should they not enjoy the free trip? Indeed, they would not even mind going to Paris if the GoI so desired.

g) A group of educated persons within the party, especially those who had recently been elected as members of the legislative

Assembly, had been assigned the job of rendering help in the finalization of the constitution. In addition to meeting the constitutional adviser in this respect, they would also act as party spokespersons on this matter and would actively participate in the debate in the Assembly when the constitution bill was introduced and discussed.

h) One Dorji Dhadul of the palace was frequently visiting Kurseong (near Darjeeling) and Siliguri during the night in the palace jeep and would return the same night. Lepcha apprehended that Dhadul was smuggling arms into Sikkim and giving these to some goondas whom the palace was hiring to create trouble.

i) One Lepcha doctor, who was earlier working in Gangtok and had shifted to Darjeeling some time back, was inciting the Lepchas of Darjeeling against the GoI. He thought that dissatisfaction amongst the Lepchas of Darjeeling would have an impact on the morale of the Lepchas of Sikkim too. The doctor also wanted to send some Lepchas from Darjeeling, to poison his mind against India. But Rinzing and his Sikkimese Lepcha friends had conveyed a message to the Darjeeling Lepchas that they should dissociate themselves from the activities of that doctor, who was doing all that at the Chogyal's behest. Rinzing wanted me to inform the IB in Kalimpong to keep a watch over the activities of this doctor.

When I asked Rinzing as to how many legislators would support the constitution bill in the Assembly, he was of the view that almost all the Sikkim Congress members should be voting for it. He gave two reasons for that. Firstly, the senior leaders were hopeful of getting cabinet posts and would keep their junior friends under control. Regarding the rest of the members, Kazi had given them the task of suggesting amendments to the draft constitution received from the constitutional adviser, and they had started feeling that they had made a lot of contributions in the finalization of the constitution bill. Rinzing's analysis was finally proved correct.

Kazi did not have permanent accommodation at Gangtok and used to stay in a room at his petrol pump. Finally, on 7 June, he was given a suite in the Sikkim PWD guest house. Khatiwada was given a room in the adjacent residence of CO Prasad. This place had some advantages. Being next to the CRPF CO's residence, the place was secure. Murari's residence was next door and thus he was available for any urgent consultation. Also, it was convenient for both Kazi and Das to meet at short notice in a secure place. However, this change had an obvious disadvantage for our spl ops. It would now not be possible for me to meet Kazi without being noticed by Murari or the CRPF personnel.

At a dinner I hosted for Election Commissioner R.N. Sengupta on 7 June, Murari told me that B.B. Gurung and R.C. Poudyal had come to see him earlier in the evening. Both had emphatically told him that they could never go against the interests of Kazi and India and that they were being unfairly maligned on this issue. Although Murari had called them separately, both of them had come together after meeting Sengupta. He was quite sure about the loyalty of everyone else, but had doubts about Rinzing Lepcha's intentions, whom he felt was behaving rather strangely. Based on my meeting with Rinzing the previous night, I told Murari that although there were reports about his meeting the Chogyal and Sonam Gyatso, these appeared to be incorrect.

I told Murari that he should call Rinzing and clear his doubts about his loyalty to Kazi. He promised to do so.

Murari further said that if the constitution bill was presented in the Assembly within the next five to six days, it would go through comfortably. But if it was going to take longer, then the Sikkim Congress legislative party members must visit New Delhi in order to stay away from the machinations of the pro-Chogyal elements. I agreed, but told him that the only criticism in that case would be that the Sikkim Congress leaders had already signed the new constitution at New Delhi, and the adoption of the same in the Assembly was a mere formality.

S.C. De, JAD (SIB), Kalimpong, was also present at the dinner. He told me that the Kazini had come to his office on 6 June and told him that Sunanda K. Datta-Ray's article in the *Statesman* of the same day was highly objectionable and that he was allegedly a CIA agent. She apparently used all sorts of adjectives for Ray and was fuming with rage. She said that she was wrongly quoted by Ray as having told him that the Sikkim Congress's ultimate objective was 'of course independence'. She further said that the PO should not have believed Ray that his report was based on what the Kazini had actually told him.

On 8 June, the PO contacted me on the secraphone (secure telephone line) at 9.15 p.m. and asked me to see him around 10.30 a.m. the next morning. On reaching India House the next day, I saw him sitting in the lawn with Constitutional Adviser Rajagopal and having discussions with Sikkim Congress leaders. The PO and Rajagopal were obviously discussing the proposed constitution bill with them. Without being noticed, I went straight to the PO's office and waited for him there. The PO prepared a brief note on his meeting with the constitutional adviser for the foreign secretary and gave me a copy.

The PO called me for a brief meeting again on 10 June, just before he left for lunch at the palace. He showed me a copy of the letter written by the Chogyal to Das on 9 June, in which he had criticized the 11 May resolution and explained the need for laying down rules and procedures for the smooth running of the House. The Chogyal did not agree to the summoning of the Assembly session till such rules and procedures were framed. It appeared that he also wanted to see the final copy of the draft constitution bill before he committed to the summoning of the next session.

The three papers shown by the PO were:

a) Note on the constitutional adviser's and PO's joint meeting with the Chogyal on 7 June.
b) Note on the constitutional adviser and PO's meeting with sixteen Sikkim Congress legislative party members on 8 June, a copy of which the PO had already given to me.
c) A copy of the demi-official letter written by the PO to the foreign secretary.

Bajpai gave me copies of the first two papers for my information.

On 11 June, I learnt that the MEA had called the Chogyal to New Delhi. The Chogyal was to leave on 12 June, along with Das, Jigdal Densapa, Auditor General M.M. Rasaily and three others, by Indian Airlines flight IC-222 from Bagdogra at 1 p.m. The plan at that stage was that the Chogyal would be given a copy of the final amended draft of the constitution bill on the morning of 13 June, and a copy of the same would be given to the Sikkim Congress leaders at Gangtok on the morning of 14 June. If the Chogyal agreed with its contents, well and good. If he

did not and threatened to abdicate, he would be told to go back to Gangtok and do it there. Meanwhile, the Sikkim Congress leaders would be suitably briefed at Gangtok to lend full support to the constitution bill. Based on the information gathered by our three-man spl ops team, it was expected that there would be a general acceptance of the proposed constitution amongst the Sikkim Congress legislators, with the exception of a few like K.C. Pradhan and B.B. Gurung. As a request for calling the session had already been received by Das, if the Chogyal did not agree to the same, the matter could be referred to the GoI under the provisions of the 8 May agreement. The Assembly session would be called within a couple of days of the Chogyal's return from New Delhi, to pass the constitution bill, thereby giving him little time for manipulations.

While the Chogyal was on his way back to Gangtok on 17 June, the Sikkim Congress had two sessions with the PO and with Das to discuss the finalization of the constitution bill. Only eleven Assembly members went to meet the PO. R.C. Poudyal. N.K. Subedi and B.P. Dahal were absent. B.B. Gurung claimed to be unwell. The PO seemed to have lost all hope of getting the draft resolution and constitution bill passed. He sent a frantic message to New Delhi asking for a freer hand to deal with the Sikkim Congress leaders. He told me that whatever I did, I must ensure that the Sikkim Congress passed the amended constitution bill.

Keeping in view the importance of the task and the PO's doubts about the passage of the bill, after consulting Banerjee, I called a meeting of our spl ops team in my office. Padam Bahadur was asked to contact his 'friends' S.K. Rai, C.S. Rai and K.C. Pradhan immediately, and inform them about the importance of the bill for the betterment of their, as well as their followers' lot. Myngma was asked to meet Kazi and Rinzing Lepcha to check the extent of support that the bill would enjoy in the Assembly if it was called within the next few days. For a change, I also called the head of the SIB, V. Vaidyalingam, to tell his staff to keep watch over the dissident activities within the Sikkim Congress legislative party and let me know if there was any possibility of any major shift in their loyalties. Given the importance of the issue, Vaidyalingam agreed to oblige me this time. But he did not come back with any information of interest. Maybe he did not have anything of interest. Maybe he had sent his report to the JAD in Calcutta through his deputy director at Calcutta and/or to the IB headquarters at New Delhi. But I did not hear from them either.

The Chogyal returned from New Delhi at 8.15 p.m. on 17 June. His flight was late by three and a half hours, and a helicopter could not be arranged by the PO's staff. The delayed arrival of the Chogyal was part of a well-thought-out plan worked out by Bajpai in consultation with Banerjee. It was felt that if the Chogyal's arrival was somehow delayed till late evening on 17 June, he would have lost one day to work on the Sikkim Congress leaders to convince them that he would be able to give them much more than what had been promised through the proposed constitution bill. It was Banerjee who got the plane's departure delayed through his Indian Airlines contacts in Calcutta, and the PO used his influence in Gangtok to see that a helicopter was not made available to the Chogyal on one pretext or another.

While the Chogyal was still in New Delhi, L.B. Chhetri, D. Lepcha and M.M. Rasaily, who had also gone to New Delhi to be available to the Chogyal for any advice he might need, had returned to Gangtok two days earlier to work on some Sikkim Congress leaders. It was learnt that Rasaily had brought with him some notes about the contents of the proposed constitution from New Delhi, copies of which were circulated amongst the vacillating Sikkim Congress members of the Assembly in order to impress upon them that if they were ready to support the Chogyal, he could provide them with much more liberal terms than contained in the proposed constitution bill. This seemed to have worked well on some Sikkim Congress leaders, especially on B.B. Gurung, K.C. Pradhan and their close associates, from the Nepalese segment of the councillors. That was one of the reasons why these persons were avoiding contact with the PO and Das.

The Chogyal's game was to create differences amongst the Lepchas and Bhutias, and the Nepalese leaders to ensure that the Nepalese did not support the new constitution, and then tell the GoI that the very segment of the population for which it had been doing so much was not willing to accept its terms. After creating doubts in the minds of the Nepalese legislators, the Chogyal would then tell New Delhi that as he had been telling the GoI, these leaders were totally unreliable and he was still a better alternative for India to protect its interests in Sikkim.

On 17 June, about 6 p.m., I received a message from Kazi through Myngma that he, accompanied by Khatiwada, would like to see me the same night at my residence. This was an unusual request as Kazi had never come to my residence for operational safety reasons. Myngma brought Kazi and Khatiwada around 10 p.m. in our ordinary-looking operational jeep to avoid detection. The purpose of their meeting was to seek clarification on some portions of the draft constitution bill, which was to be passed in the Assembly. They complained about both the PO and Das, who wanted Kazi to get the bill (received from the constitutional adviser) passed in the council without making any changes. Kazi said they didn't realize

that as party leader he had to protect his image with his followers inside and outside the Assembly to ensure that he continued to receive their unstinted support. If his followers came to know that he was willing to get such an important bill passed without discussing it with his legislature party members, he would lose face and the passage of the bill would become difficult. To ensure their support in the Assembly, he had to clear their doubts as far as possible. Further, the Chogyal, through his men, had planted some doubts in the minds of some Sikkim Congress MLAs which needed to be cleared. He had already had a couple of sessions with his party colleagues on this issue. But as no satisfactory response was forthcoming from the PO and Das, he had to come to me.

We spent about four hours going over each part of the draft constitution bill, which I had seen and discussed with Bajpai and Banerjee earlier in Darjeeling. Kazi wanted clarification on the following issues: Why was the document called a bill and not an Act? Did the legislators have powers to amend it in future? Could they remove the Chogyal with a two-thirds majority? Why chief minister and not prime minister? In section one, which defined the powers of the chief executive, why was it mentioned that the GoI could still enter into any agreement directly with the Chogyal in the future? That showed that the GoI did not trust the Sikkim Congress fully. Why couldn't the executive councillors be called cabinet ministers? Why could they not elect their own speaker rather than have the chief executive perform the dual role of speaker and chief minister? Why were the executive councillors not given charge of some crucial portfolios such as home, finance and planning?

Kazi also had serious doubts about the contents of paragraph 7 (2) of chapter III, relating to the composition and powers of the Sikkim Assembly. According to this para, 'The Government of Sikkim *may* make rules for the purpose of providing that the

Assembly adequately represents various sections of the population
. . . no single section of the population is allowed to acquire a
dominating position in the affairs of Sikkim mainly by reason of
its ethnic origin.' Kazi said that this clause was being interpreted as
a subtle way to perpetuate the old parity system, for the removal of
which his party had been fighting for a long time. It was also the main
demand during the April 1973 agitations. From the clarifications
that Kazi sought, it appeared that some Sikkim Congress leaders
had been misled by the Chogyal's men into believing that the bill
did not provide enough powers to them and that the GoI was still
keeping its option open to strike a deal with the Chogyal.

I told Kazi that this constitution drew its validity from the
8 May agreement and hence had some limitations. Further, as
mentioned by Constitutional Adviser Rajagopal in his meeting
with the Sikkim Congress leaders on 25 May, this constitution
could be amended based on the experience gained through its
implementation. Regarding the post of prime minister, it was
explained that only independent countries have a prime minister
and that Sikkim was not an independent country. Further, if the
post of chief minister was created at that stage, he would come
directly under the Chogyal, and his party would not like that.
Similarly, the speaker from the party would have to work closely
with the Chogyal in summoning Assembly sessions and other
related matters. Regarding allocations of important portfolios
to executive councillors, he was told that the provisions of the 8
May agreement would have to be kept in mind while drafting this
constitution. Also, as long as the chief executive was the head of
the administration, he had to be assigned the important portfolios.

Regarding his doubts about paragraph 7 (2), I drew his
attention to the word 'may', which indicated that the provisions
of this sub-para were not mandatory. Regarding their powers to
remove the Chogyal, I told him that it would not be possible at

that stage, but if the party remained united and the Chogyal did not willingly accept the provisions of the new constitution, such a possibility could be considered in the future. I assured them that the GoI was fully supportive of their demands and activities. It was up to them to decide their goals and that they would always have our unstinted support in achieving those targets. However, those goals had to be realistic and fixed through the experience gained over a period.

As far as the possibility of New Delhi striking a deal with the Chogyal was concerned, I told them that there was no such plan and they could rest assured that as long as I was OSD (P), nothing of this sort could happen. Such vague references to the Chogyal's position had been deliberately kept in the draft constitution to keep him hoping that he could still recover some lost ground—this would give him reason to restrain himself and not create problems in getting the bill passed by the Assembly. In the end, I requested Kazi to meet Das again and request him to make some adjustments in the draft to accommodate his party's viewpoint before it was finally passed. (From the final version, it appeared that Das was able to accommodate some of Kazi's demands.) Kazi told me that they would be meeting the PO and Das early next morning with a letter seeking clarification on some of their doubts.

The next morning, at 7 a.m., I contacted the PO on the secraphone and told him that the Sikkim Congress leaders were expected to meet him around 11 a.m. to submit some documents in connection with the constitution bill. I met the PO at India House at 9 a.m. Without telling him about my meeting with Kazi and Khatiwada the previous night, I told him that the Sikkim Congress had some doubts about some portions of the bill, which needed to be explained so that they could counter the Chogyal's propaganda relating to these very points. I shared my views on these points with the PO. I also told him that at this critical stage, the Sikkim Congress leaders needed careful handling. If they were treated well, there should be no problem in getting the bill passed in the Assembly.

Bajpai was happy with this development but was of the view that if the army was alerted and made to move into the bazaar on the day the Assembly met, it would have a sobering influence on the vacillating Sikkim Congress leaders as well as the pro-Chogyal elements who were expected to create problems. I told him that this would be an extreme step that would cause panic in the minds of the people who were already reading meaning into the presence of the large number of CRPF men in the bazaar. Also, any deployment of the army on the day the Assembly met would give an impression that the bill was passed under duress. He said that the CRPF was limited. But I suggested that as the CRPF always had a reserve contingent, they could deploy all that reserve when needed. The army could, however, be alerted and kept in the barracks as a standby, ready to move in case of an emergency.

As there was information that the pro-Chogyal crowd, mainly comprising some officers and their family members, along with some students, would disrupt the Assembly session, Bajpai also felt that it would be helpful if some supporters of the Sikkim Congress were brought in from south and west Sikkim to Gangtok on the day the Assembly met to boost the morale of their leaders and also counter the pro-Chogyal demonstrators. I told him that as long as the attitude of the Sikkim Congress leadership was favourable, there was no need to bring men from outside the town. Further, there was always a danger of the two segments of demonstrators clashing with each other, thereby creating a bigger problem. However, if the Chogyal behaved strangely, the Sikkim Congress leaders could always bring their supporters to Gangtok at a couple of days' notice. We finally agreed not to use the army and pro-Sikkim Congress crowd on the day the Assembly met and let the CRPF handle the situation.

The document that was brought by Kazi to Bajpai at 11 a.m. on 18 June had the signatures of only eighteen Sikkim Congress leaders, as most of the Nepalese members had gone to see Das to seek clarifications. Early in the morning, I had told Murari about the possibility of these leaders meeting Das and informed him of my views on those points and requested him to convey these views to Das, before the Sikkim Congress leaders met him. Further, there was a need to be extremely diplomatic and polite in handling the Sikkim Congress leaders at the moment in view of the brainwashing that the Chogyal's men had been doing during the last few days. Further, care had to be taken that they were not given the impression that they had to pass the original draft constitution bill without making any changes. Also, they might be given some credit for the efforts made in studying the draft bill and coming up with suggestions. The rest should be left for the day the bill was presented in the Assembly.

Before the Assembly met on 20 June, a large pro-Chogyal crowd of about 2000 people moved towards the Assembly hall to prevent the session from starting. The CRPF had to resort to a lathi charge followed by lobbing tear-gas shells, resulting in injuries to some demonstrators. Finally, the crowd was dispersed, and the Assembly met in the evening with B.S. Das in the chair.[1] The members moved a number of amendments to the bill, which were duly noted. Das sent the constitution bill with suggested amendments to the Chogyal on 24 June and requested him to convene another session of the Assembly to consider the passage of the Government of Sikkim Bill, after considering the suggested amendments.

Das called the next session on 28 June to let the Assembly reconsider the bill, along with the amendments suggested by the members of the Assembly and objections raised by the Chogyal. The Assembly met again and passed the bill unanimously with some amendments, with the only opposition member, Kalzang Gyatso, absent.

The Chogyal told Das that he would like the Assembly to meet once again after his return from New Delhi, after he had presented his case before the prime minister. He called on the prime minister in New Delhi on 30 June 1974 and described the constitution bill as a violation of the treaty of 1950, the Sikkimese leaders as an unreliable lot, and himself as India's best friend. The developing situation in Sikkim would not be in India's long-term interests, he said. Indira Gandhi's response was brief. She said that he could not deride the chosen representatives of the people and that he should be going by their advice. Thereafter, she bade a cold farewell to the Chogyal with folded hands.

Kazi and his men were totally opposed to the calling of any more Assembly sessions to accommodate the Chogyal's wishes. I again requested Kazi through Myngma to accommodate the Chogyal's request so that later he did not say that he was not given a chance to present his case before the Assembly. Kazi agreed and the session was held on 3 July. As Kazi did not want the Chogyal to present his legal case personally to the Assembly, the note prepared by his legal adviser was read by Das on behalf of the Chogyal. The Chogyal's pleas were rejected by the Assembly, which reiterated its earlier stand on the bill. Foreign Secretary Kewal Singh reached Gangtok early the next morning (4 July), and at a meeting at the palace later that day, the Chogyal put his seal on the bill, which then became the Government of

Sikkim Act, 1974. Kazi described this as a red-letter day in the history of Sikkim.

A new constitution, as envisaged through the Government of Sikkim Act, 1974, was promulgated on 5 July, followed by the formation of a small five-member cabinet headed by Kazi as chief minister. Khatiwada was mysteriously kept out. Kazi explained through Myngma that it was done due to opposition from within the party.

Soon after, all thirty-one Sikkim Congress MLAs went to New Delhi to call on the prime minister, foreign minister and other high-ranking dignitaries.[2] Foreign Minister Sardar Swaran Singh described them as the 'founders of the democratic set-up' in Sikkim. On the last day of their stay, they called on Indira Gandhi. Kazi thanked the prime minister for all the help rendered by her to the Sikkimese people in fulfilling their democratic aspirations, and requested her to take follow-up action as per the Government of Sikkim Act, 1974. Thereafter, K.C. Pradhan also thanked her. Khatiwada told me on 15 April 2018 that when everyone had spoken, he stood up and asked Gandhi, 'Madam, how long do we have to tolerate this nuisance (Chogyal)?' Gandhi did not answer, but just smiled.[3] Addressing the Sikkimese delegation, she said that the main purpose behind India helping them was to support the 'unfolding of the new "great experiment" of democracy in Sikkim'. And now it was 'for the leaders and the people of Sikkim to visualize the kind of Sikkim that they want . . . India's "sympathy", "cooperation" and good "neighbourliness" would be offered to Sikkim and its new politicians to help with this endeavour.'

According to Khatiwada, within an hour or so of his returning to his room at The Ashoka Hotel, where all the Sikkim Congress MLAs were put up, Joint Secretary N.B. Menon came to his room and asked him to accompany him for some important meeting. Without telling Khatiwada anything, Menon took him to the prime minister's office, where Indira Gandhi, responding to Khatiwada's question from earlier that day, said, 'Don't worry, we have taken note of your query.'

Although Kazi had verbally requested Indira Gandhi to take follow-up action as per the provisions of the 1974 Act, I sent a written note to Kazi through Myngma, requesting him to put in a formal request to Das, with a copy to the PO, asking the GoI to urgently implement the provisions of the Government of Sikkim Act, especially relating to Sikkim's participation and representation in the political and economic institutions of India. As advised, Kazi submitted a written request in this respect to Das on 24 July. Kazi sent a reminder to Das on 12 August, requesting him to expedite action on his request.

Pursuant to the above request received by the GoI from Kazi through Das and the PO, a draft of the thirty-fifth Constitutional Amendment Bill, 1974, was circulated amongst members of the Indian parliament on 31 August 1974. The bill made provisions for associate status for Sikkim and the election of two members by its Assembly—one to the Rajya Sabha and another to the Lok Sabha.

The Constitution Amendment Bill was introduced in the Indian parliament on 2 September.[4] External Affairs Minister Sardar Swaran Singh, who moved the bill in the parliament, said that the Indian Constitution was a dynamic and living constitution. He said that the erstwhile Part A and B states had gone, and India was, more or less, a unified and integrated country. This could be achieved through amendment of the Constitution and wishes of the people. The Lok Sabha passed the bill on 4 September and the Rajya Sabha on 7 September, thereby granting Sikkim the status of an associate state of India.

As expected, there was some criticism from China and Pakistan. In Kathmandu, there were some student demonstrations against

India's action. The Nepalese foreign minister also made some critical remarks, which were toned down after the intervention of the local Indian Embassy. Other than the Calcutta-based *Statesman*, which was known for its pro-Chogyal stance, the rest of the Indian press was supportive.

On 11 September, the US Secretary of State Henry Kissinger sent a message to the US Embassy in New Delhi and some others.[5] It contained the following questions raised on Sikkim and the answers given by the US department of state's spokesman in a press conference on 9 September.

Q. What about the principle, though, of a large country taking over a smaller one?

A. I don't wish to comment on the affair between Sikkim and India here.

Q. Are you saying in effect [that] we are not concerned when a large country takes over a small one?

A. This is a very complicated parliamentary question that is being taken up in New Delhi, and I don't wish to comment on the merits of it. Nor on the deliberations of [the] national assembly of Sikkim.

I think you can read some of the details of that yourself.

In New Delhi, on 11 September, Joint Secretary Menon called the political counsellor from the US Embassy over to his office to inform him that 'the foreign ministry had noted with care with which the states department's spokesperson responded to questions about Sikkim on 9 September. The ministry wished to express appreciation for the sensitivity of the USG to GoI concerns on this issue.'[6]

Late in the evening of 24 July, we received the shocking news that my immediate boss, P.N. Banerjee, had died of a massive heart attack at a hotel in Dhaka during his clandestine visit to the capital city of Bangladesh. He had guided me during the initial period of my assignment in Gangtok. Over a period, he had developed confidence in my handling of the job, and in certain situations had given me the liberty to take action in anticipation of his approval.

Due to important developments taking place in the erstwhile East Pakistan, and thereafter in Sikkim, he continued to be the joint head of the IB and R&AW set-ups at Calcutta till his death, even after the IB's bifurcation in September 1968. He played a very significant role in launching some of the most sensitive operations relating to the liberation of Bangladesh, including the raising of the Mukti Bahini under Maj. Gen. Uban's (retd) leadership and building internal resistance against the Pakistani army. With his death, the thread that tied the IB and R&AW together in the eastern region was finally broken. The R&AW office there was taken over by Deputy Director Pranab Kumar Sen, and Deputy Director R.K. Mookerji became the head of the IB in Calcutta.

The perils of working in the R&AW can be judged from the fact that Banerjee was travelling to Bangladesh under an assumed name and his post-mortem had to be carried out in his real name to rule out the possibility of any foul play, and also for the release of pension for his family. Our man in Dhaka, C.N. Bhattacharya, had to pull many strings to get the job done before his mortal remains were quietly airlifted to Calcutta.

With Sikkim becoming an associate state, two significant changes happened with respect to our merger-related special operations.

PO Bajpai, who had spent over four years in Gangtok, was transferred to The Hague as India's ambassador. He left in September 1974. I stopped meeting the Chogyal as there was no reason or justification for the same.

It would, however, be highly unfair on my part to close this chapter without expressing my gratitude to PO Bajpai, and also noting the grace and equanimity exhibited by the Chogyal during my meetings with him. In addition to his good background, outstanding service record and other qualities, Bajpai was extremely hard-working person. I would get calls from him at odd hours, sometimes in the middle of the night, to clear some doubts.

The Chogyal considered Bajpai his nemesis, as he used to constantly give him trouble on one account or the other. Soon after he took charge in Gangtok in September 1971, Bajpai made New Delhi aware that the situation in Gangtok was not as hopeless as they had perceived. In fact, it was manageable to India's advantage, if New Delhi exhibited firmness and consistency in its approach towards him. Bajpai stood up to the Chogyal at a time when New Delhi was totally confused as to how to deal with him. He reversed the tide that was in the Chogyal's favour until then.

With time, I observed that Bajpai's and the Chogyal's health and happiness were interlinked but diametrically opposite. When one of them appeared happy, the other would lose his sleep and do his best to identify the reason for the smile on the other's face. With Bajpai, the immediate effect used to be an increase in the intake of antacid tablets, which he took liberally. Thereafter, he would call me to ascertain the facts behind his adversary's happiness. I am sure he must have been detailing his two first secretaries to ascertain the reasons for the same through their Sikkimese contacts.

The Chogyal seemed to have a better capacity to absorb those shocks, and with the passage of time, he had learnt to live with things. Although occasionally unfavourable events troubled him, which he drowned with heavy doses of alcohol, he seemed to have become reconciled to his fate. I saw him going through ups and downs. But one thing that needs to be mentioned is that even under the worst of circumstances and the gravest of provocations from the GoI, the Chogyal was extremely polite and gracious to me. However, keeping his past conduct in view, even under those circumstances I used to suspect that he might be up to some mischief. How else could a man be so polite and outwardly calm under the worst of circumstances? There were occasions when we used to feel sorry for him and sympathize with his lot. But we were aware of our limitations. We knew about his ultimate fate right from the beginning, but we were helpless. In fact, with some subdued guilt, we were the ones who were working to hasten his ultimate downfall. We could, however, rationalize our actions keeping in view the cause of the Sikkimese people and the larger interest of the nation.

During his four-year stay as PO in Gangtok, Bajpai suffered from three distinct disadvantages. Firstly, during T.N. Kaul's tenure as foreign secretary, he tried his best to convince the MEA, directly and through contacts with Haksar and Kao, that the situation in Gangtok was manageable and there was no need to give any concessions to the Chogyal beyond what had been granted through the 1950 treaty. Despite that, he had to go along with his boss Kaul's policy of offering permanent association status to Sikkim, which, to the Chogyal's misfortune, he refused to accept unconditionally.

Secondly, when India's policy towards the Chogyal was reversed during Kewal Singh's time as foreign secretary, his new boss, for security reasons, did not tell him that depending upon the response from his followers both inside and outside the popularly elected Assembly, Kazi could even go to the extent of seeking Sikkim's merger with India. It was mainly due to that

that Bajpai (and even B.S. Das) continued to follow India's old policy of backing the Chogyal, by making him adhere strictly to the terms of the 1950 treaty. That was also the reason why Bajpai and Das were planning to manage things so that the April 1974 elections produced a healthy opposition to the Kazi-led pro-democratic forces, in order to contain their democratic aspirations within acceptable limits. The need for Kazi's party securing a minimum two-thirds majority in the Sikkim Assembly to pass the constitution bill was, therefore, nowhere in their action plan. It was due to this dilemma that some of Bajpai's reporting before those elections attracted adverse comments from Kewal Singh.

Thirdly, unlike the Chogyal—who, due to his long association with most political leaders, knew how to handle each one of them and plant doubts in their minds that India was still negotiating with him behind their backs—Bajpai could not fully comprehend the true nature of the ever-shifting loyalties of some Sikkim Congress leaders and the R&AW's capacity to keep such characters on the designated track and securing the desired results. They would say different things to different people at different times and places to keep their options open. It was, therefore, difficult to understand as to where the loyalties of these vacillating characters lay. Insofar as the R&AW was concerned, in some cases these leaders were willing and even enthusiastic partners, while in some others we had to use all our resources to keep them on track. This made Bajpai apprehensive and insecure at times in carrying out Kewal Singh's instructions. Given my experience of working as ASP in Kanpur, additional SP in Agra, and finally as SP in Barabanki, I had some knowledge and experience of dealing with political figures of varying backgrounds. In addition, I had handled quite a few serious law-and-order problems in Uttar Pradesh. Both these experiences came in handy as OSD (P), Gangtok. It was mainly due to Bajpai's commitment to the cause and the way he treated me that we did whatever was possible to help him, without jeopardizing the operational aspect of our work. In emergencies, we did help Bajpai, mostly without his knowledge, as otherwise he would have increased his demands thereby exposing our contacts with various 'friends' from political parties. On important matters, we used to seek Banerjee's approval before carrying out the tasks assigned by Bajpai. In other cases, he would use his excellent relationship with my bosses Banerjee and Kao to get things done.

I have had the privilege of working in a couple of Indian missions abroad, where I enjoyed the cover of the local Indian mission. In Sikkim, I had a separate office but given the nature of my job, we worked as closely as possible with the PO. Over time, I discovered that the IFS had some of the finest officers who were chosen on the basis of their ranking in the merit list of the common competitive civil services examination. But unlike the All India Services officers (AIS), such as the IAS and IPS, who were given independent charge of district administrations in the fourth or fifth year of their service, the responsibility of an independent charge devolved rather late on the IFS officers. Therefore, AIS officers were better prepared to handle such situations, as we had to face in Sikkim, at a much younger age. Besides, working in an environment, like that in Sikkim, was a once in a lifetime experience for an IFS officer. For AIS officers, these were part of their normal duties. Kewal Singh had that advantage. Before shifting to the foreign office, he had worked in the field, including as deputy commissioner in charge of a district in Punjab, both undivided and post-independence.

A couple of times, Foreign Secretary Kewal Singh used the R&AW's online cypher communication for faster and real-time communication with Bajpai. These messages, which were critical of some of his actions, were to be personally handed to Bajpai by me. When Bajpai read those messages, I could see the pain on his face. He would inquire as to whether I had seen the contents. I would say that I could not help it, as these came to me soon after they were received and I had to personally put these in the envelope. But I often wondered if that was the way the head of an organization should be treating one of its most hard-working and dedicated officers, especially when he was having sleepless nights trying to handle a difficult situation to the best of his capabilities. Going by the standards of some other IFS officers, with whom I had the privilege of interacting later, he was head and shoulders above many of them. It would be relevant to mention here that within days of sending these unpleasant messages to Bajpai through us, Kewal Singh would send letters of appreciation to him for a certain job well done. I had seen a couple of these letters with Bajpai during my meeting with him on 19 April 2018. Bajpai enjoyed an excellent relationship with Banerjee and Kao. According to Bajpai, the biggest compliment that Kao paid him was when he went to visit him at The Hague on his return journey from London. Kao told him that 'he was badly missed' in Gangtok during the period leading up to the merger of Sikkim.

I am grateful to Bajpai for keeping me posted about information on crucial developments, which he acquired through frequent meetings with members of various political parties and senior officers from the Chogyal's set-up, and sometimes from the Chogyal himself. Without this input, the implementation of certain aspects of the second phase of the R&AW's spl ops would not have been that smooth. This became evident to me when his replacement, Gurbachan Singh, joined in September 1974, a couple of months after Sikkim became an associate state in July 1974. This issue will be discussed later in the book.

After offering my comments on the IFS officers, it would be unfair not to say anything about the AIS officers like me. For AIS officers, things started changing after the declaration of the

Emergency by Indira Gandhi in 1975, after which most of the institutions started crumbling. Even before that, the success of a civil servant was to some extent linked to the flexibility of his spinal cord. But there used to be a limit up to which the majority of them would bend. During the Emergency and the years that followed, a large number of civil servants started taking cover under the safety of the political umbrella by becoming a willing tool in the hands of their political masters. Conformity and pliability, rather than professional competence and compliance of service rules, procedures and the law became the yardstick for success. With the honourable exceptions of some diehards who continued to carry their services' flags high under the worst of circumstances, and to the detriment of their health and family life, a large number of AIS officers gradually became victims of the changing culture until such conduct became the norm. In that respect, in the fast-changing services environment, I considered myself lucky that I did not have to work in my state cadre for long and opted to join the R&AW, where there was little scope for political interference.

Chapter XII

Moves towards a Merger

The passage of the Government of Sikkim Act, 1974, was a significant milestone in the history of Sikkim. Though the Chogyal by then was convinced that India would not be satisfied with this halfway measure, nobody else, including Das and Bajpai, had thought that India would place so much trust in the Kazi-led Sikkim Congress as to totally demolish a time-tested regime that had served its strategic interests so well in this sensitive area since Independence in 1947. This belief was mainly based on the fact that the provisions of the Government of Sikkim Act, which granted Sikkim the status of an associate state, went much beyond what India was willing to give to the Chogyal through the offer of permanent association. In view of that, it was generally felt that a chastened Chogyal, with his powers significantly curtailed through a new constitution, would serve India's security interests better. But keeping in mind his past behaviour, it was felt at the highest level in India that the Chogyal could no longer be trusted. For that matter, associate status was just halfway to the final destination of merger. But as mentioned earlier, this secret was kept closely guarded till the very end.

From an operational point of view, the situation in Gangtok, in the aftermath of Sikkim becoming an associate state, can be summed up as follows:

a) The centre of activity had shifted from India House to Das's successor, B.B. Lal, who had to deal with the Sikkim Congress leaders on the one hand and the Chogyal, who was desperately fighting his last battle for survival, on the other.

b) Earlier, the Chogyal was the target of the Sikkim Congress's criticism with all the ills being attributed to him. But under the changed environment, the responsibility of satisfying the demands and requirements of the new government fell on Lal.

c) Contrary to the earlier situation when Kewal Singh could tell the Sikkim Congress leaders that the Chogyal was not cooperating and hence their demands could not be met, it was now for the Chogyal and his men to quietly tell the Sikkim Congress leaders that it was Lal who was not sensitive enough to the demands of the popularly elected government.

d) Unlike his predecessor, PO Gurbachan Singh had no direct role to play in the political developments in Gangtok.

It was against this background that the R&AW's spl ops entered their third and last stage. Our job during this phase was to wait for instructions from Kao, get a resolution on the merger of Sikkim with India passed in the Assembly with the maximum possible support, but not less than two-thirds of the House voting in favour of it. For this, we had to continue our efforts to keep Kazi's flock solidly behind him by neutralizing the impact of the Chogyal's divisive activities on the members of the Sikkim Congress legislative party. Kazi knew that the process of Sikkim's merger, through a resolution in the Assembly, had to be expedited before the Chogyal could succeed in weaning away some of his partymen in the Assembly. For this, he needed a suitable occasion or pretext to galvanize his party's legislative members behind him before the Assembly was called for passing the merger resolution. Though overwhelmed by the pace and scope of recent developments in Sikkim, the Chogyal did not give up. He redoubled his efforts for creating dissensions within the Sikkim Congress to sabotage the expected merger-related resolution in the Assembly, thereby discrediting Kazi and his men in the eyes of the Indian government as an undependable lot.

For our spl ops-related work in the post-associate state period, the environment had also changed significantly. Kazi became chief minister and some other Sikkim Congress 'friends' became ministers. Most of the time, they were surrounded by their followers and favour-seekers, and their meetings with members of our operational team, in a small place like Gangtok, became difficult without being noticed. PO Bajpai and Chief Executive Das were replaced by Gurbachan Singh and B.B. Lal, respectively. With the Chogyal having no role to play with respect to my real work, there was no reason for me to seek any more meetings with him. That might have also sent a signal to him that insofar as the cabinet secretariat and prime minister were concerned, he had lost relevance.

As far as Bajpai was concerned, the policy that the MEA had followed towards the Chogyal till September 1972 was still fresh in his mind. He thought that the GoI may not go all the way to merge Sikkim within the country. But it was during his tenure as PO that India was able to bring Sikkim much closer as an associate state, with its representation in Indian parliament. He had already spent four years, as compared to the usual tenure of two years, at this 'hardship' posting that saw intense and hectic political developments. Such a long tenure could have taken a toll on anybody's health. It was time for him to move on to a place where he could get a much-deserved rest. Keeping that in view, in September 1974, Bajpai was posted as India's ambassador to The Hague.

B.S. Das, who had spent only seventeen months on his job, thought that as his 'task had been completed it was time for him to leave'. Das left Gangtok on 19 September 1974 to join as chairman, International Airport Authority of India (IAAI). After handing over charge in Sikkim, Das did check with Kewal Singh as to whether a merger was the next step but could not get a clear answer.[1] The only indication that Singh gave him was that 'it had to be a political solution dependent on the will of the Sikkimese people'.

Das's successor, Lal, was an ICS officer from the same batch as the Chogyal—they had received part of their training together. He was an experienced officer who had served as chief secretary in India's biggest state—Uttar Pradesh—and thereafter as secretary to the Planning Commission of India. The Chogyal was left with the charge of only the palace establishment and the Sikkim Guards. Lal held the other important portfolios.

Though Das, much to his disappointment, did not get anything of interest from me, we used to meet occasionally at local parties and official functions. A charming lady, his wife was a gracious host. I attended quite a few lunches and dinners at his residence. On some occasions, Das did share useful information with me. Unlike Das, Lal, who had handled important assignments in India, generally remained aloof. In his interaction with persons of my rank (he was chief secretary in UP when I was serving in the cadre. But I was too junior to be known to him), he had a stiff upper lip. Being a widower and a teetotaller, parties at Mintokgang—the official residence of the erstwhile diwans and later the chief executive—reduced in frequency and to some extent in popularity with an obvious watch over the consumption of liquor.

Gurbachan Singh belonged to an illustrious Sikh family from west Punjab (now Pakistan). He was briefly joint secretary (liaison) with the R&AW immediately before his posting to Gangtok. I soon found that Singh had one thing in common with Bajpai. Both were extremely good hosts and served excellent food. Everyone, especially the locals who loved abundant free rounds of Scotch, used to look forward to attending their parties. But there was one difference. Bajpai would not allow his wife, Meera, to enter the kitchen and would cook some of the delicacies himself if he really wanted to please his guests. Gurbachan Singh, on the other hand, would leave it to his wife, Shyama, who was an outstanding cook and hostess.

Keeping his background in mind, I thought my relations with Singh would be productive for both of us, as was the case with Bajpai. But that was not to be. With his arrival, my interaction with the PO completely stopped. In my very few meetings with him, in connection with some official work, I found him to be extremely cagey with an enigmatic smile on his face. Also, he did not want to prolong the meetings, lest I may say something about the prevailing political situation. My impression during those meetings was that he knew something that he did not want to share with me. Very soon, I started suspecting that maybe Kewal Singh had told him in confidence about our final goal of merger and he wanted to keep that a secret from me. Maybe his short stint as JS (L) in the R&AW had made him aware of the 'need to know' policy, which he was using on me.

The mystery around Singh's silence was recently solved by Ranjit Gupta (Devare's successor), another of my batchmates and a friend who had served as first secretary, both with Bajpai and Singh, during that period.[2] When I met him at the local Gymkhana Club recently, I asked him about the reason behind Singh's silence. According to Gupta, Bajpai used to proactively communicate all the developments of interest in Sikkim to the JS (N) of the MEA or Kewal Singh. Bajpai would give his opinion on every issue, especially about the activities of the Chogyal or his protégés in hampering the activities of the Sikkim Congress leaders, which was not always to the liking of the ministry. On the other hand, Singh communicated with the JS (N) or Kewal Singh only when it was absolutely necessary. Rather than prodding the ministry to react to his communications on various issues, as was the case with Bajpai, Gurbachan Singh waited for instructions to act. Under such circumstances, Singh might have felt that there was no use talking to me about the developments of interest in Sikkim, lest he might have to report those to the ministry after verifying what I had told him. He might have also felt that information originating from me would ultimately reach the foreign office through Kao, and if they had any instructions on that, he would hear from Kewal Singh in due course.

With the posting of B.B. Lal as chief executive and Gurbachan Singh as PO, the equations between them, and also the Chogyal, changed considerably. Though belonging to two different services, B.S. Das was a couple of years Bajpai's senior in terms of service and age. Also, when Das joined as chief executive on 10 April 1973, the Chogyal still enjoyed all the powers on paper. Most of his confrontations used to be primarily with Bajpai. Further, Bajpai had been there as PO for almost three years before Das came to Sikkim. It was Bajpai who was in the driving seat in this triangular relationship, both in terms of experience as well as the PO. On the other hand, Lal as a former ICS officer was very senior to Gurbachan Singh. Also, the Government of Sikkim Act had made the post of the chief executive the fulcrum of the new administrative set-up. Further, compared to the POs during the earlier periods, the Chogyal now was in direct confrontation with Lal. Their differences, which were many, were referred to New Delhi through PO Gurbachan Singh, to which Singh seemed to have happily reconciled. Further, the Sikkim Congress leaders were in power now. Their main interaction was confined to Lal. In that new arrangement, there was no scope for the Sikkim Congress leaders to meet Gurbachan Singh. In fact, any such meeting would not have been taken kindly by Lal. It was also possible that Kewal Singh might have told Gurbachan Singh to let Lal handle the situation in Sikkim, including the Chogyal. But under the changed scenario, Lal became fully responsible for satisfying the demands of the Sikkim Congress leaders. He was held directly responsible by them for shortcomings, if any, in that respect.

With the Chogyal powerless but desperate to salvage some of his lost prestige and power, the new PO clammed up, B.B. Lal of no use operationally, the Sikkim Congress leaders enjoying their new-found perks and power, and the IB not sharing intelligence inputs with us as usual, our spl ops team had to devise new ways of trying to keep tabs on developments of interest in Gangtok. So far as my spl ops-related work was concerned, the lack of information from the PO was compensated to some extent by the opening of another channel. On Kazi assuming charge as chief minister, my IAS batchmate Murari, who was posted in April 1973 as OSD in-charge of the east and north districts with Gangtok as headquarters, was assigned the job of secretary to the chief minister. In his new avatar, he had access to Kazi and most of the senior

Sikkim Congress leaders, some of whom had become ministers in the cabinet, on a day-to-day basis. From him, I was able to get a lot of information that helped us to monitor the activities of the Sikkim Congress leaders from time to time. There was, however, one problem with that. In the case of Bajpai, the information was shared by him with me within the actionable time frame, allowing us to take remedial measures as and when required. In Murari's case, we used to meet at parties only, which though fairly frequent were not held daily. Therefore, information received through him was sometimes late and hence used to lose its relevance. Kazi had no dearth of official help. Therefore, there was no further need for us to send draft letters, memos or resolutions to him, which had come in handy for him in the past. To compensate for this loss of intelligence avenues, Padam Bahadur was asked to increase the frequency of his meetings with 'friends' like C.S. Rai, S.K. Rai and sometimes the maverick and mercurial K.C. Pradhan, without bothering too much about his cover. Myngma had to frequently carry my messages to or from our 'friends', including Kazi.

Our main focus during this period continued to be to keep a close watch over the activities of the Sikkim Congress leadership and the Chogyal's efforts to create differences amongst them. For the Chogyal, it was the most crucial moment for his dynasty's survival as a ruling class. He was desperately in need of enlisting the support of the vacillating and disgruntled Sikkim Congress leaders of questionable loyalty to Kazi. These included K.C. Pradhan and B.B. Gurung, who tried to sabotage Kazi's move for getting a merger-related resolution passed in the Assembly. For the Chogyal, that was also the last opportunity to discredit the Sikkim Congress in the eyes of Indira Gandhi and make her think of a course correction by reverting to her old policy of reposing full faith in him. In his desperation, he even tried to use the Kazini (an incident covered later in this chapter) to further his interests.

Our three-member team had a strategy session sometime in the third week of December 1974 to work out a plan of action to deal with the issues mentioned above. It was felt that we could not do anything to prevent the Chogyal from indulging in his self-preserving divisive activities, aimed at splitting and discrediting the Sikkim Congress. We could, however, keep a close watch over such divisive activities and take suitable action to contain, if not neutralize, their impact on the unity and credibility of the Sikkim Congress.

We divided the Sikkim Congress legislative members into three categories—Nepalese, Lepchas and Bhutias—and assessed each group's chance of being infiltrated and won over by the Chogyal. We felt that the Lepchas, being a minority which had been exploited by the Bhutias over the years to build their numbers against the ever-increasing Nepalese population, had realized that they had nothing to lose but a lot to gain if they threw in their lot with the GoI and let it decide their future. Also, Kazi was a Lepcha himself and had inducted Rinzing Lepcha, one of our close 'friends' who enjoyed support from the rest of the Lepcha MLAs. The lone Bhutia minister in Kazi's cabinet, Dorji Tshering, was also a Kazi loyalist and was not expected to go against him as and when the time came to pass the merger resolution. Also, the majority of the Bhutias were still economically, socially and educationally backward. The power and prosperity amongst the Bhutias was limited to a thin upper crust. In view of that, in the April 1974 elections, they had taken a conscious decision to split their votes equally amongst the Sikkim Congress and the pro-Chogyal candidates.

It was the Nepalese group, comprising sixteen of the thirty-two MLAs, which was a cause of concern for us. K.C. Pradhan was the most difficult of them. He had a well-known past connection with the Chogyal, which could be revived as and when the interests of the two coincided. He was ambitious and wanted to replace Kazi as the chief minister. He also did not like being denied (at our instance), the post of deputy leader of the Sikkim Congress legislative party, which he could have used as a natural stepping stone to fulfil his ambitions. B.B. Gurung was not happy at his exclusion from Kazi's cabinet despite his seniority. He was still maintaining clandestine contact with the Chogyal and his men. Khatiwada had played a major role in mobilizing large crowds for the April 1973 anti-Chogyal agitations and, therefore, expected to be rewarded with some post of responsibility in the new political dispensation. Having failed to secure any such thing, he too was sulking. Meanwhile, he had also fallen out of favour with the Kazini. His place in the Kazi household was taken over by other younger Nepalese leaders. We, therefore, felt that the combined impact of this group could have serious implications for the unity of the Sikkim Congress and could hamper our plans to see the merger resolution passed in the Assembly with a comfortable majority.

We considered various options as to how each of these three leaders could be handled. Pradhan, though well known to Padam Bahadur, was a stubborn customer. Where his own political ambitions were concerned, he might not listen to Padam Bahadur. On a couple of occasions in the past, we were able to bring him around through S.K. Rai, general secretary of the Sikkim Congress and a co-founder of the Janata Congress. It was decided that we would keep this option open in case Pradhan did not listen to Padam Bahadur. Gurung was always known to play a double game by keeping his line open with the Chogyal. With Kazi keeping him out of the cabinet, our scope of manoeuvrability with him had reduced considerably. We felt that we should watch his activities through other dependable friends in the party. If needed, I could meet him and have a frank talk to tell him that all this time we were aware of his secret link with the Chogyal but had overlooked it thinking that he would take time to sever old connections. It would be in his interest to cut off with the Chogyal now and extend unstinted support to Kazi. It was also felt that he should be told that by closely aligning with Pradhan, he was spoiling his own political future. Further, given his seniority, he was Kazi's natural successor. Also, he was an obvious claimant for a cabinet post as and when a vacancy occurred or the cabinet was expanded. He could also become a member of the Indian parliament when the party decided its candidate for that. It was felt that till I met Gurung again such messages should be sent to him through Myngma so as to make him cautious of the risks involved in his continued association with Pradhan.

Regarding Khatiwada, we felt that he was too shrewd and ambitious a person to burn his bridges with India. Sikkim was too small a place for a person of his ambitions and capabilities. He had his eyes on becoming a member of the Indian parliament, which could enable him to play the role of a national-level Gurkha leader. When he came to my residence with Kazi on 17 June 1974 to discuss the draft constitution bill, Khatiwada did express his desire to become a MP, as provided in the bill. Despite his tiff with the Kazini and exclusion from Kazi's cabinet, we were confident that he would continue to support pro-India moves in the Assembly and could again muster anti-Chogyal crowds from south and west Sikkim if required.

In the third week of January 1975, I had to visit New Delhi in connection with some personal work. As P.N. Banerjee was no more and Deputy Director P.K. Sen was not in a position to provide the requisite guidance at that stage, I sought a meeting with Kao during my stay in New Delhi. I met him on 23 January 1975 and informed him about the limitations under which our team was working and also about the strategy devised by our three-man team in the third week of December 1974. He was in agreement with our plan of action, but advised me to discuss it with 'Kazi Sahib' and seek his guidance on the proposed action plan, which I did soon after my arrival in Gangtok.

B.B. Lal did not take time to settle down in his job. He started cutting the Chogyal down to size, thereby conveying a message to the Sikkimese people about the shift in the power equation. The Chogyal's personal and family's financial support was significantly reduced to ensure that he did not misuse these funds in winning over Sikkim Congress leaders of dubious loyalty. The name of his family linked with various institutions was also removed.

While Lal was busy eroding the Chogyal's former power base, an opportunity which Kazi was looking for to revitalize his party and strengthen his hold over the members of the Assembly came in the form of a personal invitation received by the Chogyal on 12 January. This was from King Birendra of Nepal to attend his coronation ceremony on 24 February 1975. Kazi and his men did not approve of this visit. They felt that with Sikkim now having a chief minister and the Chogyal being reduced to a figurehead, the latter had no justification to represent Sikkim at the coronation ceremony. Initially, the Chogyal was in two minds, but finally decided to accept the invitation. Maybe he thought that the occasion would provide him with much-needed publicity that might help stall the GoI's efforts towards moving the merger resolution. If nothing else, he would attract the sympathy of the foreign dignitaries there. Even though Lal had conveyed the Sikkim government's disapproval of this visit and warned him of the likely consequences he might have to face if he visited Nepal, the Chogyal left for Kathmandu on 21 February amid protests by Sikkim Congress party workers.

Kazi, who knew that it would be difficult to dissuade the Chogyal from going to Kathmandu, had asked some of his youth congress leaders to arrange a token protest on the way to try and stop him from leaving Sikkim. The Chogyal's car was stopped at Singtam, with demonstrators shouting anti-Chogyal slogans. In the stone pelting that followed, the windscreen of his Mercedes car was slightly damaged. Following a circuitous route via Kalimpong, the Chogyal reached Kathmandu late in the evening.

In Kathmandu, the Chogyal met a number of foreign guests and told them what had happened on his way to Kathmandu. Prominent amongst those he met were Lord Mountbatten, Senator Charles Percy, the Pakistani ambassador and the Chinese Vice Foreign Minister, Chin-Hsi Liu. According to Indian intelligence reports from Kathmandu, he even sought help from both the Pakistani Ambassador and the Chinese Vice Foreign Minister. They reportedly promised help if he could get the issue raised at the UN. With King Birendra, he had a longish meeting.

The Chogyal even went to the extent of calling a press conference in Kathmandu on 1 March, where he said, 'We want to achieve separate identity, want to preserve our identity and international status. We have informed the GoI both orally and in writing about this.' He questioned the constitutionality of the Government of Sikkim Act and added that there was no responsible government in the state. He also alleged that a bomb or grenade had been thrown at his car while he was leaving his state. On the question of whether he would approach the UN, he said, 'We will leave no stone unturned.' He also demanded a free and fair referendum to decide the fate of Sikkim.

The Chogyal's remarks at the press conference in Kathmandu, especially those questioning the constitutionality of the government in Sikkim, attracted an adverse reaction from the Sikkim Congress leaders. The party's general secretary, S.K. Rai, exhorted people to receive the Chogyal on his return with 'full-throated anti-Chogyal demonstrations'.

Despite King Birendra's advice to stay back till things normalized, the Chogyal left for Calcutta by air and called another press conference there, in which he reiterated the opinions he had voiced in Kathmandu. However, the Indian press did not take his outburst very kindly. It also gave Kazi an occasion to attack the Chogyal. Kazi described it as an indication of a complete breakdown of trust between his government and the Chogyal.

On his return journey, the Chogyal faced hostile demonstrators at Rangpo bridge. The bridge was blocked and the demonstrators, led by Youth Congress leader R.C. Poudyal, were shouting slogans such as 'Chogyal, Go Back'. In the scuffle that followed between Capt. Yongda of the Sikkim Guards and Poudyal, the latter was injured, which further infuriated the crowd. The Chogyal's convoy somehow managed to cross the bridge with the help of the West Bengal police, which had escorted the convoy from Calcutta.

Anti-Chogyal sentiments were sufficiently whipped up on this issue and Kazi felt it was the right time to introduce the merger-related resolution in the Assembly. However, the Chogyal's last-ditch efforts to sow seeds of discord in the minds of some Sikkim Congress legislative party members seemed to have started bearing fruit. Some of them, especially K.C. Pradhan, B.B. Gurung and their friends, started having second thoughts about the need to remove the Chogyal without someone from their own ranks taking the place as head of state. Kazi needed more time to discipline such elements.

It was during that period that around midnight on 10 March 1975, I got a call from PO Gurbachan Singh to reach India House immediately. Singh had called an emergency meeting that was attended by his two first secretaries Ranjit Gupta and Gurdip Singh Bedi, Chief Executive B.B. Lal and his three IAS officers—Murari, Jayant Sanyal and Devi Manavalan, and me. Singh told us that earlier during the evening, the Chogyal's elder son, Tenzing, had met Kazi. The meeting had apparently been arranged by the Kazini. I had no information about this. Everyone was concerned that if the two decided to join hands, it would be a great setback to India's interests. Something had to be done to undo the damage caused by this meeting and also to ensure that no such further meetings happened. Preventing future meetings was Lal's job, but I had to solve the mystery of this sudden and unexpected development as soon as possible.

That even such tense situations could produce some interesting asides became evident during the course of the meeting. It was past midnight, and the effect of liquor on some of those who liked their evening drinks had not fully worn off. I could also see signs of sleep in the eyes of some. The chairs were placed in a U-shaped formation so that everyone could see and hear everyone else. Gurbachan Singh, with B.B. Lal on his right, was sitting in the centre. Ranjit Gupta was sitting on Lal's right and I was sitting on Gupta's right. Halfway through the discussions, Gupta started shouting at me, using the choicest words, just short of abusing me. Taken aback by this behaviour, I asked Jayant Sanyal, who was sitting on my right, as to whether Gupta was actually shouting at me. Jayant said that it appeared to be so, but he did not know the reason why. Thereafter, I told Gupta to keep quiet and be prepared to face the music when we moved out of the room. To make it brief, I uttered these words softly and in simple Hindi. Soon after the meeting was over, Gupta came apologizing profusely and told me that all that was actually for Lal, and that Lal was aware of that. According to Gupta, while he was giving his views on the issue, Lal in a low tone has asked him to shut up. Gupta said that Lal and his father, IPS officer Anand Swarup Gupta, were both from the UP cadre and did not enjoy cordial relations. As a result, Gupta felt he was being targeted by Lal.

With regard to Tenzing's meeting with Kazi on 10 March, it was alleged that it was brokered by the Kazini as Lal 'had refused to countenance the idea of an elected head of state, she realized the implications. She had spent years lampooning Thondup from Kalimpong, but retaining him as the Chogyal might be the only safeguard to ensure that her husband remained a big fish in the small Sikkimese pond.'

In that context, prodded by the Kazini, 'Kazi offered Tenzing a deal.[3] He laid down three conditions; if the Chogyal explicitly accepted the 1974 elections, recognized that the Sikkim Congress should therefore be (the) party in power and confirmed the Kazi himself in office, then—and only then—could the two men work together. He would accept the Chogyal had a continued role as a—limited—constitutional monarch. If Tenzing could agree, the Kazi said he would approach New Delhi to get them to rethink the situation.' Tenzing readily agreed to these conditions and promised to return the next evening. Oblivious of the developments since he left Kazi's house, Tenzing returned the following evening with his father's approval. The CRPF guards, who were duly alerted by then, denied Tenzing access to Kazi. He left a disappointed man.

We, however, could not believe that Kazi could allow the Kazini to broker such a deal with the Chogyal through Tenzing, that too behind our backs. Therefore, first thing on the morning of 11 April, I called Myngma and asked him to fix a meeting with Kazi immediately. In doing so, I risked blowing my cover, as we could not wait any longer to seek Kazi's views on that. We were also worried as to how Kao would react to such news when he heard about it from Kewal Singh without any input from us. Therefore, we wanted to send a message to Kao on this development before he heard it from Kewal Singh. I reached Kazi's residence around 8 a.m. in full view of the CRPF guards. Kazi knew the purpose of my visit and was smiling. Without me asking any question, Kazi told me that the drama was the creation of the Kazini's fertile mind as she was fond of playing her own little games and that we should not take her too seriously. Besides, as the Chogyal had given them a lot of trouble in the past, it was now their turn to make him dance to their tune.

I told Kazi that such activities could create confusion in the minds of his partymen, who could be exploited by the Chogyal. Kazi agreed and promised to caution the Kazini suitably. I also mentioned that he had to be watchful of the activities of people like K.C. Pradhan and B.B. Gurung, and some of their close friends who could create problems for him when he introduced the resolution on merger in the Assembly. With an enigmatic smile, Kazi said that he was aware of that and might be able to find a solution to this problem soon. For a change, he did not tell me as to how he was going to do so. Since I too was in a hurry to return to my office, I did not ask Kazi for the details of his plan.

Back in office, I sent Kao a message to inform him about the previous night's meeting at India House and the outcome of my visit to Kazi. As the message was sent through online cypher communication, I was confident that Kao would have received my message before hearing about it from Kewal Singh.

What was going on in the Kazini's mind when she decided to broker Tenzing's meeting with Kazi? I have not been able to solve this puzzle completely so far. The Kazini was a very shrewd and intelligent person. But while pursuing her little games, she was fully conscious of her limitations insofar as the GoI's interests in Sikkim were concerned. That was perhaps one of the reasons that in Kazi's proposal to the Chogyal, which was obviously drafted by the Kazini, it was specifically mentioned that if the Chogyal agreed to Kazi's proposal, the matter could be taken up with New Delhi for final approval.

We also felt that this move could have been the result of B.B. Lal's strict handling of the Sikkim Congress leaders, including Kazi. Maybe Kazi wanted to convey to Lal that he could not be taken for granted. Not long before this incident, I had attended a party where the Kazini was also present. Finding her standing alone, I went up to her and asked how things were going. To my surprise, she said, 'The father-in-law is acting difficult.' When I asked who this father-in-law was, the Kazini, with mischief in her wide, greenish-blue eyes lined with black mascara, whispered, 'Mr Sidhu, don't you know? Obviously, B.B. Lal.' As someone else came and joined us, the conversation could not proceed further. The Kazini's remarks conveyed that Lal was still behaving like the chief secretary of Uttar Pradesh and was considering the newly appointed cabinet ministers as his junior civil servants. I had already heard about his strict behaviour from the others, but I felt that as Kazi was an experienced person with hardly any ego, he would not go to that extent just to spite Lal. So, this line of thinking too was discounted.

Another thing that came to my mind was whether all that happened on the night of 10 March was Kazi's calculated plan to discredit K.C. Pradhan in the eyes of the Indian government. Incidentally, Kazi had dropped a hint about this to me on the morning of 11 March. Kazi had been directly involved in the political movement of Sikkim even before India's independence. To seek Sikkim's merger with India had been his ambition. He was so close to it and did not want to waste this opportunity due to the Chogyal's divisive activities, which appeared to be bearing fruit finally. He was suspicious of some of his colleagues, especially Pradhan, Gurung and associates, and was not totally confident of their support as and when the merger resolution was introduced in the Assembly. If that was so, Kazi wanted to kill two birds with this stone. Firstly, he wanted to convey to the Chogyal how their roles had reversed during this period. Rather than being hounded, as was the case in the past, he was now in a position to oblige the Chogyal and had the right access to New Delhi to put in a word to save the Chogyal's position. Secondly, by floating the idea of a likely compromise with the Chogyal, Kazi wanted to know how many of his partymen would willingly come out in support of this move and how far they were willing to accommodate the Chogyal's continued relevance in Sikkim. This could then help Kazi to expose, isolate and neutralize the leaders of this group before the merger resolution was introduced. None of us, including Gurbachan Singh and B.B. Lal, could understand the real intent of this master stroke. But this was the way things turned out finally.

Following Kazi's adventure of 10 March, I told Padam Bahadur to meet his friends C.S. Rai and S.K. Rai on 12 March to see what they felt about Kazi's meeting with Tenzing. Myngma also carried

my message to B.B. Gurung the same evening, reiterating my
earlier message about the need for him to keep a safe distance from
Pradhan and his anti-party activities. Gurung was specifically told
that this was the time he should be expecting to be inducted into the
cabinet. Similarly, Myngma was also told to meet Rinzing Lepcha
to convey my message to keep a watch over the developments in
this respect. Both Padam Bahadur and Myngma came back with
the news that Pradhan had already met Kazi and was collecting
signatures from the party's legislative members on a memo that he
wanted to send to New Delhi. They said that the memo supported
Kazi's move for some sort of a compromise with the Chogyal and
a reduction in the role of the chief executive and other Indian civil
servants posted in Sikkim. As Pradhan had said that the memo
was prepared with prior approval from Kazi, quite a few Assembly
members, including Rinzing, had already signed it.

I did not feel the need to meet Kazi again, but I asked Padam
Bahadur to meet Pradhan early on 13 March and firmly tell him
that the GoI was extremely serious this time. India would never
let the Chogyal regain lost ground. Such activities as were being
pursued by him and his friends would be suitably dealt with.
Therefore, it would be in his interest to stop indulging in such
activities. He also told Pradhan that he had a bright political
future, which he should not tarnish. Pradhan understood the
logic but it appeared to be too late for him to retrace his steps.
With Pradhan trapped in his own net, Kazi called a meeting of
the Sikkim Congress Working Committee on 16 March. Here,
he moved a resolution in which the role of some persons (Pradhan
and company) in preparing the 12 March 'illegal' document in an
unauthorized manner was criticized. The Chogyal and his agents
were blamed for trying to divide and discredit the popularly elected
government. The Chogyal was also accused of inciting some party
legislators to attend the unauthorized meeting of 12 March, in

which some legislators were misled into signing an unauthorized document. Pradhan was later forced to resign from his post of minister for agriculture. This resolution sent out the message that if a person of Pradhan's standing could be so unceremoniously eased out of the cabinet, the others had better not nurse any pro-Chogyal sympathies.

Chapter XIII

The Merger

With the Chogyal failing to strike a deal with Kazi through his eldest son, Tenzing, and the dissident group within the Sikkim Congress led by K.C. Pradhan having been marginalized, Kazi was now ready to move a resolution in the Assembly, demanding the merger of Sikkim with India. He wanted to do that as early as possible, as a delay might lead to erosion of the anti-Chogyal feelings that were a result of his visit to Nepal and also the impact of his shrewd move to neutralize dissident activity of the Pradhan-led group from within his legislative party. On 2 April, we received a message from Kao to seek Kazi's views on the desirability of holding a referendum to seek public approval of his merger-related resolution, as and when it was passed in the Assembly. Thereafter, I had a brief meeting with Kazi. He had no objection to that and was confident that his party would be able to get almost the same number of votes in the referendum favouring their resolutions as they had received during the April 1974 elections. I also mentioned to Kazi that it would be a good idea if his party could bring a few thousand supporters from south and west Sikkim to Gangtok on the day the Assembly met, as that would act as a morale booster for the legislators. Kazi readily agreed.

By the first week of April 1975, Murari, who was secretary to the chief minister, and the three-member spl ops team of the

R&AW were of the view that Kazi should have no problem in getting the merger-related resolutions passed in the Assembly with the requisite majority. Even Ranjit Gupta felt that way. But none of them were aware that the Sikkim Guards could be disarmed a day before the Assembly met to take up these resolutions. However, as revealed by Gupta recently, the atmosphere in the Political Office was a bit tense and there were apprehensions as to what would be the reaction of the Chogyal and his time-tested loyalists from the Sikkim Guards when they came to know about the passage of the merger-related resolutions, including the removal of the Chogyal. It was also felt that an extreme reaction from the Chogyal and/or the Sikkim Guards could necessitate the use of the Indian army to control the situation, resulting in possible physical harm to the Chogyal and others in the palace.

It was against this background that Kewal Singh landed in Gangtok on 4 April on a two-day visit. The same day, I also received a message from Kao that a three-member team of senior R&AW officers from the headquarters, led by an old IB hand known for the role he played in Jammu and Kashmir, Col (retd) Ijwant Singh Hasanwalia, along with some equipment, was reaching Bagdogra airport by a special flight on 5 April. Kewal Singh's sudden arrival and the news about the R&AW team coming left us in no doubt that New Delhi had finally decided to give Kazi the green signal to call an Assembly session and move the resolution regarding the merger of Sikkim with India.

The R&AW team comprising Hasanwalia, IPS officers Shivraj Bahadur and M.S. Bhatnagar (who retired as DGP, Haryana), along with some others, were received at Bagdogra airport on

5 April and brought straight to our office around 7.30 p.m. As requested by me, a team of two technical officers headed by Dildar Singh, with the amateur radio frequency jamming equipment, also came with them. The jamming equipment was required to jam the Chogyal's broadcasts on his ham radio if he tried to say anything against India, during or after the Assembly session in which the resolution regarding the merger was to be passed. Hasanwalia told me that although Kao had full confidence in my capabilities to handle the situation, he felt that the presence of senior officers would boost my morale—very essential for the success of such an operation.

Hasanwalia and Bahadur spent most of their time in the safe house. But Bhatnagar, a typical nondescript sleuth, started moving on the streets of Gangtok in the garb of a tourist with a camera, cap, walking stick and jogging shoes. Though eleven years my senior, he would come to my office in the morning and discuss with me the type of information I would like him to look for during the day. He would return at the end of the day, sharing with me whatever he had heard, seen or observed, especially around the bazaar. His first task was to cover the Sunday Haat and Lal Bazaar on 6 April, the day after he arrived. The Sunday Haat used to attract a lot of people, including some small-time, on-the-move shopkeepers and villagers bringing their produce from outside Gangtok. This was also the occasion when residents of Gangtok and neighbouring areas used to do their weekly shopping. It was an ideal place for Bhatnagar to brush his field espionage skills and try to collect whatever information was possible. In addition to walking around, most of the time he would sit in small restaurants and shops, and listen to or even participate in the discussions on the topic of the day.

I soon realized that in all probability, Kao had told Bhatnagar about our handicap in getting the real-time intelligence (as I had informed him on 23 January) and might have asked him to lend a helping hand during his stay in Gangtok. During the first couple of days, Bhatnagar got the impression that the common man was happy with the political change, and also with Kazi and his Sikkim Congress leadership. They were hopeful that with the change in the power equation, the lot of the average person was likely to improve. However, he found that the younger generation from the Bhutia community was not happy, and even resentful, with the loss of the Chogyal's powers and the consequent shifting of power to the Kazi-led Sikkim Congress leadership. But the number of such people, even in Gangtok, was not significant. Maybe senior members of this community did not like to share their feelings with a stranger. On 8 April, he found that there was some army movement and that the atmosphere was getting tense. That was the day we decided that Bhatnagar should no longer go around the town, lest he be marked as an intelligence operator.

Keeping in view Gurung's past loyalties towards the Chogyal, Myngma was once again asked to convey to him that this was the time for him to wash off his 'sins' and come clean with his undiluted loyalty for India through unstinted support to any resolution that Kazi may introduce in the Assembly. He was reminded that he was a senior leader, and with Pradhan having lost his cabinet post, he stood a good chance of getting that slot in the cabinet once Kazi sorted out his problems with Pradhan. Further, he might be considered as the party's nominee for membership of the Indian parliament. Gurung understood the logic behind this argument and promised to extend his support to Kazi within and outside the Assembly.

Kewal Singh had made a number of visits before the 8 May agreement was signed. He had even visited Gangtok on 13 April 1974, two days before the elections were to be held. His arrival in Gangtok on 4 April 1975 was in line with that pattern. It was obvious that this time too he had come to Gangtok to assess the situation, in consultation with B.B. Lal and Kazi, and work out details for the smooth passage of the merger-related resolutions in the Assembly, besides counselling the Chogyal to adopt a cooperative attitude towards Kazi's government.

I have had no access to the MEA papers from this period. As mentioned earlier, PO Gurbachan Singh did not share anything of interest with me, and contact with B.B. Lal was out of bounds due to my cover constraints. Ranjit Gupta knew only about Kewal Singh's meetings in Gangtok on 4 and 5 April, but did not know what transpired therein.[1] In view of that, I have tried to construct the events which took place in Gangtok and New Delhi between 4 April and 16 May 1975, based on my meetings with Depinder Singh, the then commander of the Gangtok-based 64 Brigade, Ranjit Gupta, the then first secretary in the Political Office, and Murari, the then secretary to the chief minister. For this, I have also depended on sources like the information received by our three-member spl ops team, the previous pattern of Kewal Singh's meetings with important people in Gangtok, cables issued and received by the US Embassy in New Delhi and Foreign Minister Y.B. Chavan's statements in the Indian parliament on 11 April.

On Friday, 4 April, soon after his arrival in Gangtok, Kewal Singh had a closed-door meeting with Gurbachan Singh and B.B. Lal at India House to seek their views on the matter. Although it was generally believed that Kazi had by that time neutralized opposition from within the Sikkim Congress and was confident of getting the requisite majority for passing the merger-related resolutions, the tense atmosphere at India House indicated that Lal and Singh were not sure as to how the Chogyal and his diehard loyalists from the Sikkim Guards would react. Therefore, they might have advised Kewal Singh that the Chogyal's potential for mischief had to be neutralized in one way or another before the Assembly was called to take up those resolutions.

Thereafter, Kewal Singh met Kazi at India House and sought his views on the chances of success of the resolution going through in the Assembly. Kazi assured him of his MLAs' support, but was not sure as to how the Chogyal would react to that development. Kazi's concerns in that respect have been detailed by Chavan in his statement in the Indian parliament on 11 April which is covered in a subsequent paragraph.

Armed with the information gathered during the above two meetings, and suitably briefed by the prime minister and foreign minister before his departure for Gangtok, Kewal Singh met the Chogyal on the evening of 4 April. Reminding him of his disruptive and non-cooperative attitude, especially since his visit to Nepal, Kewal Singh advised him to exercise restraint and reconcile himself to his constitutional role by adopting a more constructive attitude towards the Kazi-led Sikkim Congress government. Sensing that Kewal Singh was referring to the impending Assembly session where the merger and his removal-related resolutions could be taken up, the Chogyal expectedly told Kewal Singh that he would do everything within his means to protect his power and position. Finding the Chogyal in a defiant mood, Kewal Singh took that as a veiled threat to even use the Sikkim Guards to disrupt the Assembly. What happened in that meeting has been briefly described in the following paragraph, which is an excerpt from Chavan's statement on 11 April, through which he wanted to apprise the members of the Indian parliament of the passage of the two merger-related resolutions in the Sikkim Assembly the previous day.

In view of the sharp deterioration in relation between the elected representatives and the Chogyal, I had instructed the Foreign Secretary to visit Gangtok last week to study the situation. In particular, the Foreign Secretary did his utmost to impress upon the Chogyal that we had all along been urging patience upon the elected representatives in the hope that the Chogyal would cooperate with the government instead of seeking confrontation with it. But if these efforts to impede the functioning of the government insult the elected representatives and intimidate them with various ways continued, the situation could well reach crisis proportions. It is now unfortunately evident that this effort did not have the desired effect.

Referring to the 8 May 1973 agreement and the Government of Sikkim Act, 1974, Chavan further mentioned that the 'Chogyal's statements and actions (indicate) that he was not reconciled to his constitutional role and that he was determined to obstruct the functioning of the democratically elected government, through all means at his disposal'.

On his return from the palace, Kewal Singh held another meeting with Gurbachan Singh and B.B. Lal at India House. In view of the Chogyal's defiant mood, it was decided that to avoid any unforeseen development, it would be essential to disarm the Sikkim Guards before the Assembly met.

Following that, Lal called Kazi to his office-cum-residence and sought his views on disarming of the Sikkim Guards, to which Kazi readily agreed in view of his past known antipathy towards the Guards. After that, Lal advised Kazi to write, or sign, two letters. The first requested the GoI to disarm the Sikkim Guards and the second was addressed to Lal for calling an emergency session of the Sikkim Assembly. The request received from Kazi for disarming the Sikkim Guards is corroborated by the following portion of Chavan's above-mentioned statement in the parliament. There is also a reference to a conspiracy to assassinate Kazi and other leaders, which is covered in another paragraph.

It is in the context of the deteriorating law and order situation and the suspicion of the imminent threat to the lives of some leaders in Sikkim that an urgent request was received from Chief Minister for the immediate disarming and disbanding of Sikkim Guards. Even earlier, the government of India had been approached by the Chief Minister that the government of Sikkim should not be expected to support with public funds the presence of several hundred armed personnel for the exclusive use of the Chogyal . . . The evidence of the possible conspiracy against the Chief Minister and his colleagues indicating complicity of some Sikkim Guards added urgency to the request, in view of the pressing appeal from the Chief Minister and of the Government of India's responsibility to ensure law and order in the state, the government took necessary steps to disarm the Sikkim Guards on the afternoon of 9 April. Before I conclude I would like to mention another demand by the political leaders in Sikkim, which has been made earlier on many occasions and has been reiterated in recent weeks, for according to the elected government full rights and responsibilities on par with a constituent unit of the Indian union . . . It has again been repeated, along with the demand for the abolition of the institution of Chogyal, in the resolution passed unanimously by the Sikkim assembly at its meeting on April 10, the implications of which are being studied by the government of India.

Late at night, PO Gurbachan Singh contacted the commander of the Siliguri-based 33 Corps and the GOC of the Gangtok-based

17 Mountain Division and requested them to attend a meeting at India House the next morning, i.e., 5 April.[2]

On 5 April, Kazi told Murari that he would like to move two resolutions in the Assembly regarding the merger of Sikkim with India and the consequent removal of the Chogyal.[3] I got to know this during a recent meeting with him. He also mentioned that once these resolutions were passed, he would like to get public approval of these resolutions through a statewide referendum. Kazi specifically told Murari that he was resorting to that measure lest he be accused later of having kept his party leaders in the dark about the intended resolutions of such far-reaching consequences. Thereafter, Kazi asked Murari to call a meeting of all his party MLAs and senior civil servants so that he could seek their views on the advisability or otherwise of placing these resolutions before the Assembly. As desired, Murari called the meeting to which some known pro-Chogyal civil servants, including C.D. Rai and L.B. Chhetri, were also invited. Kazi briefly explained the reason behind calling that meeting and invited their views on the matter. As expected, the civil servants vehemently opposed Kazi's suggestions. But the Sikkim Congress legislative group, including K.C. Pradhan and B.B. Gurung, wholeheartedly supported Kazi.

I realized very early during my interaction with Kazi that, as a shrewd and seasoned politician, he did not take any step without a well-thought-out plan to achieve his goals. Kazi was aware that the senior civil servants were beholden to the Chogyal, and hence would oppose his suggestions even in a closed-door meeting, as they and their families had done in April 1974 by demonstrating outside the Assembly hall, when the Government of Sikkim Bill was being discussed. Therefore, by calling that meeting, he actually wanted to assess the magnitude of support for these resolutions from within his party's legislative group in the face of opposition from civil servants. In case any of his partymen were opposed to these resolutions, suitable measures could have been taken in time to neutralize his opposition.

I had an over two-hour debriefing session with Depinder Singh (who eventually retired as GOC-in-C, Southern Command) at the Gymkhana Club in New Delhi on 18 December 2017. Thereafter, I sought a number of clarifications from him over the telephone. Most of the information in this chapter regarding the planning and execution of the Sikkim Guards' disarming operation conducted under his command, and some of his actions thereafter, is based on my interaction with him.

According to Depinder Singh, he came to know about the decision to disarm the Sikkim Guards only on the morning of 5 April from the Commander of 33 Corps, Lt Gen. Gurbachan Singh just before a closed-door meeting was held at India House that day. The meeting was attended by Foreign Secretary Kewal Singh, PO Gurbachan Singh and Kishan Rana (director [north], MEA), Lt Gen. Gurbachan Singh, Maj. Gen. H.S. Khullar, who was GOC of the 17 Mountain Division, and he himself as the Commander of 64 Mountain Brigade. Addressing the meeting, the PO informed the attendees that Kazi wanted to call an Assembly session on 10 April to move a resolution regarding the merger of Sikkim with India and the consequent removal of the Chogyal. It was, therefore, felt that the Chogyal and his loyalists from the Sikkim Guards could disturb the proceedings or revolt against that resolution, which would require the Indian army's intervention. To avoid such an eventuality, which could also be dangerous for the Chogyal and his family members, it had been decided to disarm the Sikkim Guards a day before the Assembly met.

At that stage, Depinder Singh mentioned that the Chogyal was rather well known to him both personally and professionally (the Chogyal was an honorary major general of the Indian army and the colonel-in-chief of 8 Gurkha Regiment, to which Depinder Singh belonged), and that he might be able to convince him to order the Sikkim Guards to voluntarily lay down their arms and surrender. That suggestion was made to avoid launching a full-fledged army operation and the likely loss of life and property as a result. PO Gurbachan Singh then asked Depinder Singh whether he was absolutely sure that the Chogyal would listen to his advice. To this, Depinder Singh replied that he could not give a 100 per cent guarantee, but that he was 90 per cent sure that the Chogyal would listen to him. But that was not acceptable to the PO. With that, the disarming of the Sikkim Guards through army action was the only alternative left.

On 6 April, Kewal Singh returned to New Delhi and soon after appeared before India's highest political body, the Political Affairs Committee (PAC),[4] comprising Prime Minister Indira Gandhi and three of her senior cabinet colleagues, including Foreign Minister Y.B. Chavan and Defence Minister Sardar Swaran Singh. Kewal Singh informed them about the outcome of his visit to Gangtok and described the situation there as serious and requiring urgent action. The PAC gave approval for the disarming of the Sikkim Guards by the Indian army.

Another meeting took place at India House later during the day after the return of the PO from Bagdogra airport, where he had gone to see off Kewal Singh. By that time, Kewal Singh had already informed the PO about the PAC's decision and the army top brass was given the go-ahead by Defence Minister Swaran Singh. The 6 April meeting was attended by all the officers present at the 5 April meeting, minus Kewal Singh, but with three more—Chief Executive B.B. Lal, First Secretary Ranjit Gupta and Deputy Chief of Army Staff (DCOAS) Lt Gen. Jaswant Singh—who had flown in from New Delhi the same morning. Depinder Singh specifically remembered Lal's presence at that meeting, as the proceedings were conducted in Punjabi, with due apologies to him. When Gupta asked as to why Col Kishen Singh Gurung, CO of the Sikkim Guards, was not being taken into confidence, Gurbachan Singh told him to let the army handle that problem. As the decision to disarm the Sikkim Guards by the Indian army had already been approved by the PAC, only broad outlines and ramifications of the army action planned for 9 April were discussed in that meeting. All those present there agreed that the operation should be conducted in a manner that caused the least possible damage to the life and property of the Sikkim Guards and other residents of the palace complex.

On 7 April, to keep the Chogyal out of harm's way when the Sikkim Guards were disarmed, it was decided that he would be taken to New Delhi on 9 April on the pretext of an urgent meeting with Indira Gandhi. PO Gurbachan Singh, who was to accompany him, was extremely nervous and apprehensive as to how the Chogyal would react when he found out that there was actually no meeting fixed. That plan was, however, dropped on the morning of 9 April on the plea that no helicopter was available for their trip from Gangtok to Bagdogra.

Based on information received by the local police about a conspiracy being hatched by some Chogyal loyalists, including Capt. Yongda of the Sikkim Guards, to assassinate Kazi and some senior Sikkim Congress leaders, Yongda was arrested on 7 April. He reportedly told the police the next day that the conspiracy to assassinate the Sikkim Congress leaders was hatched under the Chogyal's instructions. That helped in removing from the scene a committed potential troublemaker had the Chogyal decided to use the Sikkim Guards to create problems on the day the Assembly met.

From the afternoon of 6 April to the evening of 8 April, Depinder Singh worked on his operational plan to disarm the

Sikkim Guards. Some army movement was observed in Gangtok on 8 April, which was explained to a startled Chogyal by PO Gurbachan Singh as part of a routine military exercise.

It was on the morning of 9 April that Depinder Singh called Col Gurung to the 64 Brigade headquarters and asked him to stay there till the operation ended. Similarly, Adjutant Sikkim Guards, Major Bagota, and another captain-rank officer on deputation from the Indian army appeared to have been suitably tipped off by their local army friends and sought refuge at their houses. The Sikkim Guards were thus left under the charge of Captain Roland Chhetri.

Col Gurung, like Depinder Singh, was also from the 8 Gurkha Regiment. He was in fact Singh's senior but had been superseded and even worked as his second in command at one point. Depinder Singh was well aware of Gurung's temperament. He felt that if Gurung was present at the Guards headquarters during the army action, he would certainly lead his men to resist, irrespective of how heavily the odds were stacked against him, and even if he got killed in the process.

All the three battalions—First Paratroopers, JAT and J&K Militia—attached to 64 Mountain Brigade headed by Depinder Singh, were deployed in the operation on 9 April. Around noon, the CRPF took position on the ridge towards the Political Office, and army troops started moving towards the main entrance gate (Tsuklakhang) of the palace, which was manned by two Sikkim Guards sentries. Seeing the Indian army move towards the gate, one of the two sentries—Basant Kumar Chhetri—challenged them and asked them to stop. He had just pointed his rifle towards them when he was shot dead by the approaching Indian troops. The other sentry was also hit in the right arm, which had to be amputated later. The Chogyal, in panic, called PO Gurbachan Singh to inquire as to what was happening, but the phone was passed on to General Khullar who was sitting with the PO. General Khullar asked the Chogyal to order the Sikkim Guards to lay down their arms. Thereafter, the Sikkim Guards were surrounded and made to surrender with their arms raised. The entire operation was over in about twenty minutes.

Lt Col Sudarshan Singh of the First Paratroopers entered the palace with a small contingent. Approaching the place where the Chogyal and his elder son, Tenzing, were standing, he asked them to hand over all their personal weapons. Depinder Singh told me that after the disarming of the Sikkim Guards, PO Gurbachan Singh had asked him to bring the Chogyal to India House so that he could be informed of the reasons for the disarming of the Sikkim Guards. But Depinder Singh told Gurbachan Singh that he should speak to his senior, General Khullar, in this regard. Things did not work out that way as General Khullar himself went to the palace later during the day and informed the Chogyal that the Sikkim Guards had to be disbanded in keeping with the orders received from his seniors. He asked the Chogyal to remain confined to the palace in the interest of his personal safety. After some time, PO Gurbachan Singh also came to the palace but was asked to leave by an angry Chogyal. Thereafter, in the evening, the Chogyal, dressed in the Sikkim Guards uniform, and in full view of the Indian army personnel deployed there, went to where sentry Basant Kumar Chhetri's body was lying. He dipped his finger in Chhetri's blood and applied it as a tilak in recognition of the dead soldier's loyalty. Later that night, the surrendered Sikkim Guards personnel were taken to Siwan army detention camp near Singtam. The Indian army personnel on deputation were, however, asked to report to the local division headquarters.

Three days after the operation, Depinder Singh went to Col Gurung's house and told his wife, in her husband's presence, the actual reason behind her husband's virtual confinement at the brigade headquarters on 9 April. While Col Gurung was still furious as to why he was kept confined when his men were being disarmed, his wife appreciated Depinder Singh's decision. After four more days, Depinder Singh received a call from Coo Coo La's daughter, who told him that the Chogyal had expressed his desire to meet him. Depinder Singh went to the palace. Thondup told him that he could understand his compulsions in carrying out the orders of his seniors to disarm the Sikkim Guards, and hence bore no grudge against him. Thereafter, they hugged each other.

Till late morning on 9 April, we did not know that the Indian army had been asked to disarm the Sikkim Guards. Just before noon, we observed an unusual movement of a number of army jongas fitted with VHF antennae in front of our office. Our technical officer, Arora, was told to start monitoring the wireless communication linked to those antennae. Within minutes, we discovered that the Indian army had launched an operation to disarm the Sikkim Guards. We also started recording the conversation taking place on that network.

Soon after, R.T. Nagrani, staff officer to Kao, telephoned me from New Delhi. He wanted a 'blow by blow account' of the operation to disarm the Sikkim Guards. It was obvious that Kewal Singh had told Kao about it. We were lucky that our VHF monitoring had started producing the required information. Nagrani had called me on the normal post and telegraph line. We were about to shift to the secraphone connected to this line, but to my horror, PO Gurbachan Singh interjected on the telephone line and said, 'Sidhu, you cannot talk to anybody from New Delhi on this telephone line.' The line went dead. We opened our online cipher link with New Delhi and started sending regular messages to Nagrani based on the information obtained through monitoring the army VHF network.

On 10 April, or 11 morning, I requested Ranjit Gupta to join me for a cup of tea as I had something important to discuss with him. I also asked him to request Kishan Rana on my behalf to join us. They came around 5.30 p.m. I told them that my purpose in inviting them was to inform them that I had recorded all the conversation on the army network during the disarming of the Sikkim Guards on 9 April. In view of that, I thought it would be better if I told them in advance that the report that they or the army officers would be preparing on this operation, should be as truthful as possible.

The Chogyal used to operate a ham radio under the call sign AC3PT. He had used it briefly during the April 1973 demonstrations in Gangtok. There was, therefore, every possibility of him using it again when the merger-related resolution was taken up in the Assembly. On my request, Kao had sent a two-man team headed by Dildar Singh with equipment to jam the Chogyal's radio transmissions. They started their operation from the evening of 7 April. For the next two days, there was no sign of AC3PT communicating with anybody. On 9 April afternoon, due to the ongoing army operation to disarm the Sikkim Guards, I sent a message to Dildar Singh that his team needed to be extra vigilant. There was no activity till late evening that day. It was only around 9 p.m. that our team was able to pick up voice calls on AC3PT. They heard the Chogyal broadcasting that this country was under attack. Soon after, Dildar Singh was able to lock on to that frequency and jam it. Thereafter, our team continuously tracked it and jammed every frequency the Chogyal chose to broadcast his messages.

However, before his radio communication could be traced and jammed, the Chogyal was able to communicate with some ham operators from other countries for a few minutes.[5] He had conveyed to them that his country was being invaded. He requested that someone should convey that to the 'International League for the Rights of Man'. Early on 10 April, this ham radio equipment was confiscated by the Indian authorities concerned.

The same day (9 April 1975), the Sikkim Congress issued a statement in Gangtok saying that 'it has now become evident that the people of Sikkim can realize their full rights only if Sikkim becomes a unit of the Union of India'.[6] The party also called for the abolition of 'the oppressive and undemocratic institution of the Chogyal for all times'. The Indian press reported on 9 April that Kazi had sent a telegram (presumably after Yongda's confession) to Indira Gandhi, calling for the removal of the Chogyal. The telegram is said to mark the first formal request from Kazi for the Chogyal's deposition.

On 10 April, extracts from a letter sent by Mrs Gandhi the previous day or so to Kazi were made available to the press in New Delhi.[7] The prime minister said that the government of India was 'deeply disappointed' to note the 'critical' situation which had arisen. She indicated that the Government of India had received a number of reports and representations from Sikkim about the 'obstructive methods' that had been used against the elected Sikkimese representatives. 'We were particularly shocked to know of the stabbing of members of the Sikkim Assembly and reports of assassination attempts against popular leaders.' She extended the government's 'full support to the elected representatives of the Government of Sikkim, especially when the preservation and strengthening of democratic government and the welfare of the people of Sikkim are concerned'.

At the same time, the press in New Delhi also reported extracts from a letter sent by Foreign Minister Chavan to the Chogyal in response to the latter's recent letter to the prime minister.[8] In the letter, Chavan had cited numerous representations coming from the Sikkimese leaders in which they had mentioned that 'they had found the Chogyal not only to be wanting in his duty to function as a constitutional head of the government but all his actions and statements in recent months have been in complete disregard of that role'. Chavan further said that 'we have all along been hopeful that you would show understanding and keep pace with the march towards democratization. These hopes have been belied.' In perhaps the key sentence, Chavan declared, 'While the government will do all it can to protect the institution of the Chogyal, its primary duty is towards the welfare of the common people and their aspiration for democratic reforms and for speedy social and economic development.'

On 10 April, on Kazi's request, Chief Executive B.B. Lal called an emergency session of the Assembly. A total of twenty-nine Sikkim Congress legislators, including the chastened K.C. Pradhan and the hopeful B.B. Gurung, attended it. Soon after the session was declared open by Lal, two resolutions were introduced. The Hindi version was read out by Rinzing Lepcha and the English by Gurung. The first resolution was about the abolition of the institution of the Chogyal, and the consequent merger of Sikkim with India. The second was about the holding of a referendum on the first resolution. The resolutions were adopted unanimously by all twenty-nine party members present.

As I had discussed with Kazi, about 3000 supporters from south and west Sikkim arrived in Gangtok on the morning of 10 April and continued to march on the streets shouting anti-Chogyal and pro-Kazi slogans. On 11 April, a larger public meeting attended by over 10,000 Sikkim Congress supporters was held at Singtam. After Kazi's speech, the crowd overwhelmingly supported the resolutions passed by the Assembly on 10 April.

In Washington, the minister (political) Indian Embassy, Eric Gonsalves, called on Deputy Assistant Secretary Adolph Dubs, informing him about the two resolutions passed by the Sikkim

Assembly on 10 April.[9] Referring to that meeting, Secretary of State Henry Kissinger sent a message to US Ambassador William Saxbe on 11 April 1975 asking him for continued reporting on Sikkim developments.

In New Delhi, Foreign Minister Chavan took note of these resolutions in his 11 April statement in the parliament. Relevant extracts of that statement have already been reproduced in the preceding paragraphs. Interestingly, the observation made by Chavan in the following portion of his statement was the first public acknowledgement by an Indian leader that the country's policy towards Sikkim in the post-independence period had been—as described earlier in this book—a policy of 'apparent appeasement of the Chogyal and cautious containment of the pro-democracy forces'.

> The Government of India has been requested on several occasions in the past twenty years, by political leaders and people of Sikkim, for the abolition of the institution of Chogyal. The Government of India's endeavour has been, to protect the institution, although in the case of princely states the princely order has been abolished in deference to the democratic process in the country. The deviation in the case of Sikkim was motivated by our desire to show special consideration to the Chogyal in the hope that he would play a responsible role.

On 14 April, in compliance with the second resolution of 10 April, a referendum was held. A total of 61,169 votes out of the total electorate of approximately 97,000 were polled. As many as 59,637 (97 per cent) votes were polled in favour of the merger of Sikkim with India and the consequent removal of the Chogyal. In this context, Kishan Rana told me that he had to travel from Gangtok to New Delhi a couple of times to attend meetings, wherein the modalities of holding the referendum were discussed. One of the issues which was deliberated at length was whether the referendum should have two separate questions on the removal of the Chogyal and the merger of Sikkim with India, or if both these questions should be merged into one to avoid conflicting outcomes resulting from the confusion in the minds of the voters, the majority of whom were illiterate. It was finally decided to have only one question, which also had the Political Office and Kishan Rana's support. Murari also told me separately that during that period Kewal Singh took him to Indira Gandhi's office, where she showed him a paper on which two questions had been typed separately. Murari suggested the merger of the two questions and assured her that there would be overwhelming support of the people of Sikkim for the issue projected through a single question.

The Chogyal held a press conference at the palace on 14 April in which he called for an immediate meeting with Indira Gandhi and members of the Sikkim Assembly to discuss the issue of an independent identity of Sikkim and the formation of a responsible government.[10] He also levelled various charges against the Indian and Sikkimese authorities, saying he had been placed under house arrest. About the 14 April referendum, he reportedly commented that it would only have meaning if it was held under the supervision of a neutral agency.

PO Gurbachan Singh, who was subsequently contacted by the press for comment, denied that the Chogyal was under house arrest, saying that he would not have been able to hold a press conference in that case.[11]

As per the US Embassy's assessment, the Chogyal's above comments not only stirred further controversy, but probably served to harden official opinion in New Delhi against undertaking any new initiatives aimed at reaching a Sikkim compromise.[12]

Between 16 and 17 April, the Sikkim Congress delegation comprising Kazi, C.S. Rai, party general secretary S.K. Rai, Rinzing Lepcha and N.B. Khatiwada reached New Delhi to call on Indira Gandhi and the others to request them to take immediate follow-up action on the 10 April resolutions. The prime minister reportedly assured them on 16 April that her government would take the necessary steps to facilitate an early implementation of the Sikkim's Assembly resolutions endorsed by the 14 April referendum. She also explained that the GoI would soon introduce a new constitution amendment bill to make Sikkim a constituent unit of the Union of India. Kazi told journalists after the meeting that his delegation was satisfied with the assurances given by the prime minister. Indira Gandhi and Foreign Minister Chavan met the opposition leaders on 17 April and found wide support for the current situation in Sikkim.[13]

Chavan introduced the thirty-sixth constitution amendment bill in the Lok Sabha on 21 April, seeking incorporation of Sikkim as the twenty-second state of the Union of India. During the debate that followed, he said on 23 April amid cheers, 'It is a political fact today that the institution of the Chogyal, by the assembly resolution and people's mandate, has been abolished.' He also said, 'We are not dealing with some sort of normal legalistic situation. We are dealing with, if I may say so, some sort of revolutionary political situation.' In referring to the Chogyal, Chavan contended that the GoI had tried to affect reconciliation between the Chogyal and the people, but it was not successful since the Chogyal was an anachronistic feudal head. Thereafter, the Lok Sabha passed the bill on 23 April by 299 votes to eleven. The Rajya Sabha cleared it on 26 April by 158 to three votes.

The bill was sent for the President's assent, which was granted on 15 May. With that, Sikkim became the twenty-second state of India. Chief Executive B.B. Lal was appointed the first governor of Sikkim on 16 May. After that, the Chief Justice of Sikkim, Rajendra Sachar, administered oath to Lal, who then administered the oath of office and secrecy to five members of Kazi's cabinet. Consequent to the Presidential assent to the thirty-sixth amendment to the Indian Constitution, the abolition of the institution of the Chogyal became a political reality and Thondup became an ordinary citizen of India.

News reports mentioned that Indira Gandhi wrote a letter in response to the Chogyal's messages. She had reportedly urged him to adopt a realistic attitude and accept the people's wishes. The letter reiterated the GoI's goodwill towards the Chogyal and his family, despite his recent activities.[14]

The MEA spokesman reacted sharply on 13 April to a Pakistani foreign ministry statement that said India had annexed Sikkim. The spokesman said the GoI was not surprised at Pakistan's attempts to misconstrue the events in Sikkim. He said, 'Pakistan's own record of dealing with former princely states is amply demonstrated by its unilateral action in Hunza,' and added, 'We deplore this attitude and we have always refrained from commenting on Pakistan's own internal affairs though there is much that could be said about them.'[15]

Although on the morning of 15 April the New Delhi press reported that 'official sources' were not unduly exercised by Beijing's comments on Sikkim's alleged annexation by India, the Indian wire services reported late afternoon on 15 April that Indira Gandhi had made caustic comments about the journalists who mentioned the Chinese reaction to developments in Sikkim the same day. She was quoted as saying that 'China has been saying many things (but) they did not say anything when Pakistan moved into Hunza'. She then reportedly asked the journalists, 'What have they (the Chinese) done to Tibet?'[16]

At the height of the Cold War, and against the background of the improving relationship with China following US President Richard Nixon's visit to Beijing in 1972, in his cable dated 16 April to the US Department of State, US Ambassador William Saxbe mentioned that since the GoI had traditionally exercised strict control over its inner line and borderland areas 'we do not expect that the Soviets will have any greater access to Sikkim or sensitive areas within Sikkim as a result of the current political turmoil or Sikkim's total absorption into India. Our exchanges with Soviets here suggest that in fact conditions in Sikkim had attracted no more attention on their part than conditions in other border lands.' Also, on the basis 'of information now available here we do not think the Soviets have a notably active interest in Sikkim or for that matter, Bhutan, at this time'.[17]

According to the US Embassy in Kathmandu, press commentary on the events in Sikkim continued to be remarkably low-key. The official press had totally ignored the issue and had given no publicity to any local protest either by the Sikkimese or the Nepalese. In special comments on the situation in Nepal, it said that 'while there can be no doubt about the strength of Nepalese private opinions on the subject of Sikkim, the government has been successful in defusing it as (a) public issue. There will probably continue to be some criticism of Indian policy in the vernacular press but it will be kept within bounds as government of Nepal continues its efforts to prevent recurrence of last summer's confrontation in Indo-Nepalese relations.' In a message dated 11 April, the embassy had commented that the 'Government of Nepal has apparently learnt lessons from last year's events: that it can confront India on matters of political sensitivity to the GoI only to its peril.'[18]

At this stage it would be relevant to examine whether it was absolutely essential or even desirable to disarm the Sikkim Guards with the help of the Indian army one day before the Assembly met to take up those resolutions.

Neither Murari nor any of the three members of our R&AW's spl ops team had any information that the Chogyal or any of the Sikkim Guards would do anything to disturb the proceedings of the Assembly or revolt against it in the palace. Senior Indian army officers posted in Gangtok shared an excellent relationship with the Chogyal. Col Gurung, Adjutant Bagota, one company commander and about sixty JCOs and other ranks were on deputation from the Indian army to the Sikkim Guards (out of an effective total strength of about 270 on the day). Nothing of this kind could have escaped their notice. In addition, there were three Int. Corps officers (Major Chiklekar, Captains Tejpal and A.J. Singh) who were feeding information of interest to the GOC of 17 Mountain Division on a daily basis. And this was important information. Had they known about this, Maj. Gen.

Khullar or Brig. Depinder Singh would have surely shared it with the others present on 5 April in India House. As explained in an earlier chapter, unlike his predecessor Bajpai, PO Gurbachan Singh had completely cut himself off from the monitoring of day-to-day political developments and left that job entirely to B.B. Lal. That left Lal and a large IB staff posted in Sikkim (whose main duty was to keep tabs on such activities) who could have the requisite information. It was possible that the IB headquarters had sent a report containing such information to the MEA. In the alternative, on his arrival in Gangtok on 4 April, Kewal Singh was briefed by Lal about such a possibility.

The main function of the Sikkim Guards was to provide security to the palace premises and ensure the personal safety of the Chogyal and his immediate family members. Yongda, the only diehard pro-Chogyal Sikkim Guards officer, had already been arrested on 7 April for suspected complicity in a criminal conspiracy to assassinate Kazi. The other company commander, Capt. Chhetri, could hardly have defied the orders of Col Gurung or his adjutant. In view of this, there was very little chance of the Sikkim Guards personnel going out of the palace premises or even out of their barracks to disturb the proceedings of the Sikkim Assembly while it was discussing the merger resolution. The Chogyal himself was an honorary major general in the India army. He was well aware of the implications of him or his son leaving the palace with the Sikkim Guards personnel to disturb the proceedings of the Assembly. It would have been a serious offence inviting court martial for himself and the concerned Sikkim Guards personnel, and the arrest of his son, Tenzing.

In contrast to 1974, there was no information about pro-Chogyal public demonstrations outside the Assembly hall on 10 April 1975. If there was any specific information that the

Chogyal himself or through his men would disrupt the Assembly proceedings on 10 April, the army could have been deployed at crucial locations, including the Assembly premises in Gangtok, to prevent access to the Assembly. However, going by past experience, the deployment of the CRPF in full strength in the city and around the Assembly hall, with the army on full alert in the barracks, as was the case in April 1974, and Col Gurung suitably briefed to maintain strict control over the movements of the Sikkim Guards, would have been good enough to handle the situation on 10 April also.

Army action on the evening of 10 April, after the passage of these resolutions in the Assembly, would have looked like a natural consequence of these resolutions, had Depinder Singh's efforts to convince the Chogyal to order the Sikkim Guards to surrender failed. Had the Chogyal shown any signs of resistance to the Assembly's moves to pass the merger resolutions, army action could have been justified. However, the disarming of the Sikkim Guards a day before the Assembly passed the resolutions, made the whole operation look as if it was undertaken to neutralize opposition from within the Sikkim Congress legislative group to the proposed passing of merger-related resolutions in the Assembly on 10 April, which was far from the truth.

When the decision to merge as many as 565 princely Indian states into the Union of India was being taken on the eve of India's independence, despite objections raised by Sardar Patel, Nehru decided to allow Sikkim to retain its separate identity for reasons stated earlier. A request from the popular leaders, including Tashi Tshering and Kazi, made in December 1948, for the accession of Sikkim to India was parried by Nehru. India helped the then maharaja ward off serious challenges to his authority, and even his rule, especially during the 'no tax', 'no rent' campaign led by Tshering. Relations with Sikkim were finally formalized in the form of the 1950 treaty and Sikkim became a protectorate of India. India continued to follow the terms of that treaty in letter as well as in spirit.

But Thondup was not satisfied with what he had got courtesy of Nehru. He wanted to secure an independent status for Sikkim, and in doing so, he was a man in a hurry. He wanted to see his concerted efforts bearing fruit during his lifetime. That proved to be his undoing. In this context, the following extracts from a note dated 4 December 1953, prepared by the then diwan J.S. Lall, as a backgrounder for Prime Minister Nehru, for his meeting with Maharaj Kumar Thondup are extremely relevant and prophetic:[19]

This baffling character (Maharaj Kumar) plays an important role in the internal politics. Highly intelligent and involved with a sense of mission, he can also be an extremely difficult customer. He shows an astonishing gift for political manipulations. As such, and as he is the future maharaja, every effort has to be made to retain his confidence. When confidence has been created, I found that he generally plays the game.

The Maharaj Kumar once remarked that the state is the ruler. When he becomes the ruler himself, he will probably try to put this into effect, and thus set forces into motion which might well annihilate him and his dynasty. He is in practice the ruler now. Unless held in check, his period might well mark the downfall of the dynasty and its replacement by the rule of the Nepalese majority. Because of the repercussions any such development may have on the Bhutia–Lepcha and our frontier in this area, care has to be

taken to guide the Maharaj Kumar and restrain him firmly
if necessary.

But no such advice was acceptable to Thondup. He wanted
to maintain his autocratic rule with absolute hold over the
administration of Sikkim through a discriminatory political and
economic regime in which a very small coterie would enjoy the
perks. Located next to a vibrant and democratic India, such a
discriminatory system was artificially sustained due to India's
protective cover, induced mainly due to its strategic interest in
that region. Such a regime was bound to collapse once that cover
was gone.

Thondup was like a man possessed. He was possessed with
the idea of securing independent status for Sikkim like the one
enjoyed by neighbouring Bhutan, whose king was a relative of
his. But in doing so, he became totally oblivious to the changed
geopolitical realities and India's security interests in Sikkim. He
became a victim of his own insatiable and unrealistic ambitions.
When he felt his goal was near, he found in Indira Gandhi a
much more rejuvenated, confident and formidable person. Only
in December 1971 she had been able to break Pakistan into two
parts, which led to the liberation of Bangladesh. Soon thereafter,
she secured a landslide victory in the general elections. She did not
take the Chogyal's refusal of her offer of permanent association
kindly, and she could not go any further. Fortunately for her,
she had the advantage of the services of Kao-led, newly created,
upbeat and vibrant R&AW, which had honed its skills through a
not so insignificant role in the liberation of Bangladesh. Hence,
her 180-degree policy reversal towards Sikkim.

Some Indian officers who saw the Chogyal immediately after
the disbanding of the Sikkim Guards and the 10 April 1975
Assembly resolutions for Sikkim's merger and abolition of the

institution of the Chogyal, found his condition similar to that of a child who had seen his most precious toy, passed down generations, shattered to pieces before his own eyes. When the time came to rationalize the reasons thereof, he might have realized that no one else but he himself was responsible, as he was the one who pushed that toy to the precipice, from where a fall was the natural consequence.

Going by what has been explained above, it was Thondup himself who was responsible for the end of the Namgyal dynasty's rule in Sikkim. India continued to play by the rules till the very end. It was his ungrateful acts of insatiable ambition that led Indira Gandhi to undo the damage caused by her father in 1947. Only when the water went over her head did she decide to lift India's protective cover from over the Chogyal's head. She used the R&AW to send a signal to the pro-democratic and pro-independence forces in Sikkim that India would no longer stand in their way for the fulfilment of their long-cherished desire to secure for the residents of Sikkim, the same rights and privileges as were being enjoyed by residents of other Indian states. Such a signal given in the beginning of February 1973 provided Kazi Lhendup Dorji a much-awaited opportunity to translate his lifelong dream of seeing his state become a part of independent India and open new avenues of freedom, equality and prosperity for every citizen of this small but strategic state, without any discrimination based on ethnic, religious and socio-economic background, into a reality.

Chapter XIV

The Aftermath

The R&AW's twenty-seven-month involvement in the merger-related special operations came to an end with Sikkim becoming the twenty-second state of India in May 1975. As a result, the three-man operational team was wound up and the R&AW was no longer involved in the internal affairs of the state. The officially non-existent IB staff that had been posing as R&AW employees since the IB's bifurcation and R&AW's creation in September 1968 assumed independent and legitimate existence. On 5 June, one of my IPS batchmates Maloy Krishna Dhar was posted as assistant director, SIB, Gangtok. Though after the merger we were left with only China and Tibet-related work, I had to deal with some other issues too that are described below:

A couple of days after the results of the referendum were announced, Murari came to my residence around 10 p.m. He said that as per his information there were a number of names under consideration for the post of governor of Sikkim. Two of the contenders happened to be Nari Rustomji (a close friend of

Thondup's who had served as the diwan in the 1950s) and Chief Executive B.B. Lal. Murari said that Lal had been chief executive for over a year and was well aware of all the problems of the state, including its politics. Further, he had also established a good rapport with the civil servants, including Murari. In view of that, it would be better if we had a known person as a governor rather than a total stranger, and that too a person who was a friend of the former Chogyal. Murari then came to the main point. He suggested that I request Kazi to pass a resolution in the cabinet, requesting Indira Gandhi for Lal's appointment as the governor. The rest, he said, he would handle as secretary to the chief minister. Though I had some reservations about Lal being an ideal choice as the first governor of Sikkim, on Murari's insistence I met Kazi the next morning and requested him to pass such a resolution. Kazi, too, had some reservations. He described Lal as lacking warmth and somewhat aloof, and a bit tough to deal with. But on my request, he agreed to do the needful. The resolution was adopted and a copy was sent by hand through Rinzing Lepcha to Indira Gandhi. The announcement of Lal as governor came on 16 April, when I hosted dinner at my residence. Lal was one of the guests. He was felicitated by everybody present at the party.

It soon became clear that we had made a mistake in getting Lal appointed as governor. Even Murari realized it. One of the cabinet ministers later told me that when Kazi was discussing the matter of Lal's appointment as governor, he had had one drink too many. He thought that it was the name of the other Lal, i.e., Murari, which was being discussed as the likely governor. Perhaps that was why he was the most enthusiastic supporter of that proposal. This may be an unlikely, and certainly unverifiable, story but it indicates the widespread lack of enthusiasm for B.B. Lal.

Soon after the results of the referendum were declared, I was asked by Kao to send him a note on some issues that would require the GoI's special attention in the post-merger period. It took me three days to prepare that nine-page note. As per my recollection, some of the contents of that note were as follows:

a) Indian tax laws, both direct and indirect, should not be made applicable to the residents of Sikkim for a certain number of years. As they were not paying any income tax as subjects of Sikkim, implementation of any such tax would be an added burden. Also, tax holiday on the indirect front could encourage some Sikkimese to start their industries and generate employment.

b) Establish small-scale industries and vocational training centres for the Sikkimese people to generate employment, which in turn could bring prosperity to the lowest segments of the society.

c) Care needs to be taken to retain the existing social structure of the society in general, and not to destroy the upper-class and privileged segment, as had happened in the erstwhile states absorbed in the Union of India in 1947. This could be done by creating alternative sources of income, if needed, for the members of this segment of the population. This would also help in winning over the sympathy, and possibly support, of former pro-Chogyal elements.

d) Improvement in infrastructure and communication to open up remote areas of Sikkim. While doing so, care had to be taken that the funds were not siphoned off and the projects didn't remain on paper only.

e) With a population of less than 3,00,000, and the attention that the new state was bound to receive from India, care had to be taken that the state was not swamped by outsiders, especially persons of Nepalese origin from the neighbouring areas. That would neutralize all the efforts made towards bringing prosperity to the people of the newly created Indian state.

f) The way Sikkim had remained polarized for long on sectarian and religious lines, a certain segment of the population was bound to be dissatisfied with the merger. Therefore, the Chinese sitting across the border could subvert the loyalty of such people, especially those in north and east Sikkim. The activities of such elements, especially those living in close proximity to the army units deployed in that area, had to be kept under close watch and preventive actions taken wherever needed.

It appeared that Kao had sent a copy of this note to the PMO, which in turn sent it to the ministry of home affairs. It finally landed on the table of Governor Lal. One day, I got a call from Raj Bhawan to see Lal. On reaching his office, he showed me a copy of the note lying on his table and wanted to know if I had written it. After glancing through the first couple of pages, I said that I had written it on Kao's instructions. I asked Lal if he would like to discuss it with me. He had no question on that. Maybe he thought that I was too junior a person for him to engage in any meaningful discussion on those issues. That happened to be my first and last official contact with him.

When the R&AW was created in September 1968, some officers and staff members of the IB posted in New Delhi and its regional offices and forward posts had joined R&AW. But the IB, being the parent office, retained all the office and residential accommodation. The R&AW had to shift to new locations. Due to reasons explained earlier, that did not happen in Gangtok. With Sikkim becoming a state of India, it was time to do the same in Gangtok.

Fortunately for us, a large number of buildings and houses belonging to the former Political Office estate had fallen vacant with the transfer of their India-based occupants out of Sikkim.

For the distribution of these assets, which were formally taken over by the ministry of home affairs from the MEA, a team of two officers from the former—Joint Secretary Shivinder Singh Sidhu and his Deputy Secretary Prabhat Kumar—were deputed to visit Gangtok and give their recommendations to the GoI in this respect. I happened to know both of them well from my UP days. In view of that we did not face any problem in getting the requisite office and residential accommodation allotted to us. On my request, Kazi suggested Diki Khang (House of Peace) as the name for the house allotted to the OSD (P).

The Special Frontier Force (SFF), an Indian paramilitary force, was created in November 1962. Mainly comprising young men of Tibetan origin, its main job was to conduct covert operations behind Chinese lines in the event of another Sino–Indian War. With its headquarters in Chakrata, Uttarakhand, it came under the charge of the secretary, R&AW, after the IB's bifurcation in 1968. On the eve of Sikkim's merger with India, the SFF had no presence from the western tip of the Nepal–Tibet–Indian border to the eastern tip of the Sikkim–Tibet–Bhutan tri-junction. From the SFF's point of view, Sikkim provided an ideal location and filled a crucial gap. It was against this background that within ten days of Sikkim's merger, I received a letter from Kao asking me to meet the chief minister and seek his views on the deployment of one battalion of the SFF in Sikkim.

The SFF was at that time headed by Maj. Gen. Bhardwaj (retd) as its inspector general. He had already identified an area of about 30 acres in Ravangla, adjacent to Temi Tea Estate, for the location of the battalion. I met Kazi and discussed this with him. Kazi had some idea about the purpose behind the raising of the SFF and appreciated the plan of its deployment in south Sikkim. It was not the SFF's job to stop Nepalese influx into Sikkim, but Kazi felt its mere presence in that area would act as a deterrent to such activities. With Kazi's permission sought, I informed Kao that he could send Bhardwaj with a formal request to the chief minister for the allotment of the required piece of land in the Ravangla area. Within a few days, Bhardwaj came with a letter from Kao and accompanied me to Kazi's office. The land was allotted soon thereafter.

Similarly, the Special Service Bureau (SSB) was also set up by the legendary director of the IB, B.N. Mullick, in December 1963, following the Sino–Indian War. Its primary task was to inculcate feelings of national spirit in the border population and assist them in developing their capabilities for resistance to any future Chinese aggression through a continuous process of motivation, training, development, welfare programmes and activities. The SSB also came under the charge of the R&AW secretary. With Sikkim becoming a part of India, in consultation with me, an advance party comprising a company of the SSB moved into Sikkim. I helped them locate a place near Singtam. Soon after my departure from Sikkim, I learnt that the entire SSB battalion had moved into Sikkim. With the possibility of the Chinese threat diminishing, in January 2001, the SSB was transferred from the cabinet secretariat to the ministry of home affairs. Renamed the Sashastra Seema Bal, the force was thereafter assigned the duties of manning the Nepal and Bhutan borders.

As everything had happened so fast after the merger, it was difficult for anybody to fully comprehend its implications, especially insofar as the roles of the two central intelligence agencies in Sikkim were concerned. From being very actively involved in political developments in Sikkim between February 1973 and April 1975, we suddenly cut off our link with the internal developments of Sikkim. This role had passed on to the SIB, Gangtok, headed by Maloy Dhar. I had realized the implications of this change for our 'friends' from the Sikkim Congress well in time. Within days of the merger, I wrote a personal letter to Kao in which I requested that in view of the changed situation in Sikkim, it would be better for us to introduce our 'friends' to Maloy. And before doing that, explain to them why we were doing so. I felt that it would make our 'friends' aware of our changed role and also help them protect their political interests by aligning their future with the IB. But Kao felt otherwise. I was informed that rather than exposing our operational details to the IB, it would be better if the IB was allowed to take care of their operational needs on their own. It appeared that Kao had discussed this matter with the DIB.

Unlike the R&AW, which had no separate section or junior officer dealing with Sikkim in New Delhi, the IB had a separate desk dealing with the affairs of Sikkim and Bhutan. Soon after the merger, the IB's officer looking after this desk was shifted to another area to bring about a complete break from the past. Kao's decision on my request, therefore, might have been a part of that strategy. But to avoid confusion in the minds of our friends, which was bound to occur as a result of the sudden change of responsibility, we briefed all our 'friends' that their interests thereafter, as in any other state of India, would be looked after by the IB, which had posted its own officer and who would function from the same office complex that I occupied earlier.

I was transferred from Gangtok in February 1976 and got stuck in transit in New Delhi as my predecessor at that station wanted to stay a bit longer. I finally took charge of my new assignment in September 1976. It was in a place where there was no scope of keeping abreast with what was happening in Sikkim. But one day in 1979, I was surprised to know that Kazi had lost the elections (including his own seat) and that too to a known pro-Thondup protégé, Nar Bahadur Bhandari. During my stay in Sikkim, prompted, encouraged and also financed by Thondup and his men, Bhandari, as the leader of the newly created pro-Chogyal party SIUF, had contested the April 1974 elections on two planks. Firstly, he attacked Kazi as a desh bechoa. Secondly, he demanded immediate withdrawal of the Indian officers brought on deputation to Sikkim in the wake of the April 1973 anti-Chogyal agitations. He had miserably failed and could not get even a single seat in those elections, even though Thondup was still the Chogyal. Given his background, how Bhandari could replace a man of Kazi's stature as chief minister in 1979, and that too after Sikkim had become a part of India, was an enigma for me.

To understand what had really happened that led to Kazi's ignominious defeat, I recently discussed this matter with my old friends[1]—Murari, Sanyal and Manavalan (former OSDs in Sikkim) and the still going strong Nar Bahadur Khatiwada[2]—at my residence on 15 April 2018. I also read the relevant chapters of the book *Open Secrets: India's Intelligence Unveiled* by Maloy Krishna Dhar.[3]

The merger brought a sudden change in Gangtok. There was a complete break with the past, insofar as Sikkim's relations with India were concerned. Before the merger, the Sikkimese politicians, irrespective of their affiliations, used to receive special and privileged treatment from the PO and other diplomats posted in Gangtok. They were taken on 'familiarization' trips around India and sometimes meetings were arranged with the prime minister and foreign minister, where they were received cordially. The Political Office was a hub of various activities, including lavish lunches, cocktails and dinners, which they used to attend as honoured guests. After the merger, they had to wait on a strict governor like B.B. Lal. Social interaction and the frequency and level of entertainment dropped considerably at the former Political Office-turned-Raj Bhawan. Very soon, most of the Sikkim Congress leaders and their followers started showing signs of frustration at this treatment they were receiving from the governor and New Delhi. With the passage of time, they started feeling that that was not the deal they had made. These feelings of neglect and frustration were fully exploited by the former Chogyal and his men—if for nothing else but to take revenge on Kazi for having dispossessed them of their position and privileges.

Since February 1973, when the R&AW and its spl ops team in Gangtok got involved in Sikkim's internal affairs, the MEA and R&AW, under the charge of two separate ministers (the foreign minister and the prime minister respectively), worked in total cohesion and coordination both in New Delhi and Gangtok. As the matter was personally handled by Kewal Singh and Kao, respectively, decisions on issues raised by the PO and OSD (P) were received within a day or two and sometimes the same day. Though, as mentioned by Maloy Dhar, the R&AW's OSD (P) was not an adjunct of the Political Office, but we made ourselves look like one so as to convey to the Sikkim Congress leaders that both the ministry and R&AW were working together and supported their cause for democratic reforms and finally the merger of Sikkim with India.

During the pre-merger days, in view of India's security interests, delegations of anti-Chogyal parties—first the Tashi Tshering-led SSC and later the Kazi-led SSC/SNC—generally returned from New Delhi empty-handed. Even during their agitations in Sikkim for pro-democratic reforms, India's interventions had mostly been in favour of the maharaja. But there was a certain degree of sophistication and finesse in handling the anti-maharaja leaders. They were made to feel important and wanted due to India's long-term interest in their survival. As late as 1972, Sikkim's six-member executive council was taken on a familiarization tour of some places of interest in India by First Secretary Sudhir Devare, culminating in their call on the foreign minister and Prime Minister Indira Gandhi.

After the merger, the affairs of Sikkim came directly under the charge of the ministry of home affairs, with the home minister controlling both the home ministry and the IB. In view of that, there should have been greater cohesion and coordination between the two set-ups insofar as their dealing with Sikkim's affairs was concerned. But unfortunately, the home ministry neither had the time nor the finesse in dealing with the members of the Sikkim legislature or even cabinet ministers. For it, Sikkim was a tiny state with a population of less than 3,00,000. The state was seen as a minuscule addition to the already heavy workload relating to the other twenty-one much bigger states. Also, due to the fast-changing political situation in India, the parties in power started using the IB/SIB to further their respective interests. The need for maintenance of political stability in Sikkim was relegated to the background. There was hardly any coordination between the home ministry and the IB/SIB in Gangtok, with the latter playing a subordinate role. In fact, the head of the SIB in Gangtok had a poor impression of the functioning of the IB and its senior officials.

The relationship between the members of R&AW's spl ops team and the anti-Chogyal and pro-democracy leaders was of a collaborative nature, to the exclusion of the pro-former Chogyal parties and persons. After the merger, they lost this exclusivity when Maloy Dhar started meeting their opponents, including the former Chogyal, thereby creating confusion in their minds. While the R&AW delivered what it promised to the Sikkim Congress leaders in their march towards Sikkim's 'delayed' independence, the IB was soon reduced to its primary role of collecting intelligence. India's decision makers and the IB's representative in Sikkim lost sight of the fact that any attack on Kazi as a desh bechoa was in fact an attack on India's decision to help Kazi and his men fight for their freedom from the former Chogyal's yoke, and thus allowed Thondup to have his revenge on Kazi.

In order to consolidate the gains of the merger, it was incumbent upon the Indian officers and institutions concerned to first identify the nature of the gains, then mark the persons who could nullify these gains, and finally take suitable action to neutralize the impact of their destabilizing activities. The gains were obvious. Sikkim became a part of India and India's security interests in that state were no longer at the mercy of a Chogyal who had started nursing ambitions of becoming the head of an independent country. As Sikkim's merger took place through an amendment to the Indian Constitution, nobody had the power to undo that Act. In fact, there is no provision for voluntary cessation of Indian territory in the Constitution. In that case, the only thing they had to do was ensure political stability in the state, which had been the cornerstone of the Government of India's policy towards Sikkim since its independence. On the contrary, all such considerations were forgotten soon after the merger. Everybody concerned, namely Indira Gandhi egged on by her son Sanjay, Morarji Desai, Governor B.B. Lal, the ministry of home affairs and the IB (directly and through Maloy Dhar), in pursuit of their own narrow political interests (in the case of Maloy and the IB, due to their inability to convince their political masters to take a balanced view of the situation) or due to unmindfulness or even sheer ignorance of the consequences of their actions, made their respective contributions.

As the former Chogyal had lost everything after the merger, the threat to Kazi's government and the resulting political instability could have mainly emanated from him and his son and their close advisers such as Jigdal Densapa, M.M. Rasaily, Karma Topden, etc. They were expected to use the services of disgruntled Sikkim Congress leaders such as K.C. Pradhan, B.B. Gurung, N.K. Subedi and even N.B. Khatiwada, who had gained nothing from the merger. In addition, the services of pro-Thondup anti-Kazi Nepalese leaders like Bhandari were always available to them.

Rather than observing the activities of this group for some time, and taking action to curb their anti-Kazi activities (which should have been considered as anti-India and anti-merger in the aftermath of the merger), in his desire to consolidate the gains of the merger and to bring the Sikkimese people closer to India, the head of the IB in Sikkim established contact with the former Chogyal and his men, including his elder son Tenzing (reportedly with the approval of his headquarters but to the utter dislike of the Kazini), within months of his arrival in Gangtok. He called on the former Chogyal, encouraged Tenzing to visit his residence and started visiting the houses of former Chogyal-loyalists, including N.B. Bhandari, and also the disheartened and rebellious Khatiwada. But he failed to appreciate the real impact of such meetings on the minds of the Sikkim Congress leadership, their followers and the sagging morale of the former Chogyal and his trusted friends, who had almost deserted him and started currying favour with anyone who could protect their interests. Thondup was too shrewd a man to let Maloy Dhar gauge his real intentions. And so were his trusted former employees. The irony of Dhar's new-found confidence in his supposed proximity to the former Chogyal could be judged from one incident, which he has described in his book.

Dhar received information through a known visiting journalist that New Delhi would like him to get a letter signed from the former Chogyal saying that he had no objection to the merger of Sikkim and that he accepted Indira Gandhi's leadership. Without waiting for clearance from his bosses, Dhar met Thondup and conveyed this message to him. Thondup's reaction was predictable. He told Dhar that though he liked the messenger, he should tell New Delhi that he had killed the message.

Thondup and his men might have also presumed that Dhar's meetings with him were indicative of some sort of a shift in the Government of India's policy of total neglect of the former Chogyal. Similarly, Dhar pulled Bhandari out of the dumps and unwittingly helped him resurrect and continue his anti-Kazi activities, in which the former Chogyal might have lent more than a helping hand. Dhar's improved relations with Khatiwada helped him build his independent base at the cost of Kazi's position. Without any proper guidance from or control of the SIB Gangtok over the fast-moving political developments in Gangtok, the cohesiveness of Kazi's party started dissipating. Kazi, without Khatiwada, felt helpless, and Khatiwada (he later resigned from Kazi's party) without Kazi's sane advice became rudderless.

The R&AW, in the past, had helped Kazi come out of a number of difficult situations to continue with his anti-Chogyal, pro-democracy and pro-merger campaign. The last one, and the most serious challenge to his position, which came from a 12 March 1975 signature campaign led by K.C. Pradhan, was nipped in the bud by Kazi, with support from us. It was now Dhar's turn as the IB's representative to do the needful, but it appeared that he was helpless.

The situation in Gangtok became more confusing when soon after the merger, Indira Gandhi mounted pressure on Kazi to join her party, Indian National Congress, or INC (I). Governor B.B. Lal played a leading role in convincing Kazi to listen to Gandhi. Lal packed off all thirty-one Sikkim Congress members of the legislative assembly on an Indian Airlines flight from Bagdogra to attend the INC (I) annual session at SAS Nagar, Mohali in December 1975 to formally join the party. Kazi did as advised.

In November 1976, when Prime Minister Gandhi visited Gangtok to celebrate her birthday with her family, her younger son Sanjay called Maloy Dhar and asked him to produce Khatiwada before him. He said that he wanted to make him in-charge of the Youth Congress in Sikkim. When Dhar said, and rightly so, that it would be advisable to consult Kazi, Sanjay retorted that if Kazi objected, he would change the chief minister of Sikkim. Dhar sought the IB's advice, but the desk officer in charge of Sikkim chided him and told him that 'you don't live another day by antagonizing' Sanjay. Khatiwada was produced before Sanjay late at night, and he gladly accepted the offer. With that, Khatiwada got an opportunity to build his own base at the cost of Kazi's hold over the party.

Indira Gandhi's party lost the 1977 general elections to the Janata Party-led coalition due to the excesses committed by her government during the Emergency. She was replaced by Morarji Desai as the prime minister. Kazi soon came under pressure from the Janata Party leaders to join their party. As advised by his IB bosses, Maloy Dhar called on the home minister, who told him to 'get Kazi to join my party'. Despite protests from Kazi, B.B. Lal pushed Kazi into the Janata Party's lap.

The unkindest cut of all to Kazi's leadership came from the new Prime Minister, Morarji Desai, when on 7 March 1978, in his misconceived idealism, he described the merger of Sikkim as an undesirable step that could not be undone. Further, it was wrong for a big country to do so, as most of the smaller neighbouring states were concerned about that. He, however, conceded that it could only be accomplished as most of the Sikkimese people wanted it, and the former Chogyal was not popular with the majority.

India washed its hands of its past commitment to the cause for which Kazi had devoted his life and let him fend for himself. Other Sikkim Congress leaders, who had enthusiastically participated in their struggle for freedom from the Chogyal, without any protective cover from the new Indian dispensation, started looking for cover in the wake of the former Chogyal-inspired and Bhandari-led desh bechoa campaign. Rather than feeling proud of what they had achieved, they were made to feel guilty as if they had committed some sort of sin by fighting for the delayed independence of their state.

Actually, it was Dhar's policy of running with the hare and hunting with the hounds that had led to such a situation. In his misconceived notion of strengthening the post-merger relations between New Delhi and Gangtok, Maloy rejuvenated the hounds and allowed the protective shield around the hare to wither away, thereby letting the hounds pounce upon the hare. According to him, 'some mysterious forces' started influencing members of the Sikkim Assembly to press for a vote against the merger of Sikkim. To handle such a grim situation, Dhar requested his regional head in Calcutta and the IB headquarters to provide him with the latest electronic interception gadgets and other facilities with permission to use those, which was summarily rejected. This left him dependent solely on Humint (intelligence collected through human assets). Having realized that New Delhi had lost its bearings, Dhar kept himself confined to honest reporting.

Khatiwada told me that despite Kazi's best efforts, the parity formula could not be removed or even changed before the April 1974 elections. However, the Nepalese continued to support him as they felt that what was being offered through the new method of distribution of seats (fifteen each for the Nepalese and Bhutia–Lepchas and one reserved seat each for the monasteries and scheduled castes) was a significant improvement on what was earlier available to them. However, a decision taken by the Government of India towards the end of 1978 to declare the Bhutia–Lepchas scheduled tribes, giving them some concessions in terms of jobs, etc., created certain apprehensions in the minds of the Nepalese population. Thereafter, a new seat allocation formula for the next elections was announced in early 1979. Through this, even parity was abolished and the new distribution formula, highly in favour of the Bhutia–Lepchas, was announced. A total of thirty-two seats were divided into seventeen for the general category, twelve for scheduled tribes, two for scheduled castes and one for sangha. It meant that the Bhutia–Lepchas, as a scheduled-tribe segment comprising only 25 per cent of the population, got almost 40 per cent of the Assembly seats reserved for them if the sangha seat was added to their group. On the other hand, the Nepalese segment comprising 75 per cent of the population got the remaining 60 per cent if the two scheduled-caste seats were added to this group. Even out of these nineteen seats, the seventeen which belonged to the general category were open for everyone, including the Bhutia–Lepchas, to contest.

With that Kazi lost whatever respect he had left amongst the Nepalese. Even the Lepchas were not very happy, as the better-educated Bhutias took advantage of those concessions. Kazi remained honest to the core, but the corrupt practices of most of his cabinet ministers increased. Kazi's party started crumbling as dissidence grew. As a result, R.C. Poudyal, N.B. Khatiwada,

B.B. Gurung and others left Kazi and his Janata Party. They
floated their own parties. Finding that the growing resentment
against Kazi was leading to political instability in Sikkim, in
August 1979, Governor B.B. Lal recommended the dismissal of
Kazi's government and imposition of President's rule in the state,
which was accepted by the central government.

It was under these circumstances that the first elections in
Sikkim in the post-merger period were held in October 1979.
Poudyal, leader of the Sikkim Congress (R) personally stayed out
of the elections as a mark of protest against this 'discriminatory'
distribution of seats, although his party contested the elections. In
the elections, the Bhandari-led Sikkim Janata Parishad (SJP) got
fifteen seats, the Poudyal-led Sikkim Congress (R) got eleven, the
Sikkim Prajatantra Congress (SPC) won four and an independent
candidate got the last seat. Kazi and his Janata Party could not get
even a single seat, with Kazi himself losing badly to a newcomer
Athup Lepcha from the Djongu scheduled-tribe seat. Khatiwada
won his seat as SPC candidate. B.B. Gurung, who won from two
constituencies, vacated one seat. Bhandari as leader of the party
having sixteen seats (with the support of the lone sangha member)
was called by Governor Lal to form the government.

The former Chogyal's eldest son, Tenzing Kunzung Namgyal,
died in an accident in Gangtok on 11 March 1978, two days
short of his twenty-sixth birthday.[4] Driving fast and following a
short but narrow winding road to the petrol pump, he tried to
avoid a head-on collision with a truck coming from the opposite
side, but his car swerved to the left and fell into a gorge. Devi
Manavalan, one of the three OSDs from West Bengal, who

came to Sikkim in April 1973 to help restore law and order, had become commissioner in charge of the four districts by then. He had developed a good rapport with Tenzing and used to watch him play football. Manavalan told me that Tenzing, as the captain of the Sikkim state team, had plans of taking his team to play at that year's national-level Santosh Trophy football tournament (September 1978).

Heartbroken by Tenzing's death, worried about the serious illness of his eldest daughter in New York and financially in bad shape, Thondup, accompanied by his friend Rustomji, went to New Delhi to call on Morarji Desai and to seek a financial settlement with the GoI. As the written undertaking given by Thondup did not satisfy Desai about his potential for future mischief, Desai refused to release funds and foreign exchange for his children's education and medical expenses.[5]

According to Manavalan, a similar attempt was also made by Thondup when Morarji Desai visited Gangtok on 9 April 1979. But since Thondup was not willing to give written assurances that he recognized Sikkim as a part of India, and that he would leave Sikkim and would not directly or indirectly interfere in its internal affairs, no such deal could be worked out. Further, encouraged by Desai's statement of 7 March 1978, in which he had criticized the merger of Sikkim, Thondup had prepared a petition for submission to Desai during that visit, in which he had requested suitable action for restoring the protectorate status accorded to Sikkim as per the 1950 treaty. When Desai expressed his inability to do anything in that respect due to the absence of any such provision in the Indian Constitution, the petition was not presented.

In September 1981, a medical check-up found that Thondup was suffering from carcinoma of the oesophagus. He was taken to New York for chemotherapy but the treatment did not work.

The twelfth and last Chogyal, Palden Thondup Namgyal, died on 29 January 1982 at the Memorial Sloan Kettering Cancer Center in New York. Indira Gandhi made arrangements for his mortal remains to be flown to Gangtok, and also for the funeral which took place on 19 February 1982. It was attended by approximately 20,000 people.

In May 1995, the Sikkim government, led by Pawan Kumar Chamling as chief minister, organized a function in Gangtok to mark the twentieth anniversary of the merger. Kazi was an honoured guest. After the function, a leaflet in the form of a press release signed by Kazi was distributed outside the venue.[6] In the leaflet, Kazi had expressed his anguish at the growing corruption, the yawning gap between the rich and the poor, politically motivated rifts between the various segments of the Sikkimese society and the Government of India's inaction despite repeated complaints (against the previous government led by Nar Bahadur Bhandari as chief minister till 17 June 1994). In the end, in his frustration, Kazi 'called upon the Union Government to immediately restore to us—the people of Sikkim—the status of "protectorate state" guaranteed to the Sikkimese people by the Indo–Sikkim treaty of 1950, thereby abrogating all the instruments of merger like the Thirty-sixth Constitutional Amendment Act, 1975, that reduced us to a part of India. This is because we have waited long enough and eventually lost our patience. We, therefore, feel confident that we are competent to govern ourselves better according to our political genius and outside the framework of the Constitution of India.'

In November 1996, Kathmandu-based journalist Sudheer Sharma met Kazi in Kalimpong for an interview for *Jana Astha*

Weekly.[7] In that interview, Kazi went even further by saying, 'Everybody accuses me of selling the country. Even if it is true, should I alone be blamed? I went out of my way to ensure the merger of Sikkim with India, but after the work was done, the Indians just ignored me . . . Earlier, I used to be given red carpet welcome. Now I have to wait for weeks even to meet second grade leaders.' Sharma again met Kazi at Kalimpong in 2000. In this meeting Kazi said that 'Money was made available to me through the Intelligence Bureau (IB). The people from IB used to visit me twice or thrice a year. An IB agent, Tejpal Singh, used to hand over money personally to me.'

These were the views of a person deeply hurt at the treatment meted out to him by the Indian establishment, after the merger. It is noteworthy that Kazi, even during his hour of grief, did not name the R&AW as the agency responsible for encouraging him to launch his anti-Chogyal campaign, which finally resulted in Sikkim's merger. Maybe it was because of the way I treated Kazi. I always felt that I was his political assistant, sent by the GoI, to help him achieve his goal. In fact, here again, like the Chogyal and his sister, Coo Coo La, Kazi blamed the IB and its head of the Sikkim set-up (much before my arrival in Sikkim), Tejpal Singh, of meddling in Sikkim's internal affairs. In criticizing Tejpal Singh, Kazi absolved the R&AW of any involvement in merger-related operations in Sikkim.

While the former Chogyal and his sister's complaints against the IB had resulted mainly due to their ignorance of the R&AW's involvement, and due to unwarranted or even careless exposure by Tejpal Singh and his men, Kazi knew about the R&AW's involvement in the merger-related operations. In that light, accusations about the IB's agents making payments to him at regular intervals were wilful and deliberate. In the post-merger period, for Kazi, the IB was the equivalent of the R&AW, which could not protect his honour when the former Chogyal's men branded him a desh bechoa. He had observed and the Kazini had protested against Maloy Dhar's growing contacts with the former Chogyal and his protégés, including Nar Bahadur Bhandari. He also missed the exclusivity that he and his party had enjoyed during the period leading up to the merger. He felt abandoned after his ignominious defeat in 1979 and found that there was nobody there to help restore his honour. Thereafter, a dejected Kazi tried his best to return to the INC (I) fold after Indira Gandhi's return to power in 1980. Typical of her, she did not forget Kazi's joining the Janata Party in 1977 and did not even meet him despite repeated requests.

It appears that, though belated, the grant of the nation's second-highest award—Padma Vibhushan—to Kazi in 2002 (at the age of ninety-eight), helped soothe his feelings to some extent. Thereafter, in recognition of his outstanding contribution to and for ushering in democracy in Sikkim, the government of Sikkim also decorated Kazi with the title of 'Sikkim Ratna' (Jewel of Sikkim) on the occasion of India's Independence Day, 15 August 2004. Kazi died on 28 July 2007 at the ripe old age of 103.

Before I end, I would like to discuss the accusations made by some pro-former Chogyal protégés, including N.B. Bhandari, that in helping the merger of Sikkim, Kazi had sold his country. In that context, an important thing that needs to be considered is: Whose country had Kazi sold? Sikkim at that time did not belong to its people at large. It belonged to the Chogyal and his family only. He ran the affairs of the state with the help of a coterie that benefited directly from his autocratic rule, while the majority of the Sikkimese people lived in poverty and denial of basic rights. One of Thondup's ancestors, Khye Bumsa (which in Sikkimese means 'superior of the thousand warriors'), came from Tibet in the thirteenth century and entered into a blood brotherhood treaty with a local Lepcha chieftain called Thekong Tek. Though Khye Bumsa returned to Chumbi Valley, it was this treaty that finally led to Phuntsog Namgyal establishing the Namgyal dynasty in Sikkim in 1642.

Kingdoms are created by force, military might, brotherhood treaties or deceit. They crumble when people realize that the unpopular king has become powerless, as the very power (in this case India's protective cover) which had propped up the king or even sustained his unpopular rule, had disappeared or withdrawn its protection and was now willing to make amends for its past acts of omission or commission. Thondup's Namgyal dynasty lasted for 333 years. It could have survived longer had there been an enlightened ruler willing to adjust to the changing environment by trying to accommodate the democratic aspirations of his people. But Thondup was not a person made out of that mould.

Given that background, Kazi emerged as the modern-day Lepcha equivalent of Khye Bumsa and retrieved Sikkim from the claws of the last of the Namgyals. But unlike the Namgyals, Kazi achieved his objective through popular support and democratic means, and handed over Sikkim to its rightful owners, i.e., the people of Sikkim at large, to let them carve out their own future through a democratically elected government that could run the affairs of the state for the combined welfare of all its people, unmindful of their ethnic and religious identity.

The Sikkimese people should be grateful to Kazi for having acted as a desh *bachau* (saviour). The phrase 'desh bechoa' was obviously coined by those who had lost their privileges, or by some of their paid touts, given the threat they may have felt because of

Kazi's untiring efforts for the cause of the people of Sikkim. In the post-merger period the proponents of this accusation were obviously encouraged and abetted by the former Chogyal to take revenge on Kazi, for having deprived him and his family of the most precious possession they had inherited.

It is now the turn of the Sikkimese people, especially the younger generation, to show their gratitude to Kazi and wash off the sins committed by some persons of the previous generation. Whenever the subject of Sikkim's merger with India came up for discussion with Kazi, I could see a glimmer of hope and expectation, especially for the younger generation, in his eyes. As head of the R&AW's spl ops team in Sikkim, I had always felt that I was dealing with Sikkim's freedom fighters under the overall inspiring leadership of Kazi, who for reasons explained earlier, had missed the freedom bus in 1947. It was now our job to help them attain what was their due. In view of that, all the SSC/SNC/Sikkim Congress leaders who actively participated in its struggle for freedom, first under Tashi Tshering and later under Kazi, truly qualify to be designated as freedom fighters on the lines of their compatriots from the rest of India. A few of them, who are still alive, deserve to walk with their heads held high and be proud of what they achieved in 1975.

Notes

Chapter I. Kao's Call

1. Nehru Memorial Museum and Library, New Delhi, 'P.N. Haksar Papers', vol. III, subfiles no. 161 and 179, on policy difference between T.N. Kaul and P.N. Haksar.
2. P.N. Dhar, *Indira Gandhi, the 'Emergency' and Indian Democracy,* Oxford University Press, 2001.
3. Recent discussions with former secretary (R) Ajit Singh Sayali and Padam Bahadur.
4. Recent discussions with IAS officer (retd) Rana Banerjee.
5. V.H. Coelho, *Sikkim And Bhutan,* Indian Council for Cultural Relations, 1970.

Chapter II. Namgyals and the British Imperialism

1. Government of Sikkim Census Report (2011), Directorate of Census Operations, Sikkim.
2. The New Encyclopaedia Britannica, 15th edition, vol. 21, published by Encyclopaedia Britannica, Inc.
3. Recent discussions with N.B Khatiwada.

4. Barun Roy, *Gorkhas and Gorkhaland: A Socio-Political Study of the Gorkha People and the Gorkhaland Movement*, published by Barun Roy, December 2012.
5. P.K. Parmar, *The Gorkhas*, Deep and Deep Publication, New Delhi, January 1990.
6. Government of Sikkim Census Report (2011).
7. National Archives of India, Ministry of External Affairs, file no. 7 (7) NEF-1947, New Delhi.
8. Claude Arpi, 'China Is on a Sticky Wicket in Bhutan', IDR blog, 13 July 2017.
9. Andrew Duff, *Sikkim: Requiem for a Himalayan Kingdom*, Penguin Random House India, 2015.
10. Coelho, *Sikkim and Bhutan*.
11. Dhar, *Indira Gandhi, the 'Emergency' and Indian Democracy*.
12. National Archives of India, Ministry of States, PR branch, file no. 5-PR/47-1947, New Delhi.
13. National Archives of India, Ministry of External Affairs, file no. 7 (7) NEF-1947, New Delhi.

Chapter III. The Sikkim of Tashi Tshering's Dreams (1947–53)

1. Sunanda K. Datta-Ray, *Smash and Grab: Annexation of Sikkim*, Tranquebar Press by Westland Ltd, Chennai, 2013.
2. Recent discussions with Ambassador (retd.) Sudhir T. Devare.
3. National Archives of India, Ministry of External Affairs, file no. 13 (14) NEF-49, New Delhi.
4. 'Sikkim: Darjeeling', compendium of documents.
5. National Archives of India, Ministry of States, PR branch, file no. 5-PR/1947, New Delhi.
6. National Archives of India, Ministry of External Affairs, file no. 11 (30) NEF-1947.
7. National Archives of India, Ministry of External Affairs, file no. 13 (14) NEF-49, 1949.
8. Ibid.

9. Coelho, *Sikkim and Bhutan.*

10. Ibid.

11. Ibid.

12. Ibid.

13. Duff, *Sikkim: Requiem for a Himalayan Kingdom.*

14. National Archives of India, DIB UO note no. 154/For/53(1), dated 21 January 1953; Ministry of External Affairs, file no. N/53/4611/103, NEF, 1953.

15. Coelho, *Sikkim and Bhutan.*

16. National Archives of India, Ministry of External Affairs, MEA file no. N/53/1421/103, 1953.

17. National Archives of India, Ministry of External Affairs, file no. N/53/1395/103 NEF branch.

18. Ibid.

19. Ibid.

20. National Archives of India, New Delhi. DIB UO note no. 154/For/53(1), dated 21 January 1953. MEA file no.- N/53/4611/103(NEF Br.) 1953.

21. Ibid.

22. National Archives of India, New Delhi: MEA file no. N/53/1421/103 of 1953.

23. National Archives of India, 'Monthly Report of the PO' (May 1954), paragraph 13, Ministry of External Affairs, file no. 54/1321/103, on Tashi Tshering's death.

Chapter IV. Kazi's Political Ascendance (1953–66)

1. National Archives of India, Ministry of External Affairs, file no. N/53/1521, NEF, 1953.

2. National Archives of India, DIB UO note no. 154/FOR/53(1), dated 2 December 1953, Ministry of External Affairs, file no. N/53/1521/103, NEF, 1953.

3. National Archives of India, 'Monthly Report of the PO' (April 1954), Ministry of External Affairs, file no. N/54/1321/103(S).

4. National Archives of India, 'Monthly Report of the PO' (June 1954), Ministry of External Affairs, file no. N/54/1321/103(S).

5. Recent discussions with Karma Topden, the Chogyal's former intelligence chief.

6. Nehru Memorial Museum and Library, 'P.N. Haksar Papers', vol. III, subfile no. 179.

7. National Archives of India, Ministry of External Affairs, file no. 7 (7), NEF, 1947.

8. Recent discussions with A.S. Sayali.

9. Duff, *Sikkim: Requiem for a Himalayan Kingdom*.

Chapter V. Demands for the Revision of 1950 Treaty (1967–72)

1. Recent discussions with Karma Topden.

2. Dhar, *Indira Gandhi, the 'Emergency' and Indian Democracy*.

3. A.C. Sinha, *Politics of Sikkim*, Thompson Press, 1973.

4. Duff, *Sikkim: Requiem for a Himalayan Kingdom*.

5. Dhar, *Indira Gandhi, the 'Emergency' and Indian Democracy*.

6. Datta-Ray, *Smash and Grab: Annexation of Sikkim*.

7. Ibid.

8. Discussions with Ambassador (retd) K.S. Bajpai.

9. Nehru Memorial Museum and Library, 'P.N. Haksar Papers', vol. III, subfile no. 161, November 1970.

10. Discussions with Ambassador (retd) Devare.

11. Nehru Memorial Museum and Library, 'P.N. Haksar Papers', vol. III, subfile no. 179, March 1972.

12. Duff, *Sikkim: Requiem for a Himalayan Kingdom*.

13. Ibid; recent discussions with Ambassador (retd) Bajpai.

Chapter VI. My Two and a Half Avatars

1. B.S. Das, *The Sikkim Saga*, Vikas Publishing House, New Delhi, 1983.

2. Discussions with A.S. Sayali.

3. Recent discussions with Karma Topden.

4. Datta-Ray, *Smash and Grab: Annexation of Sikkim*; Duff, *Sikkim: Requiem for a Himalayan Kingdom*.

5. Ashok Raina, *Inside RAW: Story of India's Secret Service*, Vikas Publishing House, New Delhi, 1981; Duff, *Sikkim: Requiem for a Himalayan Kingdom*.

6. Duff, *Sikkim: Requiem for a Himalayan Kingdom*; Datta-Ray, *Smash and Grab: Annexation of Sikkim*.

7. Raina, *Inside RAW: Story of India's Secret Service*; Duff, *Sikkim: Requiem for a Himalayan Kingdom*.

Chapter VII. The 8 May 1973 Agreement: Chogyal Contained

1. Recent discussions with Ambassador (retd) Devare.

2. Recent discussions with IAS officer (retd) Jayant Sanyal.

3. Recent discussions with IAS officer (retd) D.K. Manavalan.

4. Recent discussions with N.B. Khatiwada.

5. Sinha, *Politics of Sikkim*.

6. Recent telephonic discussions with Padam Bahadur.

7. Duff, *Sikkim: Requiem for a Himalayan Kingdom*.

8. Recent discussions with Ambassador (retd) Devare.

9. Recent discussions with Ambassador (retd) Bajpai.

10. Recent discussions with N.B. Khatiwada.

11. Recent discussions with Ambassador (retd) Devare.

12. Lt Gen. P.N. Hoon (retd), *The Untold Story*, Mohindra Publishing House, Chandigarh, 2015

13. Recent discussions with Ambassador (retd) Gurdip Singh Bedi.

14. Dhar, *Indira Gandhi, the 'Emergency' and Indian Democracy*.

15. Das, *The Sikkim Saga*.

16. Ibid.

17. Recent discussions with Ambassador (retd) Devare.

18. Ibid.

Chapter VIII. March towards Democracy

1. Recent discussions with Ambassador (retd) Devare.
2. Recent discussions with Karma Topden.

Chapter IX. April 1974 Elections: Democracy Institutionalized

1. Das, *The Sikkim Saga.*

Chapter X. The Resolution of 11 May 1974: Demand for Closer Ties with India

1. Das, *The Sikkim Saga.*
2. Ibid.

Chapter XI. Halfway House: Sikkim as an Associate State

1. Das, *The Sikkim Saga.*
2. Dhar, *Indira Gandhi, the 'Emergency' and Indian Democracy.*
3. Recent discussions with N.B. Khatiwada.
4. Dhar, *Indira Gandhi, the 'Emergency' and Indian Democracy.*
5. WikiLeaks, US State Department Cable, 1974STATE197329_b, 11 September 1974.
6. WikiLeaks, US Embassy, New Delhi Cable: 1974NEWDE12115_b, 11 September 1974.

Chapter XII. Moves towards a Merger

1. Das, *The Sikkim Saga.*
2. Recent discussions with Ambassador (retd) Ranjit Gupta.
3. Duff, *Sikkim: Requiem for a Himalayan Kingdom.*

Chapter XIII. The Merger

1. Recent discussions with Ambassador (retd) Ranjit Gupta.

2. Recent discussions with Lt Gen. (retd) Depinder Singh.
3. Recent discussions with IAS officer (retd) K.M. Lal.
4. WikiLeaks Cable, Sikkim (W. Saxbe), US Embassy Wiki Leaks Cable 1975NEWDE04815_b, 10 April 1975.
5. Duff, *Sikkim: Requiem for a Himalayan Kingdom*; National Archives of the UK, 'Political Situation in Sikkim', fol. no. 86, 26 August 1975.
6. WikiLeaks Cable, Sikkim (W. Saxbe), US Embassy Wiki Leaks Cable 1975NEWDE04815_b, 10 April 1975.
7. WikiLeaks Cable, Sikkim (W. Saxbe), US Embassy 1975NEWDE04921_b, 11 April 1975.
8. Ibid.
9. WikiLeaks Cable, Sikkim (W. Saxbe), US Embassy 1975STATE082154_b, 11 April 1975.
10. WikiLeaks Cable, Sikkim (W. Saxbe), US Embassy: 1975NEWDE05050_b, 15 April 1975.
11. Ibid.
12. WikiLeaks Cable, Sikkim (W. Saxbe), US Embassy: 1975NEWDE05120_b, 16 April 1975.
13. WikiLeaks Cable, Sikkim (W. Saxbe), US 1975NEWDE0524_b, 18 April 1975.
14. WikiLeaks Cable, Sikkim (W. Saxbe), US Embassy 1975NEWDE5516_b, 24 April 1975.
15. WikiLeaks Cable, Sikkim (W. Saxbe), US Embassy: 1975NEWDE04994_b.
16. WikiLeaks Cable, Sikkim (W. Saxbe), US Embassy: 1975NEWDE05050_b, 15 April 1975.
17. WikiLeaks Cable, Sikkim (W. Saxbe), US Embassy: 1975NEWDE05120_b, 16 April 1975.
18. WikiLeaks Cable, Nepalese Reaction: 1975KATHMA01743_b. April 11; 1975KATHMA01852_b, 22 April 1975.
19. National Archives, Ministry of External Affairs, file no. N/53/1395/NEF.

Chapter XIV. The Aftermath

1. Recent discussions with three retired IAS officers: K.M. Lal, Jayant Sanyal and D.K. Manavalan.
2. Recent discussions with N.B. Khatiwada.
3. Maloy Krishna Dhar, *Open Secrets: India's Intelligence Unveiled*, Manas Publications, New Delhi, 2005.
4. Duff, *Sikkim: Requiem for a Himalayan Kingdom.*
5. Ibid.
6. Obituary of L.D. Kazi, *Nepal*, September 2007, https://blog. cm.np/2013/01/31 the-pain-of-losing-a-nation-story-of-lhendupdo rjicomment-page-1.
7. Ibid.

Index

Abell, George, Sir, 43
accession, 37–40, 45–6,
51–4, 56, 72, 80, 117,
319–20, *see also* Instrument
of Accession; bilateral
instrument of, 37–8, 45, 53
accusations, 125, 342–43, 345
agitations: anti-durbar, 45; in
April 1973, 22, 221, 223,
258; for pro-democratic
reforms, 331
All India Congress Committee
(AICC), 74, 77–9
Alley, Rishi Prasad, 59
All-India State People's
Conference, 51
Anglo-Chinese Convention of
Calcutta in March 1890, 30
Anglo–Nepal war, 27
Anglo–Sikkim treaty of peace
and friendship, 28
annexation of Sikkim, 33

anti-Chogyal: agitations, 8, 19,
22, 80, 87, 123, 125–6,
131, 134–35, 138–39, 142,
145–46, 150–53, 157–59,
163, 169–70, 174–75, 285,
311; forces, 17, 47, 166;
JAC leaders, 164; operation,
134; parties, 20, 123, 146,
148, 175, 331; sentiments,
150, 286; Sikkim Congress
leaders, 132
anti-durbar parties, 46–7
anti-India: conspiracy,
243; procession, 106;
propaganda, 102
anti-Kazi activities, 334–35
anti-Tenzing slogans, 160
army, Indian, 1, 33, 157, 295,
304–06, 308, 317
Arora, 308
Arpi, Claude, 32
assassination attempts, 310